1,000,000 Books

are available to read at

Forgotten Books

www.ForgottenBooks.com

Read online
Download PDF
Purchase in print

ISBN 978-1-332-51250-8
PIBN 10107648

This book is a reproduction of an important historical work. Forgotten Books uses state-of-the-art technology to digitally reconstruct the work, preserving the original format whilst repairing imperfections present in the aged copy. In rare cases, an imperfection in the original, such as a blemish or missing page, may be replicated in our edition. We do, however, repair the vast majority of imperfections successfully; any imperfections that remain are intentionally left to preserve the state of such historical works.

Forgotten Books is a registered trademark of FB &c Ltd.
Copyright © 2018 FB &c Ltd.
FB &c Ltd, Dalton House, 60 Windsor Avenue, London, SW19 2RR.
Company number 08720141. Registered in England and Wales.

For support please visit www.forgottenbooks.com

1 MONTH OF
FREE
READING

at
www.ForgottenBooks.com

By purchasing this book you are eligible for one month membership to ForgottenBooks.com, giving you unlimited access to our entire collection of over 1,000,000 titles via our web site and mobile apps.

To claim your free month visit:
www.forgottenbooks.com/free107648

* Offer is valid for 45 days from date of purchase. Terms and conditions apply.

English
Français
Deutsche
Italiano
Español
Português

www.forgottenbooks.com

Mythology Photography **Fiction**
Fishing Christianity **Art** Cooking
Essays Buddhism Freemasonry
Medicine **Biology** Music **Ancient Egypt** Evolution Carpentry Physics
Dance Geology **Mathematics** Fitness
Shakespeare **Folklore** Yoga Marketing
Confidence Immortality Biographies
Poetry **Psychology** Witchcraft
Electronics Chemistry History **Law**
Accounting **Philosophy** Anthropology
Alchemy Drama Quantum Mechanics
Atheism Sexual Health **Ancient History**
Entrepreneurship Languages Sport
Paleontology Needlework Islam
Metaphysics Investment Archaeology
Parenting Statistics Criminology
Motivational

WELLINGTON

After a painting by JOHN SIMPSON

DEEDS THAT WON
THE EMPIRE

HISTORIC BATTLE SCENES

BY

THE REV. W. H. FITCHETT
("VEDETTE")

WITH PORTRAITS AND PLANS

SMITH, ELDER, & CO., 15 WATERLOO PLACE
1897

WELLINGTON

After a painting by John Hoppner

DEEDS THAT WON
THE EMPIRE

HISTORIC BATTLE SCENES

BY

THE REV. W. H. FITCHETT

("VEDETTE")

WITH PORTRAITS AND PLANS

LONDON
SMITH, ELDER, & CO., 15 WATERLOO PLACE
1897

DA
65
F54

Printed by BALLANTYNE, HANSON & Co.
At the Ballantyne Press

PREFACE

THE tales here told are written, not to glorify war, but to nourish patriotism. They represent an effort to renew in popular memory the great traditions of the Imperial race to which we belong.

The history of the Empire of which we are subjects —the story of the struggles and sufferings by which it has been built up—is the best legacy which the past has bequeathed to us. But it is a treasure strangely neglected. The State makes primary education its anxious care, yet it does not make its own history a vital part of that education. There is real danger that for the average youth the great names of British story may become meaningless sounds, that his imagination will take no colour from the rich and deep tints of history. And what a pallid, cold-blooded citizenship this must produce!

War belongs, no doubt, to an imperfect stage of society; it has a side of pure brutality. But it is not all brutal. Wordsworth's daring line about "God's most perfect instrument" has a great truth behind it. What examples are to be found in the tales here retold, not merely of heroic daring, but of even finer qualities— of heroic fortitude; of loyalty to duty stronger than the love of life; of the temper which dreads dishonour more than it fears death; of the patriotism which makes love of the Fatherland a passion. These are the elements of robust citizenship. They represent some, at least, of the qualities by which the Empire, in a sterner time than ours, was won, and by which, in even these ease-loving days, it must be maintained.

These sketches appeared originally in the *Melbourne Argus*, and are republished by the kind consent of its proprietors. Each sketch is complete in itself; and though no formal quotation of authorities is given, yet all the available literature on each event described has been laid under contribution. The sketches will be found to be historically accurate.

CONTENTS

	PAGE
THE FIGHT OFF CAPE ST. VINCENT	1
THE HEIGHTS OF ABRAHAM	13
THE GREAT LORD HAWKE	27
THE NIGHT ATTACK ON BADAJOS	39
THE FIRE-SHIPS IN THE BASQUE ROADS	51
THE MAN WHO SPOILED NAPOLEON'S "DESTINY"!	62
GREAT SEA-DUELS	74
THE BLOOD-STAINED HILL OF BUSACO	88
OF NELSON AND THE NILE	99
THE FUSILEERS AT ALBUERA	114
THE "SHANNON" AND THE "CHESAPEAKE"	126
THE GREAT BREACH OF CIUDAD RODRIGO	138
HOW THE "HERMIONE" WAS RECAPTURED	151
FRENCH AND ENGLISH IN THE PASSES	163
FAMOUS CUTTING-OUT EXPEDITIONS	175
MOUNTAIN COMBATS	188
THE BLOODIEST FIGHT IN THE PENINSULA	199
THE BATTLE OF THE BALTIC	211

CONTENTS

	PAGE
KING-MAKING WATERLOO—	224
I. The Rival Hosts	229
II. Hougoumont	236
III. Picton and D'Erlon	239
IV. "Scotland for Ever!"	243
V. Horsemen and Squares	249
VI. The Fight of the Gunners	256
VII. The Old Guard	262
VIII. The Great Defeat	272
THE NIGHT ATTACK OFF CADIZ	278
TRAFALGAR—	
I. The Strategy	290
II. How the Fleets Met	304
III. How the Victory was Won	317

LIST OF PORTRAITS

DUKE OF WELLINGTON	*Frontispiece*
EARL ST. VINCENT	*To face page* 1
GENERAL WOLFE	,, 13
LORD HAWKE	,, 27
GENERAL PICTON	,, 39
LORD COCHRANE	,, 51
SIR SIDNEY SMITH	,, 62
LORD NELSON	,, 99
(*After a Painting by* L. F. ABBOTT)	
LORD BERESFORD	,, 114
SIR PHILIP BOWES VERE BROKE	,, 126
CAPTAIN LAURENCE	,, 130
MARSHAL SOULT	,, 163
CAPTAIN EDWARD RIOU	,, 211
NAPOLEON	,, 224
ADMIRAL SAUMAREZ	,, 278
LORD NELSON	,, 290
(*After the Portrait by* HOPPNER)	

LIST OF PLANS

	PAGE
THE BATTLE OFF CAPE ST. VINCENT	5
THE SIEGE OF QUEBEC	16
THE SIEGE OF BADAJOS	41
THE BATTLE OF THE NILE	106
THE BATTLE OF ALBUERA	118
THE SIEGE OF CIUDAD RODRIGO	148
THE COMBAT OF RONCESVALLES	168
THE BATTLE OF ST. PIERRE	200
THE BATTLE OF THE BALTIC	214
THE BATTLE OF WATERLOO	227
THE ATTACK AT TRAFALGAR	308

EARL ST. VINCENT

After a painting by SIR W. BEECHEY, R.A.

THE FIGHT OFF CAPE ST. VINCENT

THE SCEPTRE OF THE SEA.

"Old England's sons are English yet,
　　Old England's hearts are strong;
And still she wears her coronet
　　Aflame with sword and song.
As in their pride our fathers died,
　　If need be, so die we;
So wield we still, gainsay who will,
　　The sceptre of the sea.

We've Raleighs still for Raleigh's part,
　　We've Nelsons yet unknown;
The pulses of the Lion-Heart
　　Beat on through Wellington.
Hold, Britain, hold thy creed of old,
　　Strong foe and steadfast friend,
And still unto thy motto true,
　　'Defy not, but defend.'

Men whisper that our arm is weak,
　　Men say our blood is cold,
And that our hearts no longer speak
　　That clarion note of old;
But let the spear and sword draw near
　　The sleeping lion's den,
Our island shore shall start once more
　　To life, with armèd men."
　　　　—HERMAN CHARLES MERIVALE.

ON the night of February 13, 1797, an English fleet of fifteen ships of the line, in close order and in readiness for instant battle, was under easy sail off Cape St. Vincent. It was a moonless night, black with haze, and the great ships moved in silence like gigantic spectres over the sea. Every now and again there came floating from the south-east the dull sound of a far-off gun. It was the grand fleet of Spain, consisting of twenty-seven ships of line, under Admiral Don Josef de Cordova; one great ship calling to another through the night, little dreaming that the sound of their guns was so keenly noted by the eager but silent fleet of their enemies to leeward. The morning of the 14th—a day famous in the naval history of the empire—broke dim and hazy; grey sea, grey fog, grey dawn, making all things strangely obscure. At half-past six, however, the keen-sighted British outlooks caught a glimpse of the huge straggling line of Spaniards, stretching apparently through miles of sea haze. "They are thumpers!" as the signal lieutenant of the *Barfleur* reported with emphasis to his captain; "they loom like Beachy Head in a fog!" The Spanish fleet was, indeed, the mightiest ever sent from Spanish ports since "that great fleet invincible" of 1588 carried into the English waters—but not out of them!—

"The richest spoils of Mexico, the stoutest hearts of Spain."

The Admiral's flag was borne by the *Santissima Trinidad*, a floating mountain, the largest ship at that time on the sea, and carrying on her four decks 130 guns. Next came six three-deckers carrying 112 guns each, two ships of the line of 80 guns each, and seventeen carrying 74 guns, with no less than twelve 34-gun frigates to act as a flying cordon of skirmishers. Spain had joined France against England on September 12, 1796, and Don Cordova, at the head of this immense fleet, had sailed from Cadiz to execute a daring and splendid strategy. He was to pick up the Toulon fleet, brush away the English squadron blockading Brest, add the great French fleet lying imprisoned there to his forces, and enter the British Channel with above a hundred sail of the line under his flag, and sweep in triumph to the mouth of the Thames! If the plan succeeded, Portugal would fall, a descent was to be made on Ireland; the British flag, it was reckoned, would be swept from the seas.

Sir John Jervis was lying in the track of the Spaniards to defeat this ingenious plan. Five ships of the line had been withdrawn from the squadron blockading Brest to strengthen him; still he had only fifteen ships against the twenty-seven huge Spaniards in front of him; whilst, if the French Toulon fleet behind him broke out, he ran the risk of being crushed, so to speak, betwixt the upper and the nether millstone. Never, perhaps, was the naval supremacy of England challenged so boldly and with such a prospect of success as at this moment. The northern powers had coalesced under Russia, and only a few weeks later the English guns were thundering over the roofs of Copenhagen, while the united flags of France and Spain were preparing to sweep through the narrow seas. The "splendid isolation" of to-day is no novelty. In 1796, as it threatened to be in 1896, Great Britain stood singly against a world in arms, and it is scarcely too much to say that her fate hung on the fortunes of the fleet that, in the grey dawn of St. Valentine's Day, a hundred years ago, was searching the skyline for the topmasts of Don Cordova's huge three-deckers.

Fifteen to twenty-seven is enormous odds, but, on

the testimony of Nelson himself, a better fleet never carried the fortunes of a great country than that under Sir John Jervis. The mere names of the ships or of their commanders awaken more sonorous echoes than the famous catalogue of the ships in the "Iliad." Trowbridge, in the *Culloden*, led the van; the line was formed of such ships as the *Victory*, the flagship, the *Barfleur*, the *Blenheim*, the *Captain*, with Nelson as commodore, the *Excellent*, under Collingwood, the *Colossus*, under Murray, the *Orion*, under Sir James Saumarez, &c. Finer sailors and more daring leaders never bore down upon an enemy's fleet. The picture offered by the two fleets in the cold haze of that fateful morning, as a matter of fact, reflected the difference in their fighting and sea-going qualities. The Spanish fleet, a line of monsters, straggled, formless and shapeless, over miles of sea space, distracted with signals, fluttering with many-coloured flags. The English fleet, grim and silent, bore down upon the enemy in two compact and firm-drawn columns, ship following ship so closely and so exactly that bowsprit and stern almost touched, while an air-line drawn from the foremast of the leading ship to the mizzenmast of the last ship in each column would have touched almost every mast betwixt. Stately, measured, threatening, in perfect fighting order, the compact line of the British bore down on the Spaniards.

Nothing is more striking in the battle of St. Vincent than the swift and resolute fashion in which Sir John Jervis leaped, so to speak, at his enemy's throat, with the silent but deadly leap of a bulldog. As the fog lifted, about nine o'clock, with the suddenness and dramatic effect of the lifting of a curtain in a great theatre, it revealed to the British admiral a great opportunity. The weather division of the Spanish fleet, twenty-one gigantic ships, resembled nothing so much as a confused and swaying forest of masts; the leeward

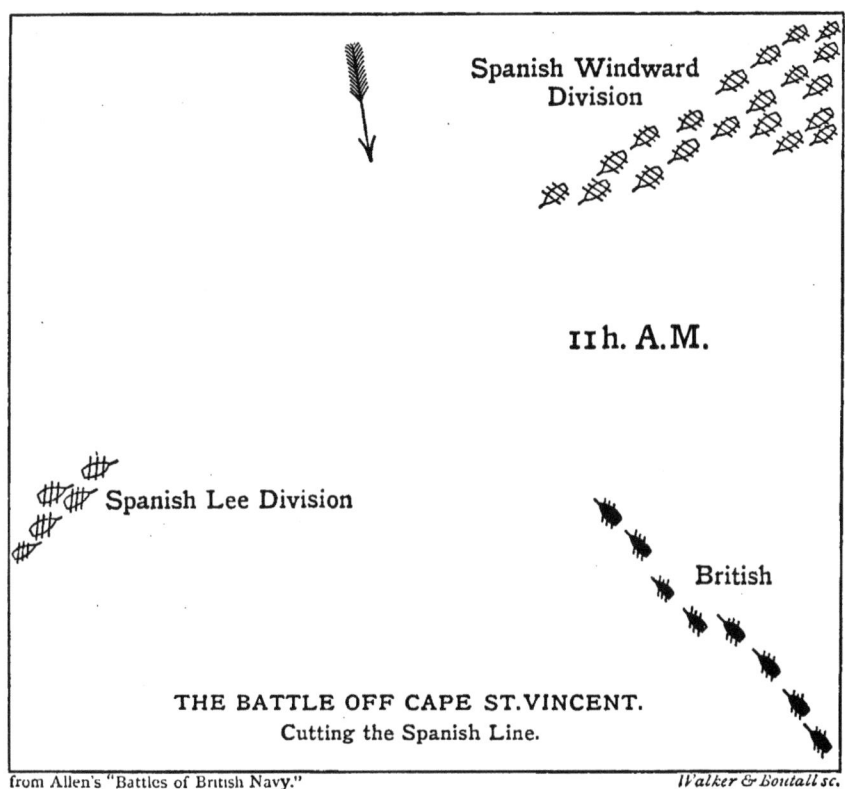

THE BATTLE OFF CAPE ST. VINCENT.
Cutting the Spanish Line.

from Allen's "Battles of British Navy." Walker & Boutall sc.

division—six ships in a cluster, almost as confused—was parted by an interval of nearly three miles from the main body of the fleet, and into that fatal gap, as with the swift and deadly thrust of a rapier, Jervis drove his fleet in one unswerving line, the two columns melting into one, ship following hard on ship. The Spaniards strove furiously to close their line, the twenty-one huge ships bearing down from the windward, the smaller squadron clawing desperately up from the leeward. But the British fleet—a long line of gliding pyramids of sails, leaning over to the pressure of the wind, with "the meteor flag" flying from the peak of each vessel, and the curving lines of guns awaiting grim and silent beneath—was too swift. As it swept through the gap, the Spanish vice-admiral, in the *Principe de Asturias*, a great three-decker of 112 guns, tried the daring feat of breaking through the British line to join the severed squadron. He struck the English fleet almost exactly at the flagship, the *Victory*. The *Victory* was thrown into stays to meet her, the Spaniard swung round in response, and, exactly as her quarter was exposed to the broadside of the *Victory*, the thunder of a tremendous broadside rolled from that ship. The unfortunate Spaniard was smitten as with a tempest of iron, and the next moment, with sails torn, topmasts hanging to leeward, ropes hanging loose in every direction, and her decks splashed red with the blood of her slaughtered crew, she broke off to windward. The iron line of the British was unpierceable! The leading three-decker of the Spanish lee division in like manner bore up, as though to break through the British line to join her admiral; but the grim succession of three-deckers, following swift on each other like the links of a moving iron chain, was too disquieting a prospect to be faced. It was not in Spanish seamanship, or, for the matter of that, in Spanish flesh and blood, to beat up in the teeth of such threatening lines of iron lips. The Spanish ships swung sullenly back to leeward, and the fleet of Don Cordova was cloven in twain, as though by the stroke of some gigantic sword-blade.

As soon as Sir John Jervis saw the steady line of his fleet drawn fair across the gap in the Spanish line, he flung his leading ships up to windward on the mass of the Spanish fleet, by this time beating up to windward. The *Culloden* led, thrust itself betwixt the hindmost Spanish three-deckers, and broke into flame and thunder on either side. Six minutes after her came the *Blenheim*; then, in quick succession, the *Prince George*, the *Orion*, the *Colossus*. It was a crash of swaying masts and bellying sails, while below rose the shouting of the crews, and, like the thrusts of fiery swords, the flames shot out from the sides of the great three-deckers against each other, and over all rolled the thunder and the smoke of a Titanic sea-fight. Nothing more murderous than close fighting betwixt the huge wooden ships of those days can well be imagined. The *Victory*, the largest British ship present in the action, was only 186 feet long and 52 feet broad; yet in that little area 1000 men fought, 100 great guns thundered. A Spanish ship like the *San Josef* was 194 feet in length and 54 feet in breadth; but in that area 112 guns were mounted, while the three decks were thronged with some 1300 men. When floating batteries like these swept each other with the flame of swiftly repeated broadsides at a distance of a few score yards, the destruction may be better imagined than described. The Spanish had an advantage in the number of guns and men, but the British established an instant mastery by their silent discipline, their perfect seamanship, and the speed with which their guns were worked. They fired at least three broadsides to every two the Spaniards discharged, and their fire had a deadly precision compared with which that of the Spaniards was mere distracted spluttering.

Meanwhile the dramatic crisis of the battle came swiftly on. The Spanish admiral was resolute to join the severed fragments of his fleet. The *Culloden*, the *Blenheim*, the *Prince George*, and the *Orion* were thundering amongst his rearmost ships, and as the British line swept up, each ship tacked as it crossed the gap in the Spanish line, bore up to windward and added the thunder of its guns to the storm of battle raging amongst the hindmost Spaniards. But naturally the section of the British line that had not yet passed the gap shortened with every minute, and the leading Spanish ships at last saw the sea to their leeward clear of the enemy, and the track open to their own lee squadron. Instantly they swung round to leeward, the great four-decker, the flagship, with a company of sister giants, the *San Josef* and the *Salvador del Mundo*, of 112 guns each, the *San Nicolas*, and three other great ships of 80 guns. It was a bold and clever stroke. This great squadron, with the breeze behind it, had but to sweep past the rear of the British line, join the lee squadron, and bear up, and the Spanish fleet in one unbroken mass would confront the enemy. The rear of the British line was held by Collingwood in the *Excellent;* next to him came the *Diadem;* the third ship was the *Captain*, under Nelson. We may imagine how Nelson's solitary eye was fixed on the great Spanish three-deckers that formed the Spanish van as they suddenly swung round and came sweeping

down to cross his stern. Not Napoleon himself had a
vision more swift and keen for the changing physiog-
nomy of a great battle than Nelson, and he met the
Spanish admiral with a counter-stroke as brilliant and
daring as can be found in the whole history of naval
warfare. The British fleet saw the *Captain* suddenly
swing out of line to leeward—in the direction from the
Spanish line, that is—but with swift curve the *Captain*
doubled back, shot between the two English ships that
formed the rear of the line, and bore up straight in the
path of the Spanish flagship, with its four decks, and
the huge battleships on either side of it.

The *Captain*, it should be remembered, was the
smallest 74 in the British fleet, and as the great Spanish
ships closed round her and broke into flame it seemed
as if each one of them was big enough to hoist the
Captain on board like a jolly-boat. Nelson's act was
like that of a single stockman who undertakes to "head
off" a drove of angry bulls as they break away from the
herd; but the "bulls" in this case were a group of the
mightiest battleships then afloat. Nelson's sudden
movement was a breach of orders; it left a gap in the
British line; to dash unsupported into the Spanish van
seemed mere madness, and the spectacle, as the *Captain*
opened fire on the huge *Santissima Trinidad*, was
simply amazing. Nelson was in action at once with
the flagship of 130 guns, two ships of 112 guns, one of
80 guns, and two of 74 guns! To the spectators who
watched the sight the sides of the *Captain* seemed to
throb with quick-following pulses of flame as its crew
poured their shot into the huge hulks on every side of
them. The Spaniards formed a mass so tangled that

they could scarcely fire at the little *Captain* without injuring each other; yet the English ship seemed to shrivel beneath even the imperfect fire that did reach her. Her foremast was shot away, her wheel-post shattered, her rigging torn, some of her guns dismantled, and the ship was practically incapable of further service either in the line or in chase. But Nelson had accomplished his purpose: he had stopped the rush of the Spanish van.

At this moment the *Excellent*, under Collingwood, swept into the storm of battle that raged round the *Captain*, and poured three tremendous broadsides into the Spanish three-decker the *Salvador del Mundo* that practically disabled her. "We were not further from her," the domestic but hard-fighting Collingwood wrote to his wife, "than the length of our garden." Then, with a fine feat of seamanship, the *Excellent* passed between the *Captain* and the *San Nicolas*, scourging that unfortunate ship with flame at a distance of ten yards, and then passed on to bestow its favours on the *Santissima Trinidad* — "such a ship," Collingwood afterwards confided to his wife, "as I never saw before!" Collingwood tormented that monster with his fire so vehemently that she actually struck, though possession of her was not taken before the other Spanish ships, coming up, rescued her, and she survived to carry the Spanish flag in the great fight of Trafalgar.

Meanwhile the crippled *Captain*, though actually disabled, had performed one of the most dramatic and brilliant feats in the history of naval warfare. Nelson put his helm to starboard, and ran, or rather drifted, on the quarter-gallery of the *San Nicolas*, and at once boarded that leviathan. Nelson himself crept through the quarter-gallery window in the stern of the Spaniard, and found himself in the officers' cabins. The officers tried to show fight, but there was no denying the boarders who followed Nelson, and with shout and oath, with flash of pistol and ring of steel, the party swept through on to the main deck. But the *San Nicolas* had been boarded also at other points. "The first man who jumped into the enemy's mizzen-chains," says Nelson, "was the first lieutenant of the ship, afterwards Captain Berry." The English sailors dropped from their spritsail yard on to the Spaniard's deck, and by the time Nelson reached the poop of the *San Nicolas* he found his lieutenant in the act of hauling down the Spanish flag. Nelson proceeded to collect the swords of the Spanish officers, when a fire was opened upon them from the stern gallery of the admiral's ship, the *San Josef*, of 112 guns, whose sides were grinding against those of the *San Nicolas*. What could Nelson do? To keep his prize he must assault a still bigger ship. Of course he never hesitated! He flung his boarders up the side of the huge *San Josef*, but he himself, with his solitary arm, had to be assisted to climb the main chains of that vessel, his lieutenant this time dutifully assisting his commodore up instead of indecorously going ahead of him. "At this moment," as Nelson records the incident, "a Spanish officer looked over the quarter-deck rail and said they surrendered. It was not long before I was on the quarter-deck, where the Spanish captain, with a bow, presented me his sword, and said the admiral was dying of his wounds. I asked him, on his honour, if the ship was surrendered. He

declared she was; on which I gave him my hand, and
desired him to call on his officers and ship's company
and tell them of it, which he did; and on the quarter-
deck of a Spanish first-rate—extravagant as the story
may seem—did I receive the swords of vanquished
Spaniards, which, as I received, I gave to William
Fearney, one of my bargemen, who put them with
the greatest *sang-froid* under his arm," a circle of
" old Agamemnons," with smoke-blackened faces, looking on in grim approval.

This is the story of how a British fleet of fifteen vessels
defeated a Spanish fleet of twenty-seven, and captured
four of their finest ships. It is the story, too, of how a
single English ship, the smallest 74 in the fleet—but
made unconquerable by the presence of Nelson—stayed
the advance of a whole squadron of Spanish three-deckers,
and took two ships, each bigger than itself, by boarding.
Was there ever a finer deed wrought under " the meteor
flag"! Nelson disobeyed orders by leaving the English
line and flinging himself on the van of the Spaniards, but
he saved the battle. Calder, Jervis's captain, complained
to the admiral that Nelson had "disobeyed orders." "He
certainly did," answered Jervis; "and if ever you commit
such a breach of your orders I will forgive you also."

GENERAL WOLFE

After a painting by SCHACK *in the National Portrait Gallery*

THE HEIGHTS OF ABRAHAM

"Sound, sound the clarion, fill the fife !
To all the sensual world proclaim,
One crowded hour of glorious life
Is worth an age without a name."
—Sir Walter Scott.

THE year 1759 is a golden one in British history. A great French army that threatened Hanover was overthrown at Minden, chiefly by the heroic stupidity of six British regiments, who, mistaking their orders, charged the entire French cavalry in line, and destroyed them. "I have seen," said the astonished French general, "what I never thought to be possible—a single line of infantry break through three lines of cavalry ranked in order of battle, and tumble them into ruin!" Contades omitted to add that this astonishing infantry, charging cavalry in open formation, was scourged during their entire advance by powerful batteries on their flank. At Quiberon, in the same year, Hawke, amid a tempest, destroyed a mighty fleet that threatened England with invasion; and on the heights of Abraham, Wolfe broke the French power in America. "We are forced," said Horace Walpole, the wit of his day, "to ask every morning what new victory there is, for fear of missing one." Yet, of all the great deeds of that *annus mirabilis*, the victory which overthrew Montcalm and gave Quebec to England—a victory achieved by the genius of Pitt and the daring of Wolfe—was, if not the most shining in quality, the most far-reaching in its results. "With the triumph of Wolfe on the heights of Abraham," says Green, "began the history of the United States."

The hero of that historic fight wore a singularly unheroic aspect. Wolfe's face, in the famous picture by West, resembles that of a nervous and sentimental boy—he was an adjutant at sixteen, and only thirty-three when he fell, mortally wounded, under the walls of Quebec. His forehead and chin receded; his nose, tip-tilted heavenwards, formed with his other features the point of an obtuse triangle. His hair was fiery red, his shoulders narrow, his legs a pair of attenuated spindle-shanks; he was a chronic invalid. But between his fiery poll and his plebeian and upturned nose flashed a pair of eyes—keen, piercing, and steady—worthy of Cæsar or of Napoleon. In warlike genius he was on land as Nelson was on sea, chivalrous, fiery, intense. A "magnetic" man, with a strange gift of impressing himself on the imagination of his soldiers, and of so penetrating the whole force he commanded with his own spirit that in his hands it became a terrible and almost resistless instrument of war. The gift for choosing fit agents is one of the highest qualities of genius; and it is a sign of Pitt's piercing insight into character that, for the great task of overthrowing the French power in Canada, he chose what seemed to commonplace vision a rickety, hypóchondriacal, and very youthful colonel like Wolfe.

Pitt's strategy for the American campaign was spacious, not to say grandiose. A line of strong French posts, ranging from Duquesne, on the Ohio, to Ticonderoga, on Lake Champlain, held the English settlements on the coast girdled, as in an iron band, from all extension westward; while Quebec, perched in almost impregnable strength on the frowning cliffs which look down on the St. Lawrence, was the centre of the French power in Canada. Pitt's plan was that Amherst, with 12,000 men, should capture Ticonderoga; Prideaux, with another powerful force, should carry Montreal; and Wolfe, with 7000 men, should invest Quebec, where Amherst and Prideaux were to join him. Two-thirds of this great plan broke down. Amherst and Prideaux, indeed, succeeded in their local operations, but neither was able to join Wolfe, who had to carry out with one army the task for which three were designed.

On June 21, 1759, the advanced squadron of the fleet conveying Wolfe came working up the St. Lawrence. To deceive the enemy they flew the white flag, and, as the eight great ships came abreast of the Island of Orleans, the good people of Quebec persuaded themselves it was a French fleet bringing supplies and reinforcements. The bells rang a welcome; flags waved. Boats put eagerly off to greet the approaching ships. But as these swung round at their anchorage the white flag of France disappeared, and the red ensign of Great Britain flew in its place. The crowds, struck suddenly dumb, watched the gleam of the hostile flag with chapfallen faces. A priest, who was staring at the ships through a telescope, actually dropped dead with the excitement and passion created by the sight of the British fleet. On June 26 the main body of the fleet, bringing Wolfe himself with 7000 troops, was in sight of the lofty cliffs on which Quebec stands; Cook, after-

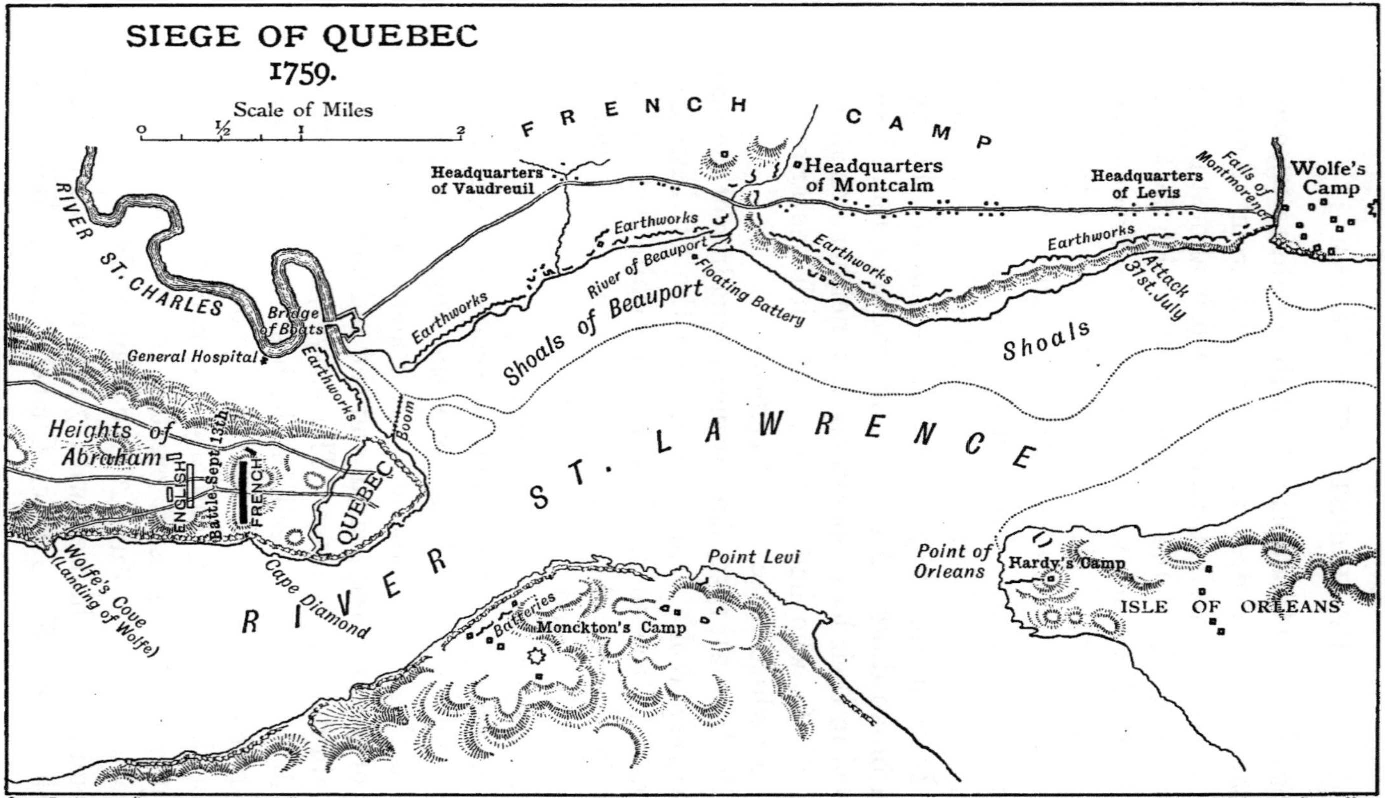

from Parkman's "Montcalm & Wolfe."

Walker & Boutall sc.

wards the famous navigator, master of the *Mercury*, sounding ahead of the fleet. Wolfe at once seized the Isle of Orleans, which shelters the basin of Quebec to the east, and divides the St. Lawrence into two branches, and, with a few officers, quickly stood on the western point of the isle. At a glance the desperate nature of the task committed to him was apparent.

Quebec stands on the rocky nose of a promontory, shaped roughly like a bull's-head, looking eastward. The St. Lawrence flows eastward under the chin of the head; the St. Charles runs, so to speak, down its nose from the north to meet the St. Lawrence. The city itself stands on lofty cliffs, and as Wolfe looked upon it on that June evening far away, it was girt and crowned with batteries. The banks of the St. Lawrence, that define what we have called the throat of the bull, are precipitous and lofty, and seem by mere natural strength to defy attack, though it was just here, by an ant-like track up 250 feet of almost perpendicular cliff, Wolfe actually climbed to the plains of Abraham. To the east of Quebec is a curve of lofty shore, seven miles long, between the St. Charles and the Montmorenci. When Wolfe's eye followed those seven miles of curving shore, he saw the tents of a French army double his own in strength, and commanded by the most brilliant French soldier of his generation, Montcalm. Quebec, in a word, was a great natural fortress, attacked by 9000 troops and defended by 16,000; and if a daring military genius urged the English attack, a soldier as daring and well-nigh as able as Wolfe directed the French defence.

Montcalm gave a proof of his fine quality as a soldier within twenty-four hours of the appearance of the

British fleet. The very afternoon the British ships dropped anchor a terrific tempest swept over the harbour, drove the transports from their moorings, dashed the great ships of war against each other, and wrought immense mischief. The tempest dropped as quickly as it had arisen. The night fell black and moonless. Towards midnight the British sentinels on the point of the Isle of Orleans saw drifting silently through the gloom the outlines of a cluster of ships. They were eight huge fire-ships, floating mines packed with explosives. The nerve of the French sailors, fortunately for the British, failed them, and they fired the ships too soon. But the spectacle of these flaming monsters as they drifted towards the British fleet was appalling. The river showed ebony-black under the white flames. The glare lit up the river cliffs, the roofs of the city, the tents of Montcalm, the slopes of the distant hills, the black hulls of the British ships. It was one of the most stupendous exhibitions of fireworks ever witnessed! But it was almost as harmless as a display of fireworks. The boats from the British fleet were by this time in the water, and pulling with steady daring to meet these drifting volcanoes. They were grappled, towed to the banks, and stranded, and there they spluttered and smoked and flamed till the white light of the dawn broke over them. The only mischief achieved by these fire-ships was to burn alive one of their own captains and five or six of his men, who failed to escape in their boats.

Wolfe, in addition to the Isle of Orleans, seized Point Levi, opposite the city, and this gave him complete command of the basin of Quebec; from his batteries on Point Levi, too, he could fire directly on the city, and destroy it if he could not capture it. He himself landed the main body of his troops on the east bank of the Montmorenci, Montcalm's position, strongly entrenched, being between him and the city. Between the two armies, however, ran the deep gorge through which the swift current of the Montmorenci rushes down to join the St. Lawrence. The gorge is barely a gunshot in width, but of stupendous depth. The Montmorenci tumbles over its rocky bed with a speed that turns the flashing waters almost to the whiteness of snow. Was there ever a more curious military position adopted by a great general in the face of superior forces! Wolfe's tiny army was distributed into three camps: his right wing on the Montmorenci was six miles distant from his left wing at Point Levi, and between the centre, on the Isle of Orleans, and the two wings, ran the two branches of the St. Lawrence. That Wolfe deliberately made such a distribution of his forces under the very eyes of Montcalm showed his amazing daring. And yet beyond firing across the Montmorenci on Montcalm's left wing, and bombarding the city from Point Levi, the British general could accomplish nothing. Montcalm knew that winter must compel Wolfe to retreat, and he remained stubbornly but warily on the defensive.

On July 18 the British performed a daring feat. In the darkness of the night two of the men-of-war and several sloops ran past the Quebec batteries and reached the river above the town; they destroyed some fireships they found there, and cut off Montcalm's communication by water with Montreal. This rendered it necessary for the French to establish guards on the line of precipices between Quebec and Cap-Rouge. On July 28 the French repeated the experiment of fire-ships on a still more gigantic scale. A vast fire-raft was constructed, composed of some seventy schooners, boats, and rafts, chained together, and loaded with combustibles and explosives. The fire-raft is described as being 100 fathoms in length, and its appearance, as it came drifting on the current, a mass of roaring fire, discharging every instant a shower of missiles, was terrifying. But the British sailors dashed down upon it, broke the huge raft into fragments, and towed them easily ashore. "Hang it, Jack," one sailor was heard to say to his mate as he tugged at the oar, "didst thee ever take hell in tow before?"

Time was on Montcalm's side, and unless Wolfe could draw him from his impregnable entrenchments and compel him to fight, the game was lost. When the tide fell, a stretch of shoal a few score yards wide was left bare on the French side of the Montmorenci. The slope that covered this was steep, slippery with grass, crowned by a great battery, and swept by the cross-fire of entrenchments on either flank. Montcalm, too, holding the interior lines, could bring to the defence of this point twice the force with which Wolfe could attack it. Yet to Wolfe's keen eyes this seemed the one vulnerable point in Montcalm's front, and on July 31 he made a desperate leap upon it.

The attack was planned with great art. The British batteries thundered across the Montmorenci, and a feint was made of fording that river higher up, so as to distract the attention of the French, whilst the boats of the fleet threatened a landing near Quebec itself. At half-past five the tide was at its lowest, and the boat-flotilla, swinging round at a signal, pulled at speed for the patch of muddy foreshore already selected. The Grenadiers and Royal Americans leaped ashore in the mud, and—waiting neither for orders, nor leaders, nor supports—dashed up the hill to storm the redoubt. They reached the first redoubt, tumbled over it and through it, only to find themselves breathless in a semi-circle of fire. The men fell fast, but yet struggled fiercely upwards. A furious storm of rain broke over the combatants at that moment, and made the steep grass-covered slope as slippery as mere glass. "We could not see half-way down the hill," writes the French officer in command of the battery on the summit. But through the smoke and the driving rain they could still see the Grenadiers and Royal Americans in ragged clusters, scarce able to stand, yet striving desperately to climb upwards. The reckless ardour of the Grenadiers had spoiled Wolfe's attack, the sudden storm helped to save the French, and Wolfe withdrew his broken but furious battalions, having lost some 500 of his best men and officers.

The exultant French regarded the siege as practically over; but Wolfe was a man of heroic and quenchless tenacity, and never so dangerous as when he seemed to be in the last straits. He held doggedly on, in spite of cold and tempest and disease. His own frail body broke down, and for the first time the shadow of depression fell on the British camps when they no longer saw the red head and lean and scraggy body of their general moving amongst them. For a week, between

August 22 and August 29, he lay apparently a dying man, his face, with its curious angles, white with pain and haggard with disease. But he struggled out again, and framed yet new plans of attack. On September 10 the captains of the men-of-war held a council on board the flagship, and resolved that the approach of winter required the fleet to leave Quebec without delay. By this time, too, Wolfe's scanty force was diminished one-seventh by disease or losses in battle. Wolfe, however, had now formed the plan which ultimately gave him success, though at the cost of his own life.

From a tiny little cove, now known as Wolfe's Cove, five miles to the west of Quebec, a path, scarcely-accessible to a goat, climbs up the face of the great cliff, nearly 250 feet high. The place was so inaccessible that only a post of 100 men kept guard over it. Up that track, in the blackness of the night, Wolfe resolved to lead his army to the attack on Quebec! It needed the most exquisite combinations to bring the attacking force to that point from three separate quarters, in the gloom of night, at a given moment, and without a sound that could alarm the enemy. Wolfe withdrew his force from the Montmorenci, embarked them on board his ships, and made every sign of departure. Montcalm mistrusted these signs, and suspected Wolfe would make at least one more leap on Quebec before withdrawing. Yet he did not in the least suspect Wolfe's real designs. He discussed, in fact, the very plan Wolfe adopted, but dismissed it by saying, "We need not suppose that the enemy have wings." The British ships were kept moving up and down the river front for several days, so as to distract and perplex the enemy. On September 12 Wolfe's plans were complete, and he issued his final orders. One sentence in them curiously anticipates Nelson's famous signal at Trafalgar. "Officers and men," wrote Wolfe, "*will remember what their country expects of them.*' A feint on Beauport, five miles to the east of Quebec, as evening fell, made Montcalm mass his troops there; but it was at a point five miles west of Quebec the real attack was directed.

At two o'clock at night two lanterns appeared for a minute in the maintop shrouds of the *Sunderland*. It was the signal, and from the fleet, from the Isle of Orleans, and from Point Levi, the English boats stole silently out, freighted with some 1700 troops, and converged towards the point in the black wall of cliffs agreed upon. Wolfe himself was in the leading boat of the flotilla. As the boats drifted silently through the darkness on that desperate adventure, Wolfe, to the officers about him, commenced to recite Gray's " Elegy ":—

> " The boast of heraldry, the pomp of power,
>   And all that beauty, all that wealth e'er gave,
>   Await alike the inevitable hour.
>   The paths of glory lead but to the grave."

"Now, gentlemen," he added, "I would rather have written that poem than take Quebec." Wolfe, in fact, was half poet, half soldier. Suddenly from the great wall of rock and forest to their left broke the challenge of a French sentinel—"*Qui vive?*" A Highland officer of Fraser's regiment, who spoke French fluently, answered the challenge. "*France.*" "*A quel regiment?*" "*De la Reine,*" answered the Highlander. As it happened the French expected a flotilla of provision boats, and after a little further dialogue, in which the cool Highlander completely deceived the French sentries, the British were allowed to slip past in the darkness. The tiny cove was safely reached, the boats stole silently up without a blunder, twenty-four volunteers from the Light Infantry leaped from their boat and led the way in single file up the path, that ran like a thread along the face of the cliff. Wolfe sat eagerly listening in his boat below. Suddenly from the summit he saw the flash of the muskets and heard the stern shout which told him his men were up. A clear, firm order, and the troops sitting silent in the boats leaped ashore, and the long file of soldiers, like a chain of ants, went up the face of the cliff, Wolfe amongst the foremost, and formed in order on the plateau, the boats meanwhile rowing back at speed to bring up the remainder of the troops. Wolfe was at last within Montcalm's guard!

When the morning of the 13th dawned, the British army, in line of battle, stood looking down on Quebec. Montcalm quickly heard the news, and came riding furiously across the St. Charles and past the city to the scene of danger. He rode, as those who saw him tell, with a fixed look, and uttering not a word. The vigilance of months was rendered worthless by that amazing night escalade. When he reached the slopes Montcalm saw before him the silent red wall of British infantry, the Highlanders with waving tartans and wind-blown plumes—all in battle array. It was not a detachment, but an army!

The fight lasted fifteen minutes, and might be told in almost as many words. Montcalm brought on his men in three powerful columns, in number double that of Wolfe's force. The British troops stood grimly silent, though they were tormented by the fire of Indians and Canadians lying in the grass. The French advanced eagerly, with a tumult of shouts and a confused fire; the British moved forward a few rods, halted, dressed their lines, and when the French were within forty paces threw in one fierce volley, so sharply timed that the explosion of 4000 muskets sounded like the sudden blast of a cannon. Again, again, and yet again, the flame ran from end to end of the steadfast line. When the smoke lifted, the French column were wrecked. The British instantly charged. The spirit of the clan awoke in Fraser's Highlanders: they flung aside their muskets, drew their broadswords, and with a fierce Celtic slogan rushed on the enemy. Never was a charged pressed more ruthlessly home. After the fight one of the British officers wrote: "There was not a bayonet in the three leading British regiments, nor a broadsword amongst the Highlanders, that was not crimson with the blood of a foeman." Wolfe himself charged at the head of the Grenadiers, his bright uniform making him conspicuous. He was shot in the wrist, wrapped a handkerchief round the wound, and still ran forward. Two other bullets struck him—one, it is said, fired by a British deserter, a sergeant broken by Wolfe for brutality to a private. "Don't let the soldiers see me drop," said Wolfe, as he fell, to an officer running beside him. An officer of the Grenadiers, a gentleman volunteer, and a private carried Wolfe to a redoubt near. He refused to allow a surgeon to be called. "There is no need," be said, "it is all over with me."

Then one of the little group, casting a look at the smoke-covered battlefield, cried, "They run! See how they run!" "Who run?" said the dying Wolfe, like a man roused from sleep. "The enemy, sir," was the answer. A flash of life came back to Wolfe; the eager spirit thrust from it the swoon of death; he gave a clear, emphatic order for cutting off the enemy's retreat; then, turning on his side, he added, "Now God be praised; I die in peace."

That fight determined that the North American continent should be the heritage of the Anglo-Saxon race. And, somehow, the popular instinct, when the news reached England, realised the historic significance of the event. "When we first heard of Wolfe's glorious deed," writes Thackeray in "The Virginians"—"of that army marshalled in darkness and carried silently up the midnight river—of those rocks scaled by the intrepid leader and his troops—of the defeat of Montcalm on the open plain by the sheer valour of his conqueror—we were all intoxicated in England by the news." Not merely all London but half England flamed into illuminations. One spot alone was dark—Blackheath, where, solitary amidst a rejoicing nation, Wolfe's mother mourned for her heroic son—like Milton's Lycidas—"dead ere his prime."

LORD HAWKE

After a painting by FRANCIS COTES, R.A.

THE GREAT LORD HAWKE

THE ENGLISH FLAG

"What is the flag of England? Winds of the world, declare!
. . . .
The lean white bear hath seen it in the long, long Arctic night,
The musk-ox knows the standard that flouts the Northern light.
. . . .
Never was isle so little, never was sea so lone,
But over the scud and the palm-trees an English flag has flown.
I have wrenched it free from the halliard to hang for a wisp on the Horn;
I have chased it north to the Lizard—ribboned and rolled and torn;
I have spread its folds o'er the dying, adrift in a hopeless sea;
I have hurled it swift on the slaver, and seen the slave set free.
. . . .
Never the lotos closes, never the wild-fowl wake,
But a soul goes out on the East Wind, that died for England's sake—
Man or woman or suckling, mother or bride or maid—
Because on the bones of the English, the English flag is stayed.
. . . .
The dead dumb fog hath wrapped it—the frozen dews have kissed—
The naked stars have seen it, a fellow-star in the mist.
What is the flag of England? Ye have but my breath to dare;
Ye have but my waves to conquer. Go forth, for it is there!"
—KIPLING.

"THE great Lord Hawke" is Burke's phrase, and is one of the best-earned epithets in literature. Yet what does the average Englishman to-day remember of the great sailor who, through the bitter November gales of 1759, kept dogged and tireless watch over the French fleet in Brest, destroyed that fleet with heroic daring amongst the sands of Quiberon, while the fury of a Bay of Biscay tempest almost drowned the roar of his guns, and so crushed a threatened invasion of England?

Hawke has been thrown by all-devouring Time into his wallet as mere "alms for oblivion"; yet amongst all the sea-dogs who ever sailed beneath "the blood-red flag" no one ever less deserved that fate. Campbell, in "Ye Mariners of England," groups "Blake and mighty Nelson" together as the two great typical English sailors. Hawke stands midway betwixt them, in point both of time and of achievements, though he had more in him of Blake than of Nelson. He lacked, no doubt, the dazzling electric strain that ran through the warlike genius of Nelson. Hawke's fighting quality was of the grim, dour home-spun character; but it was a true genius for battle, and as long as Great Britain is a seapower the memory of the great sailor who crushed Conflans off Quiberon deserves to live.

Hawke, too, was a great man in the age of little men. The fame of the English navy had sunk to the lowest point. Its ships were rotten; its captains had lost the fighting tradition; its fleets were paralysed by a childish system of tactics which made a decisive battle almost impossible. Hawke describes the *Portland*, a ship of which he was in command, as "iron-sick"; the wood was too rotten, that is, to hold the iron bolts, so that "not a man in the ship had a dry place to sleep in." His men were "tumbling down with scurvy"; his mainmast was so pulverised by dry rot that a walking-stick could be thrust into it. Of another ship, the *Ramilies* —his favourite ship, too—he says, "It became waterlogged whenever it blowed hard." The ships' bottoms grew a rank crop of grass, slime, shells, barnacles, &c., till the sluggish vessels needed almost a gale to move them. Marines were not yet invented; the navy had no uniform. The French ships of that day were better built, better armed, and sometimes better fought than British ships. A British 70-gun ship in armament and weight of fire was only equal to a French ship of 52 guns. Every considerable fight was promptly followed by a crop of court-martials, in which captains were tried for misconduct before the enemy, such as to-day is unthinkable. Admiral Matthews was broken by court-martial for having, with an excess of daring, pierced the French line off Toulon, and thus sacrificed pedantic tactics to victory. But the list of court-martials held during the second quarter of the eighteenth century on British captains for beginning to fight too late, or for leaving off too soon, would, if published, astonish this generation. After the fight off Toulon in 1744, two admirals and six post-captains were court-martialled. Admiral Byng was shot on his own deck, not exactly as Voltaire's *mot* describes it, *pour encourager les autres*, and not quite for cowardice, for Byng was no coward. But he had no gleam of unselfish patriotic fire, and nothing of the gallant fighting impulse we have learned to believe is characteristic of the British sailor. He lost Minorca, and disgraced the British flag because he was too dainty to face the stern discomforts of a fight. The corrupt and ignoble temper of English politics—the legacy of Walpole's evil régime—poisoned the blood of the navy. No one can have forgotten Macaulay's picture of New-castle, at that moment Prime Minister of England; the sly, greedy, fawning politician, as corrupt as Walpole, without his genius; without honour, without truth, who loved office only less than he loved his own neck. A Prime Minister like Newcastle made possible an admiral like Byng. Horace Walpole tells the story of how, when the much-enduring British public broke into one of its rare but terrible fits of passion after the disgrace of Minorca, and Newcastle was trembling for his own head, a deputation from the city of London waited upon him, demanding that Byng should be put upon his trial. "Oh, indeed," replied Newcastle, with fawning gestures, "he shall be tried immediately. He shall be hanged directly!" It was an age of base men, and the navy —neglected, starved, dishonoured—had lost the great traditions of the past, and did not yet feel the thrill of the nobler spirit soon to sweep over it.

But in 1759 the dazzling intellect and masterful will of the first Pitt controlled the fortunes of England, and the spirit of the nation was beginning to awake. Burns and Wilberforce and the younger Pitt were born that year; Minden was fought; Wolfe saw with dying eyes the French battalions broken on the plains of Abraham and Canada won. But the great event of the year is Hawke's defeat of Conflans off Quiberon. Hawke was the son of a barrister; he entered the navy at fourteen years of age as a volunteer, obtained the rating of an able seaman at nineteen years of age, was a third lieutenant at twenty-four, and became captain at thirty. He knew the details of his profession as well as any sea-dog of the forecastle, was quite modern in the keen and humane interest he took in his men, had something of Wellington's high-minded allegiance to duty, while his fighting had a stern but sober thoroughness worthy of Cromwell's

Ironsides. The British people came to realise that he was a sailor with the strain of a bulldog in him; an indomitable fighter, who, ordered to blockade a hostile port, would hang on, in spite of storms and scurvy, while he had a man left who could pull a rope or fire a gun; a fighter, too, of the type dear to the British imagination, who took the shortest course to the enemy's line, and would exchange broadsides at pistol-shot distance while his ship floated.

In 1759 a great French army threatened the shores of England. At Havre and Dunkirk huge flotillas of flat-bottomed boats lay at their moorings; 18,000 French veterans were ready to embark. A great fleet under the command of Conflans—one of the ablest seamen France has ever produced—was gathered at Brest. A French squadron was to break out of Toulon, join Conflans, sweep the narrow seas, and convoy the French expedition to English shores. The strategy, if it had succeeded, might have changed the fate of the world.

To Hawke was entrusted the task of blockading Conflans in Brest, and a greater feat of seamanship is not to be found in British records. The French fleet consisted of 25 ships, manned by 15,200 men, and carrying 1598 guns. The British fleet numbered 23 ships, with 13,295 men, and carrying 1596 guns. The two fleets, that is, were nearly equal, the advantage, on the whole, being on the side of the French. Hawke therefore had to blockade a fleet equal to his own, the French ships lying snugly in harbour, the English ships scourged by November gales and rolling in the huge seas of the Bay of Biscay. Sir Cloudesley Shovel, himself a seaman of the highest quality, said that "an admiral would deserve to be broke who kept great ships out after the end of September, and to be shot if after October." Hawke maintained his blockade of Brest for six months. His captains broke down in health, his men were dying from scurvy, the bottoms of his ships grew foul; it was a stormy season in the stormiest of seas. Again and again the wild north-west gales blew the British admiral off his cruising ground. But he fought his way back, sent his ships, singly or in couples, to Torbay or Plymouth for a moment's breathing space, but himself held on, with a grim courage and an unslumbering vigilance which have never been surpassed. On November 6, a tremendous westerly gale swept over the English cruising-ground. Hawke battled with it for three days, and then ran, storm-driven and half-dismantled, to Torbay for shelter on the 10th. He put to sea again on the 12th. The gale had veered round to the south-west, but blew as furiously as ever, and Hawke was once more driven back on the 13th to Torbay. He struggled out again on the 14th, to find that the French had escaped! The gale that blew Hawke from his post brought a French squadron down the Channel, which ran into Brest and joined Conflans there; and on the 14th, when Hawke was desperately fighting his way back to his post, Conflans put to sea, and, with the gale behind him, ran on his course to Quiberon. There he hoped to brush aside the squadron keeping guard over the French transports, embark the powerful French force assembled there, and swoop down on the English coast. The wild weather, Conflans reckoned, would keep Hawke storm-bound in Torbay till this scheme was carried out.

But Hawke with his whole fleet, fighting his way in

the teeth of the gale, reached Ushant on the very day Conflans broke out of Brest, and, fast as the French fleet ran before the gale, the white sails of Hawke's ships, showing over the stormy rim of the horizon, came on the Frenchman's track. Hawke's frigates, outrunning those heavy sea-waggons, his line-of-battle ships, hung on Conflans' rear. The main body of the British fleet followed, staggering under their pyramids of sails, with wet decks and the wild north-west gale on their quarter. Hawke's best sailers gained steadily on the laggards of Conflans' fleet. Had Hawke obeyed the puerile tactics of his day he would have dressed his line and refused to attack at all unless he could bring his entire fleet into action. But, as Hawke himself said afterwards, he "had determined to attack them in the old way and make downright work of them," and he signalled his leading ships to attack the moment they brought an enemy's ship within fire. Conflans could not abandon his slower ships, and he reluctantly swung round his van and formed line to meet the attack.

As the main body of the English came up, the French admiral suddenly adopted a strategy which might well have baffled a less daring adversary than Hawke. He ran boldly in shore towards the mouth of the Vilaine. It was a wild stretch of most dangerous coast; the granite Breton hills above; splinters of rocky islets, on which the huge sea rollers tore themselves into white foam, below; and more dangerous still, and stretching far out to sea, wide reaches of shoal and quicksand. From the north-west the gale blew more wildly than ever; the sky was black with flying clouds; on the Breton hills the spectators clustered in thousands. The roar of the furious breakers and the shrill note of the gale filled the very air with tumult. Conflans had pilots familiar with the coast, yet it was bold seamanship on his part to run down to a lee shore on such a day of tempest. Hawke had no pilots and no charts; but he saw before him, half hidden in mist and spray, the great hulls of the ships over which he had kept watch so long in Brest harbour, and he anticipated Nelson's strategy forty years afterwards. "Where there is room for the enemy to swing," said Nelson, "there is room for me to anchor." "Where there's a passage for the enemy," argued Hawke, "there is a passage for me! Where a Frenchman can sail, an Englishman can follow! Their pilots shall be ours. If they go to pieces in the shoals, they will serve as beacons for us."

And so, on the wild November afternoon, with the great billows that the Bay of Biscay hurls on that stretch of iron-bound coast riding shoreward in league-long rollers, Hawke flung himself into the boiling caldron of rocks and shoals and quicksands. No more daring deed was ever done at sea. Measured by mere fighting courage, there were thousands of men in the British fleet as brave as Hawke. But the iron nerve that, without an instant's pause, in a scene so wild, on a shore so perilous, and a sea sown so thick with unknown dangers, flung a whole fleet into battle, was probably possessed by no other man than Hawke amongst the 30,000 gallant sailors who fought at Quiberon.

The fight, taking all its incidents into account, is perhaps as dramatic as anything known in the history of war. The British ships came rolling on, grim and silent, throwing huge sheets of spray from their bluff bows. An 80-gun French ship, *Le Formidable*, lay in their track, and each huge British liner, as it swept past to attack the main body of the French, vomited on the unfortunate *Le Formidable* a dreadful broadside. And upon each British ship, in turn, as it rolled past in spray and flame, the gallant Frenchman flung an answering broadside. Soon the thunder of the guns deepened as ship after ship found its antagonist. The short November day was already darkening; the thunder of surf and of tempest answered in yet wilder notes the deep-throated guns; the wildly rolling fleets offered one of the strangest sights the sea has ever witnessed.

Soon Hawke himself, in the *Royal George,* of 100 guns, came on, stern and majestic, seeking some fitting antagonist. This was the great ship that afterwards sank ignobly at its anchorage at Spithead, with "twice four hundred men," a tale which, for every English boy, is made famous in Cowper's immortal ballad. But what an image of terror and of battle the *Royal George* seemed as in the bitter November storm she bore down on the French fleet! Hawke disdained meaner foes, and bade his pilot lay him alongside Conflans' flagship, *Le Soleil Royal.* Shoals were foaming on every side, and the pilot warned Hawke he could not carry the *Royal George* farther in without risking the ship. "You have done your duty," said Hawke, "in pointing out the risk; and now lay me alongside of *Le Soleil Royal.*"

A French 70-gun ship, *La Superbe*, threw itself betwixt Hawke and Conflans. Slowly the huge mass of the *Royal George* bore up, so as to bring its broadside to bear on *La Superbe,* and then the English guns broke into a tempest of flame. Through spray and mist the masts of the unfortunate Frenchman seemed to tumble; a tempest of cries was heard; the British sailors ran back their guns to reload. A sudden gust cleared the atmosphere, and *La Superbe* had vanished. Her topmasts gleamed wet, for a moment, through the green seas, but with her crew of 650 men she had sunk, as though crushed by a thunderbolt, beneath a single broadside from the *Royal George*. Then from the nearer hills the crowds of French spectators saw Hawke's blue flag and Conflans' white pennon approach each other, and the two great ships, with slanting decks and fluttering canvas, and rigging blown to leeward, began their fierce duel. Other French ships crowded to their admiral's aid, and at one time no less than seven French line-of-battle ships were pouring their fire into the mighty and shot-torn bulk of the *Royal George*.

Howe, in the *Magnanime*, was engaged in fierce conflict, meanwhile, with the *Thesée*, when a sister English ship, the *Montague*, was flung by a huge sea on the quarter of Howe's ship, and practically disabled it. The *Torbay*, under Captain Keppel, took Howe's place with the *Thesée*, and both ships had their lower-deck ports open, so as to fight with their heaviest guns. The unfortunate Frenchman rolled to a great sea; the wide-open ports dipped, the green water rushed through, quenched the fire of the guns, and swept the sailors from their quarters. The great ship shivered, rolled over still more wildly, and then, with 700 men, went down like a stone. The British ship, with better luck and better seamanship, got its ports closed and was saved. Several French ships by this time had struck, but the sea was too wild to allow them to be taken possession of. Night was falling fast, the roar of the tempest still deepened, and no less than seven huge French liners, throwing their guns overboard, ran for shelter across the bar of the Vilaine, the pursuing English following them almost within reach of the spray flung from the rocks. Hawke then, by signals, brought his fleet to anchor for the night under the lee of the island of Dumet.

It was a wild night, filled with the thunder of the surf and the shriek of the gale, and all through it, as the English ships rode, madly straining at their anchors, they could hear the sounds of distress guns. One of the ships that perished that night was a fine English seventy-four, the *Resolution*. The morning broke as wild as the night. To leeward two great line-of-battle ships could be seen on the rocks; but in the very middle of the English fleet, its masts gone, its hull battered with shot, was the flagship of Conflans, *Le Soleil Royal*. In the darkness and tempest of the night the unfortunate Frenchman, all unwitting, had anchored in the very midst of his foes. As soon as, through the grey and misty light of the November dawn, the English ships were discovered, Conflans cut his cables and drifted ashore. The *Essex*, 64 guns, was ordered to pursue her, and her captain, an impetuous Irishman, obeyed his orders so literally that he too ran ashore, and the *Essex* became a total wreck.

"When I consider," Hawke wrote to the Admiralty, "the season of the year, the hard gales on the day of action, a flying enemy, the shortness of the day, and the coast they were on, I can boldly affirm that all that could possibly be done has been done." History confirms that judgment. There is no other record of a great sea-fight fought under conditions so wild, and scarcely any other sea-battle has achieved results more decisive. Trafalgar itself scarcely exceeds it in the quality of effectiveness. Quiberon saved England from invasion. It destroyed for the moment the naval power of France. Its political results in France cannot be described here, but they were of the first importance. The victory gave a new complexion to English naval warfare. Rodney and Howe were Hawke's pupils; Nelson himself, who was a post-captain when Hawke died, learned his tactics in Hawke's school. No sailor ever served England better than Hawke. And yet, such is the irony of human affairs, that on the very day when Hawke was adding the thunder of his guns to the diapason of surf and tempest off Quiberon, and crushing the fleet that threatened England with invasion, a London mob was burning his effigy for having allowed the French to escape his blockade.

GENERAL PICTON

After a painting by SIR MARTIN ARCHER SHEE, P.R.A.

THE NIGHT ATTACK ON BADAJOS

"Hand to hand, and foot to foot:
Nothing there, save death, was mute:
Stroke, and thrust, and flash, and cry
For quarter or for victory,
Mingle there with the volleying thunder,
Which makes the distant cities wonder
How the sounding battle goes,
If with them, or for their foes;
If they must mourn, or must rejoice
In that annihilating voice,
Which pierces the deep hills through and through
With an echo dread and new.
  .   .   .   .
From the point of encountering blades to the hilt,
Sabres and swords with blood were gilt;
But the rampart is won, and the spoil begun,
And all but the after carnage done."
—BYRON.

IT would be difficult to find in the whole history of war a more thrilling and heroic chapter than that which tells the story of the six great campaigns of the Peninsular war. This was, perhaps, the least selfish war of which history tells. It was not a war of aggrandisement or of conquest: it was waged to deliver not merely Spain, but the whole of Europe, from that military despotism with which the genius and ambition of Napoleon threatened to overwhelm the civilised world. And on what a scale Great Britain, when aroused, can fight, let the Peninsular war tell. At its close the fleets of Great Britain rode triumphant on every sea; and in the Peninsula between 1808-14 her land forces fought and won nineteen pitched battles, made or sustained ten fierce and bloody sieges, took four great fortresses, twice expelled the French from Portugal and once from Spain. Great Britain expended in these campaigns more than £100,000,000 sterling on her own troops, besides subsidising the forces of Spain and Portugal. This "nation of shopkeepers" proved that when kindled to action it could wage war on a scale and in a fashion that might have moved the wonder of Alexander or of Cæsar, and from motives, it may be added, too lofty for either Cæsar or Alexander so much as to comprehend. It is worth while to tell afresh the story of some of the more picturesque incidents in that great strife.

On April 6, 1812, Badajos was stormed by Wellington; and the story forms one of the most tragical and splendid incidents in the military history of the world. Of "the night of horrors at Badajos," Napier says, "posterity can scarcely be expected to credit the tale." No tale, however, is better authenticated, or, as an example of what disciplined human valour is capable of achieving, better deserves to be told. Wellington was preparing for his great forward movement into Spain, the campaign which led to Vittoria, the battle in which "40,000 Frenchmen were beaten in forty minutes." As a preliminary he had to capture, under the vigilant eyes of Soult and Marmont, the two great border fortresses, Ciudad Rodrigo and Badajos. He had, to use Napier's phrase, "jumped with both feet" on the first-named fortress, and captured it in twelve days with a loss of 1200 men and 90 officers.

But Badajos was a still harder task. The city stands on a rocky ridge which forms the last spur of the

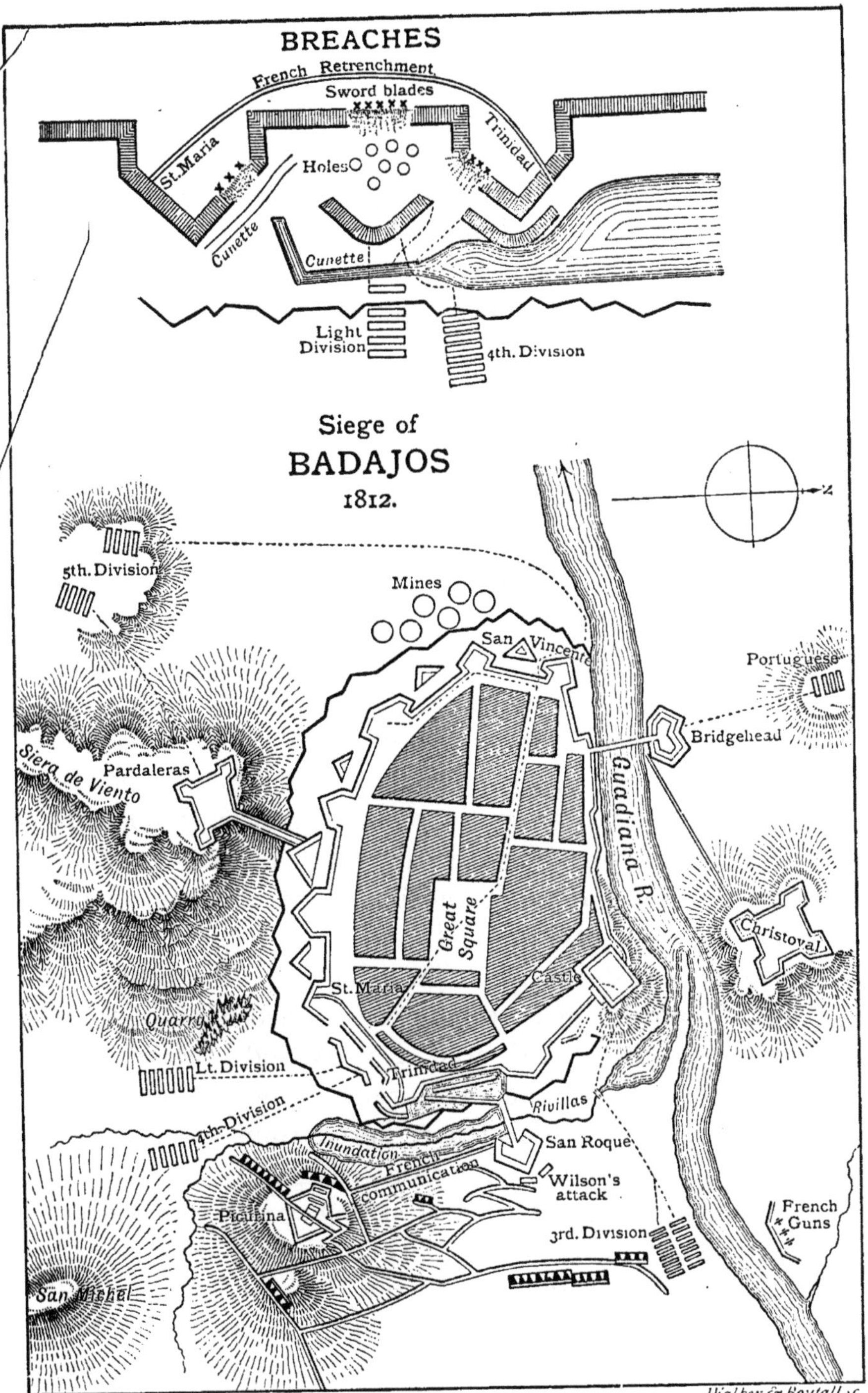

from Napier's "Peninsular War."

Walker & Boutall sc.

Toledo range, and is of extraordinary strength. The river Rivillas falls almost at right angles into the Guadiana, and in the angle formed by their junction stands Badajos, oval in shape, girdled with elaborate defences, with the Guadiana 500 yards wide as its defence to the north, the Rivillas serving as a wet ditch to the west, and no less than five great fortified outposts—Saint Roque, Christoval, Picurina, Pardaleras, and a fortified bridge-head across the Guadiana—as the outer zone of its defences. Twice the English had already assailed Badajos, but assailed it in vain. It was now held by a garrison 5000 strong, under a soldier, General Phillipson, with a real genius for defence, and the utmost art had been employed in adding to its defences. On the other hand Wellington had no means of transport and no battery train, and had to make all his preparations under the keen-eyed vigilance of the French. Perhaps the strangest collection of artillery ever employed in a great siege was that which Wellington collected from every available quarter and used at Badajos. Of the fifty-two pieces, some dated from the days of Philip II. and the Spanish Armada, some were cast in the reign of Philip III., others in that of John IV. of Portugal, who reigned in 1640; there were 24-pounders of George II.'s day, and Russian naval guns; the bulk of the extraordinary medley being obsolete brass engines which required from seven to ten minutes to cool between each discharge.

Wellington, however, was strong in his own warlike genius and in the quality of the troops he commanded. He employed 18,000 men in the siege, and it may well be doubted whether—if we put the question of equipment aside—a more perfect fighting instrument than the force under his orders ever existed. The men were veterans, but the officers on the whole were young, so there was steadiness in the ranks and fire in the leading. Hill and Graham covered the siege, Picton and Barnard, Kempt and Colville led the assaults. The trenches were held by the third, fourth, and fifth divisions, and by the famous light division. Of the latter it has been said that the Macedonian phalanx of Alexander the Great, the Tenth Legion of Cæsar, the famous Spanish infantry of Alva, or the iron soldiers who followed Cortes to Mexico, did not exceed it in warlike quality. Wellington's troops, too, had a personal grudge against Badajos, and had two defeats to avenge. Perhaps no siege in history, as a matter of fact, ever witnessed either more furious valour in the assault, or more of cool and skilled courage in the defence. The siege lasted exactly twenty days, and cost the besiegers 5000 men, or an average loss of 250 per day. It was waged throughout in stormy weather, with the rivers steadily rising, and the tempests perpetually blowing; yet the thunder of the attack never paused for an instant.

Wellington's engineers attacked the city at the eastern end of the oval, where the Rivillas served it as a gigantic wet ditch; and the Picurina, a fortified hill, ringed by a ditch fourteen feet deep, a rampart sixteen feet high, and a zone of mines, acted as an outwork. Wellington, curiously enough, believed in night attacks, a sure proof of his faith in the quality of the men he commanded; and on the eighth night of the siege, at nine o'clock, 500 men of the third division were suddenly flung on the Picurina. The fort broke into a ring of flame, by the light of which the dark figures of the stormers were seen leaping with fierce hardihood into the ditch and struggling madly up the ramparts, or tearing furiously at the palisades. But the defences were strong, and the assailants fell literally in scores. Napier tells how "the axemen of the light division, compassing the fort like prowling wolves," discovered the gate at the rear, and so broke into the fort. The engineer officer who led the attack declares that "the place would never have been taken had it not been for the coolness of these men" in absolutely walking round the fort to its rear, discovering the gate, and hewing it down under a tempest of bullets. The assault lasted an hour, and in that period, out of the 500 men who attacked, no less than 300, with 19 officers, were killed or wounded! Three men out of every five in the attacking force, that is, were disabled, and yet they won!

There followed twelve days of furious industry, of trenches pushed tirelessly forward through mud and wet, and of cannonading that only ceased when the guns grew too hot to be used. Captain MacCarthy, of the 50th Regiment, has left a curious little monograph on the siege, full of incidents, half tragic and half amusing, but which show the temper of Wellington's troops. Thus he tells how an engineer officer, when marking out the ground for a breaching-battery very near the wall, which was always lined with French soldiers in eager search of human targets, "used to challenge them to prove the perfection of their shooting by lifting up the skirts of his coat in defiance several times in the course of his survey; driving in his stakes and measuring his distances with great deliberation, and concluding by an extra shake of his coat-tails and an ironical bow before he stepped under shelter!"

On the night of April 6, Wellington determined to assault. No less than seven attacks were to be delivered. Two of them—on the bridge-head across the Guadiana and on the Pardaleras—were mere feints. But on the extreme right Picton with the third division was to cross the Rivillas and escalade the castle, whose walls rose time-stained and grim, from eighteen to twenty-four feet high. Leith with the fifth division was to attack the opposite or western extremity of the town, the bastion of St. Vincente, where the glacis was mined, the ditch deep, and the scarp thirty feet high. Against the actual breaches Colville and Andrew Barnard were to lead the light division and the fourth division, the former attacking the bastion of Santa Maria and the latter the Trinidad. The hour was fixed for ten o'clock, and the story of that night attack, as told in Napier's immortal prose, is one of the great battle-pictures of literature; and any one who tries to tell the tale will find himself slipping insensibly into Napier's cadences.

The night was black; a strange silence lay on rampart and trench, broken from time to time by the deep voices of the sentinels that proclaimed all was well in Badajos. "*Sentinelle garde à vous*," the cry of the sentinels, was translated by the British private as "All's well in Badahoo!" A lighted carcass thrown from the castle discovered Picton's men standing in ordered array, and compelled them to attack at once. MacCarthy, who acted as guide across the tangle of wet trenches and the narrow bridge that spanned the Rivillas, has left an amusing account of the scene. At one time Picton declared MacCarthy was leading them wrong, and, drawing his sword, swore he would cut him down. The column reached the trench, however, at the foot of the castle walls, and was instantly overwhelmed with the fire of the besieged. MacCarthy says we can only picture the scene by " supposing that all the stars, planets, and meteors of the firmament, with innumerable moons emitting smaller ones in their course, were descending on the heads of the besiegers." MacCarthy himself, a typical and gallant Irishman, addressed his general with the exultant remark, " 'Tis a glorious night, sir—a glorious night!" and, rushing forward to the head of the stormers, shouted, " Up with the ladders!" The five ladders were raised, the troops swarmed up, an officer leading, but the first files were at once crushed by cannon fire, and the ladders slipped into the angle of the abutments. " Dreadful their fall," records MacCarthy of the slaughtered stormers, " and appalling their appearance at daylight." One ladder remained, and, a private soldier leading, the eager red-coated crowd swarmed up it. The brave fellow leading was shot as soon as his head appeared above the parapet; but the next man to him—again a private—leaped over the parapet, and was followed quickly by others, and this thin stream of desperate men climbed singly, and in the teeth of the flashing musketry, up that solitary ladder, and carried the castle.

In the meanwhile the fourth and light divisions had flung themselves with cool and silent speed on the breaches. The storming party of each division leaped into the ditch. It was mined, the fuse was kindled, and the ditch, crowded with eager soldiery, became in a moment a sort of flaming crater, and the storming parties, 500 strong, were in one fierce explosion dashed to pieces. In the light of that dreadful flame the whole scene became visible—the black ramparts, crowded with dark figures and glittering arms, on the one side; on the other the red columns of the British, broad and deep, moving steadily forward like a stream of human lava. The light division stood at the brink of the smoking ditch for an instant, amazed at the sight. "Then," says Napier, "with a shout that matched even the sound of the explosion," they leaped into it and swarmed up to the breach. The fourth division came running up and descended with equal fury, but the ditch opposite the Trinidad was filled with water; the head of the division leaped into it, and, as Napier puts it, "about 100 of the fusiliers, the men of Albuera, perished there." The breaches were impassable. Across the top of the great slope of broken wall glittered a fringe of sword-blades, sharp-pointed, keen-edged on both sides, fixed in ponderous beams chained together and set deep in the ruins. For ten feet in front the ascent was covered with loose planks, studded with sharp iron points. Behind the glittering edge of sword-blades stood the solid ranks of the French, each man supplied with three muskets, and their fire scourged the British ranks like a tempest.

Hundreds had fallen, hundreds were still falling; but the British clung doggedly to the lower slopes, and every few minutes an officer would leap forward with a shout, a swarm of men would instantly follow him, and, like leaves blown by a whirlwind, they swept up the ascent. But under the incessant fire of the French the assailants melted away. One private reached the sword-blades, and actually thrust his head beneath them till his brains were beaten out, so desperate was his resolve to get into Badajos. The breach, as Napier describes it, "yawning and glittering with steel, resembled the mouth of a huge dragon belching forth smoke and flame." But for two hours, and until 2000 men had fallen, the stubborn British persisted in their attacks. Currie, of the 52nd, a cool and most daring soldier, found a narrow ramp beyond the Santa Maria breach only half-ruined; he forced his way back through the tumult and carnage to where Wellington stood watching the scene, obtained an unbroken battalion from the reserve, and led it towards the broken ramp. But his men were caught in the whirling madness of the ditch and swallowed up in the tumult. Nicholas, of the engineers, and Shaw, of the 43rd, with some fifty soldiers, actually climbed into the Santa Maria bastion, and from thence tried to force their way into the breach. Every man was shot down except Shaw, who stood alone on the bastion. "With inexpressible coolness he looked at his watch, said it was too late to carry the breaches," and then leaped down! The British could not penetrate the breach; but they would not retreat. They could only die where they stood. The buglers of the reserve were sent to the crest of the glacis to sound the retreat; the troops in the ditch would not believe the signal to be genuine, and struck their own buglers who attempted to repeat it. "Gathering in dark groups, and leaning on their muskets," says Napier, "they looked up in sullen desperation at Trinidad, while the enemy, stepping out on the ramparts, and aiming their shots by the light of fireballs, which they threw over, asked as their victims fell, 'Why they did not come into Badajos.'"

All this while, curiously enough, Picton was actually in Badajos, and held the castle securely, but made no attempt to clear the breach. On the extreme west of the town, however, at the bastion of San Vincente, the fifth division made an attack as desperate as that which was failing at the breaches. When the stormers actually reached the bastion, the Portuguese battalions, who formed part of the attack, dismayed by the tremendous fire which broke out on them, flung down their ladders and fled. The British, however, snatched the ladders up, forced the barrier, jumped into the ditch, and tried to climb the walls. These were thirty feet high, and the ladders were too short. A mine was sprung in the ditch under the soldiers' feet; beams of wood, stones, broken waggons, and live shells were poured upon their heads from above. Showers of grape from the flank swept the ditch.

The stubborn soldiers, however, discovered a low spot in the rampart, placed three ladders against it, and climbed with reckless valour. The first man was pushed up by his comrades; he, in turn, dragged others up, and the unconquerable British at length broke through and swept the bastion. The tumult still stormed and raged at the eastern breaches, where the men of the light and fourth division were dying sullenly, and the men of the fifth division marched at speed across the town to take the great eastern breach in the rear. The streets were empty, but the silent houses were bright with lamps. The men of the fifth pressed on; they captured mules carrying ammunition to the breaches, and the French, startled by the tramp of the fast-approaching column, and finding themselves taken in the rear, fled. The light and fourth divisions broke through the gap hitherto barred by flame and steel, and Badajos was won!

In that dreadful night assault the English lost 3500 men. "Let it be considered," says Napier, "that this frightful carnage took place in the space of less than a hundred yards square—that the slain died not all suddenly, nor by one manner of death—that some perished by steel, some by shot, some by water; that some were crushed and mangled by heavy weights, some trampled upon, some dashed to atoms by the fiery explosions—that for hours this destruction was endured without shrinking, and the town was won at last. Let these things be considered, and it must be admitted a British army bears with it an awful power. And false would it be to say the French were feeble men. The garrison stood and fought manfully and with good discipline, behaving worthily. Shame there was none on any side. Yet who shall do justice to the bravery of the British soldiers or the noble emulation of the officers? . . . No age, no nation, ever sent forth braver troops to battle than those who stormed Badajos."

LORD COCHRANE

After a painting by WALTON

THE FIRE-SHIPS IN THE BASQUE ROADS

" Ship after ship, the whole night long, their high-built galleons came ;
Ship after ship, the whole night long, with her battle-thunder and flame ;
Ship after ship, the whole night long, drew back with her dead and her shame.
For some were sunk and many were shattered, and so could fight us no more—
God of battles, was ever a battle like this in the world before?"
—TENNYSON.

ON the night of April 11, 1809, Lord Cochrane steered his floating mine against the gigantic boom that covered the French fleet lying in Aix Roads. The story is one of the most picturesque and exciting in the naval annals of Great Britain. Marryat has embalmed the great adventure and its chief actor in the pages of "Frank Mildmay," and Lord Cochrane himself—like the Earl of Peterborough in the seventeenth century, who captured Barcelona with a handful of men, and Gordon in the nineteenth century, who won great battles in China walking-stick in hand—was a man who stamped himself, as with characters of fire, upon the popular imagination.

To the courage of a knight-errant Cochrane added the shrewd and humorous sagacity of a Scotchman. If he had commanded fleets he would have rivalled the victories of Nelson, and perhaps even have outshone the Nile and Trafalgar. And to warlike genius of the first order Cochrane added a certain weird and impish ingenuity which his enemies found simply resistless. Was there ever a cruise in naval history like that of Cochrane in his brig misnamed the *Speedy*, a mere coasting tub that would neither steer nor tack, and whose entire broadside Cochrane himself could carry in his pockets! But in this wretched little brig, with its four-pounders, Cochrane captured in one brief year more than 50 vessels carrying an aggregate of 122 guns, took 500 prisoners, kept the whole Spanish coast, off which he cruised, in perpetual alarm, and finished by attacking and capturing a Spanish frigate, the *Gamo*, of 32 heavy guns and 319 men. What we have called the impish daring and resource of Cochrane is shown in this strange fight. He ran the little *Speedy* close under the guns of the huge *Gamo*, and the Spanish ship was actually unable to depress its guns sufficiently to harm its tiny antagonist. When the Spaniards tried to board, Cochrane simply shoved his pigmy craft a few yards away from the side of his foe, and this curious fight went on for an hour. Then, in his turn, Cochrane boarded, leaving nobody but the doctor on board the *Speedy*. But he played the Spaniards a characteristic trick. One half his men boarded the *Gamo* by the head, with their faces elaborately blackened; and when, out of the white smoke forward, some forty demons with black faces broke upon the astonished Spaniards, they naturally regarded the whole business as partaking of the black art, and incontinently fled below! The number of Spaniards killed and wounded in this fight by the little *Speedy* exceeded the number of its own entire crew; and when the fight was over, 45 British sailors had to keep guard over 263 Spanish prisoners.

Afterwards, in command of the *Impérieuse*, a fine frigate, Cochrane played a still more dashing part on the Spanish coast, destroying batteries, cutting off supplies from the French ports, blowing up coast roads, and keeping perspiring battalions of the enemy marching to and fro to meet his descents. On the French coast, again, Cochrane held large bodies of French troops paralysed by his single frigate. He proposed to the English Government to take possession of the French islands in the Bay of Biscay, and to allow him, with a small squadron of frigates, to operate against the French seaboard. Had this request been granted, he says, "neither the Peninsular war nor its enormous cost to the nation from 1809 onwards would ever have been heard of!" "It would have been easy," he adds, "as it always will be easy in case of future wars, so to harass the French coasts as to find full employment for their troops at home, and so to render operations in foreign countries impossible." If England and France were once more engaged in war—*absit omen!*—the story of Cochrane's exploits on the Spanish and French coasts might prove a very valuable inspiration and object-lesson. Cochrane's professional reward for his great services in the *Impérieuse* was an official rebuke for expending more sails, stores, gunpowder and shot than any other captain afloat in the same time!

The fight in the Basque Roads, however—or rather in the Aix Roads—has great historical importance. It crowned the work of Trafalgar. It finally destroyed French power on the sea, and gave England an absolute supremacy. No fleet actions took place after its date between "the meteor flag" and the tricolour, for the simple reason that no French fleet remained in existence. Cochrane's fire-ships completed the work of the Nile and Trafalgar.

Early in 1809 the French fleet in Brest, long blockaded by Lord Gambier, caught the British napping, slipped out unobserved, raised the blockades at L'Orient and Rochefort, added the squadrons lying in these two places to its own strength, and, anchoring in the Aix Roads, prepared for a dash on the West Indies. The success with which the blockade at Brest had been evaded, and the menace offered to the West Indian trade, alarmed the British Admiralty. Lord Gambier, with a powerful fleet, kept guard outside the Aix Roads; but if the blockade failed once, it might fail again. Eager to destroy the last fleet France possessed, the Admiralty strongly urged Lord Gambier to attack the enemy with fire-ships; but Gambier, grown old, had visibly lost nerve, and he pronounced the use of fire-ships a "horrible and unchristian mode of warfare." Lord Mulgrave, the first Lord of the Admiralty, knowing Cochrane's ingenuity and daring, sent for him, and proposed to send him to the Basque Roads to invent and execute some plan for destroying the French fleet. The Scotchman was uppermost in Cochrane in this interview, and he declined the adventure on the ground that to send a young post-captain to execute such an enterprise would be regarded as an insult by the whole fleet, and he would have every man's hand against him. Lord Mulgrave, however, was peremptory, and Cochrane yielded, but on reaching the blockading fleet was met by a tempest of wrath from all his seniors. "Why," they asked, "was Cochrane sent out? We could have done the business as well as he. Why did not Lord Gambier let us do it?" Lord Gambier, who had fallen into a sort of gentle and pious melancholy, was really more occupied in distributing tracts among his crews than in trying to reach his enemies; and Harvey, his second in command, an old Trafalgar sea-dog, when Cochrane arrived with his commission, interviewed his admiral, denounced him in a white-heat on his own quarter-deck, and ended by telling him that "if Nelson had been there he would not have anchored in the Basque Roads at all, but would have dashed at the enemy at once." This outburst, no doubt, relieved Admiral Harvey's feelings, but it cost him his flag, and he was court-martialled, and dismissed from the service for the performance.

Cochrane, however, set himself with characteristic daring and coolness to carry out his task. The French fleet consisted of one huge ship of 120 guns, two of 80 guns, eight seventy-fours, a 50-gun ship, and two 40-gun frigates—fourteen ships in all. It was drawn up in two lines under the shelter of powerful shore batteries, with the frigates as out-guards. As a protection against fire-ships, a gigantic boom had been constructed half a mile in length, forming two sides of a triangle, with the apex towards the British fleet. Over this huge floating barrier powerful boat squadrons kept watch every night. Cochrane's plan of attack was marked by real genius. He constructed three explosion vessels, floating mines on the largest scale. Each of these terrific vessels contained no less than *fifteen hundred* barrels of gunpowder, bound together with cables, with wedges and moistened sand rammed down betwixt them; forming, in brief, one gigantic bomb, with 1500 barrels of gunpowder for its charge. On the top of this huge powder magazine was piled, as a sort of agreeable condiment, hundreds of live shells and thousands of hand grenades; the whole, by every form of marine ingenuity, compacted into a solid mass which, at the touch of a fuse, could be turned into a sort of floating Vesuvius. These were to be followed by a squadron of fire-ships. Cochrane who, better, perhaps, than any soldier or sailor that ever lived, knew how to strike at his foes through their own imagination, calculated that when these three huge explosion vessels, with twenty fire-ships behind them, went off in a sort of saltpetre earthquake, the astonished Frenchmen would imagine *every* fire-ship to be a floating mine, and, instead of trying to board them and divert them from their fleet, would be simply anxious to get out of their way with the utmost possible despatch. The French, meanwhile, having watched their enemy lying inert for weeks, and confident in the gigantic boom which acted as their shield to the front, and the show of batteries which kept guard over them on either flank and to the rear, awaited the coming attack in a spirit of half-contemptuous gaiety. They had struck their topmasts and unbent their sails, and by way of challenge dressed their fleet with flags. One ship, the *Calcutta*, had been captured from the English, and by way of special insult they hung out the British ensign under that ship's quarter-gallery, an affront whose deadly quality only a sailor can understand.

The night of the 9th set in stormily. The tide ran fast, and the skies were black and the sea heavy—so heavy, indeed, that the boats of the English fleet which were intended to follow and cover the fire-ships never left the side of the flagship. Cochrane, however, had called the officers commanding the fire-ships on board his frigate, given them their last instructions, and at half-past eight P.M. he himself, accompanied only by a lieutenant and four sailors, cut the moorings of the chief explosion vessel, and drifted off towards the French fleet. Seated, that is, on top of 1500 barrels of gunpowder and a sort of haystack of grenades, he calmly floated off, with a squadron of fire-ships behind him, towards the French fleet, backed by great shore batteries, with seventy-three armed boats as a line of skirmishers. "It seemed to me," says Marryat, who was an actor in the scene, "like entering the gates of hell!"

The great floating mine drifted on through blackness and storm till, just as it struck the boom, Cochrane, who previously made his five assistants get into the boat, with his own hand lit the fuse and in turn jumped into the boat. How frantically the little crew pulled to get clear of the ignited mine may be imagined; but wind and sea were against them. The fuse, which was calculated to burn for twelve minutes, lasted for only five. Then the 1500 barrels of gunpowder went simultaneously off, peopling the black sky with a flaming torrent of shells, grenades, and rockets, and raising a mountainous wave that nearly swamped the unfortunate boat and its crew. The fault of the fuse, however, saved the lives of the daring six, as the missiles from the exploding vessel fell far *outside* them. "The effect," says Cochrane, who, like Cæsar, could write history as well as make it, "constituted one of the grandest artificial spectacles imaginable. For a moment the sky was red with the lurid glare arising from the simultaneous ignition of 1500 barrels of powder. On this gigantic flash subsiding the air seemed alive with shells, grenades, rockets, and masses of timber, the wreck of the shattered vessel." Then came blackness, punctuated in flame by the explosion of the next floating mine. Then, through sea-wrack and night, came the squadron of fire-ships, each one a pyramid of kindling flame. But the first explosion had achieved all that Cochrane expected. It dismissed the huge boom into chips, and the French fleet lay open to attack. The captain of the second explosion vessel was so determined to do his work effectually that the entire crew was actually blown out of the vessel and one member of the party killed, while the toil of the boats in which, after the fire-ships had been abandoned, they and their crews had to fight their way back in the teeth of the gale, was so severe that several men died of mere fatigue. The physical effects of the floating mines and the drifting fire-ships, as a matter of fact, were not very great. The boom, indeed, was destroyed, but out of twenty fire-ships only four actually reached the enemy's position, and not one did any damage. Cochrane's explosion vessels, however, were addressed not so much to the French ships as to the alarmed imagination of French sailors, and the effect achieved was overwhelming. All the French ships save one cut or slipped their cables, and ran ashore in wild confusion. Cochrane cut the moorings of his explosion vessel at half-past eight o'clock; by midnight, or in less than four hours, the boom had been destroyed, and thirteen French ships—the solitary fleet that remained to France—were lying helplessly ashore. Never, perhaps, was a result so great achieved in a time so brief, in a fashion so dramatic, or with a loss so trifling.

When the grey morning broke, with the exception of two vessels, the whole French fleet was lying helplessly aground on the Palles shoal. Some were lying on their bilge with the keel exposed, others were frantically casting their guns overboard and trying to get afloat again. Meanwhile Gambier and the British fleet were lying fourteen miles distant in the Basque Roads, and Cochrane in the *Impérieuse* was watching, with powder-blackened face, the curious spectacle of the entire fleet he had driven ashore, and the yet more amazing spectacle of a British fleet declining to come in and finally destroy its enemy. For here comes a chapter in the story on which Englishmen do not love to dwell. Cochrane tried to whip the muddy-spirited Gambier into enterprise by emphatic and quick-following signal. At six A.M. he signalled, "*All the enemy's ships except two are on shore,*" but this extracted from drowsy Gambier no other response than the answering pennant. Cochrane repeated his impatient signals at half-hour intervals, and with emphasis ever more shrill—"*The enemy's ships can be destroyed*"; "*Half the fleet can destroy the enemy*"; "*The frigates alone can destroy the enemy*"; but still no response save the indifferent pennant. As the tide flowed in, the French ships showed signs of getting afloat, and Cochrane signalled, "*The enemy is preparing to heave off*"; even this brought no response from the pensive Gambier. At eleven o'clock the British fleet weighed and stood in, but then, to Cochrane's speechless wrath, re-anchored at a distance of three and a half miles, and by this time two of the French three-deckers were afloat.

Gambier finally despatched a single mortar-vessel in to bombard the stranded ships, but by this time Cochrane had become desperate. He adopted a device which recalls Nelson's use of his blind eye at Copenhagen. At one o'clock he hove his anchor atrip and drifted, stern foremost, towards the enemy. He dare not make sail lest his trick should be detected and a signal of recall hoisted on the flagship. Cochrane coolly determined, in a word, to force the hand of his sluggish admiral. He drifted with his solitary frigate down to the hostile fleet and batteries, which Gambier thought it scarcely safe to attack with eleven ships of the line. When near the enemy's position he suddenly made sail and ran up the signal, "*In want of assistance*"; next followed a yet more peremptory message, "*In distress.*" Even Gambier could not see an English frigate destroyed under the very guns of an English fleet without moving to its help, and he sent some of his ships in. But meanwhile, Cochrane, though technically "in distress," was enjoying what he must have felt to be a singularly good time. He calmly took up a position which enabled him to engage an 80-gun ship, one of 74 guns, and, in particular, that French ship which, on the previous day, had hung the British flag under her quarter-gallery. For half-an-hour he fought these three ships single-handed, and the *Calcutta* actually struck to him, its captain afterwards being court-martialled and shot by the French themselves for surrendering to a frigate. Then the other British ships came up, and ship after ship of the French fleet struck or was destroyed. Night fell before the work was completed, and during the night Gambier, for some mysterious reason, recalled his ships; but Cochrane, in the *Impérieuse*, clung to his post. He persuaded Captain Seymour, in the *Pallas*, to remain with him, with four brigs, and with this tiny force he proposed to attack *L'Ocean*, the French flagship of 120 guns, which had just got afloat; but Gambier peremptorily recalled him at dawn, before the fight was renewed. Never before or since was a victory so complete and so nearly bloodless. Five seamen were killed in the fire-ships, and five in the attack on the French fleet and about twenty wounded; and with this microscopic "butcher's bill" a great fleet, the last naval hope of France, was practically destroyed. For so much does the genius and daring of a single man count!

That the French fleet was not utterly destroyed was due solely to Gambier's want of resolution. And yet, such is the irony of history, that of the two chief actors in this drama, Gambier, who marred it, was rewarded with the thanks of Parliament; Cochrane, who gave to it all its unique splendour, had his professional career abruptly terminated!

That wild night in the Aix Roads, and the solitary and daring attack on the French fleet which followed next day, were practically Cochrane's last acts as a British sailor. He achieved dazzling exploits under the flag of Chili and Brazil; but the most original warlike genius the English navy has ever known, fought no more battles for England.

THE MAN WHO SPOILED NAPOLEON'S "DESTINY"!

> "Oh, who shall lightly say that Fame
> Is nothing but an empty name!
> Whilst in that sound there is a charm
> The nerves to brace, the heart to warm.
> As, thinking of the mighty dead,
>   The young from slothful couch will start,
> And vow, with lifted hands outspread,
>   Like them to act a noble part?"
>   —JOANNA BAILLIE.

FROM March 18 to May 20, 1799—for more than sixty days and nights, that is—a little, half-forgotten, and more than half-ruined Syrian town was the scene of one of the fiercest and most dramatic sieges recorded in military history. And rarely has there been a struggle so apparently one-sided. A handful of British sailors and Turkish irregulars were holding Acre, a town without regular defences, against Napoleon, the most brilliant military genius of his generation, with an army of 10,000 war-hardened veterans, the "Army of Italy"—soldiers who had dared the snows of the Alps and conquered Italy, and to whom victory was a familiar experience. In their ranks military daring had reached, perhaps, its very highest point. And yet the sailors inside that ring of crumbling wall won! At the blood-stained trenches of Acre Napoleon experienced his first

SIR SIDNEY SMITH

After a painting by Sir R. K. Porter

defeat; and, years after, at St. Helena, he said of Sir Sidney Smith, the gallant sailor who baffled him, "That man made me miss my destiny." It is a curious fact that one Englishman thwarted Napoleon's career in the East, and another ended his career in the West, and it may be doubted which of the two Napoleon hated most —Wellington, who finally overthrew him at Waterloo, or Sidney Smith, who, to use Napoleon's own words, made him "miss his destiny," and exchange the empire of the East for a lonely pinnacle of rock in the Atlantic.

Sidney Smith was a sailor of the school of Nelson and of Dundonald—a man, that is, with a spark of that warlike genius which begins where mechanical rules end. He was a man of singular physical beauty, with a certain magnetism and fire about him which made men willing to die for him, and women who had never spoken to him fall headlong in love with him. His whole career is curiously picturesque. He became a middy at the tender age of eleven years; went through fierce sea-fights, and was actually mate of the watch when fourteen years old. He was a fellow-middy with William IV. in the fight off Cape St. Vincent, became commander when he was eighteen years of age, and captain before he was quite nineteen. But the British marine, even in those tumultuous days, scarcely yielded enough of the rapture of fighting to this post-captain in his teens. He took service under the Swedish flag, saw hard fighting against the Russians, became the close personal friend of the King, and was knighted by him. One of the feats at this period of his life with which tradition, with more or less of plausibility, credits Sidney Smith, is that of swimming by night through the Russian fleet, a distance of two miles, carrying a letter enclosed in a bladder to the Swedish admiral.

Sidney Smith afterwards entered the Turkish service. When war broke out betwixt France and England in 1790, he purchased a tiny craft at Smyrna, picked up in that port a hybrid crew, and hurried to join Lord Hood, who was then holding Toulon. When the British abandoned the port—and it is curious to recollect that the duel between Sidney Smith and Napoleon, which reached its climax at Acre, began here—Sidney Smith volunteered to burn the French fleet, a task which he performed with an audacity and skill worthy of Dundonald or Nelson, and for which the French never forgave him.

Sidney Smith was given the command of an English frigate, and fought a dozen brilliant fights in the Channel. He carried with his boats a famous French privateer off Havre de Grace; but during the fight on the deck of the captured ship it drifted into the mouth of the Seine above the forts. The wind dropped, the tide was too strong to be stemmed, and Sidney Smith himself was captured. He had so harried the French coast that the French refused to treat him as an ordinary prisoner of war, and threw him into that ill-omened prison, the Temple, from whose iron-barred windows the unfortunate sailor watched for two years the horrors of the Reign of Terror in its last stages, the tossing crowds, the tumbrils rolling past, crowded with victims for the guillotine. Sidney Smith escaped at last by a singularly audacious trick. Two confederates, dressed in dashing uniform, one wearing the dress of an adjutant, and the other that of an officer of still higher rank, presented themselves at the Temple with forged orders for the transfer of Sidney Smith.

The governor surrendered his prisoner, but insisted sending a guard of six men with him. The sham adjutant cheerfully acquiesced, but, after a moment's pause, turned to Sidney Smith, and said, if he would give his parole as an officer not to attempt to escape, they would dispense with the escort. Sidney Smith, with due gravity, replied to his confederate, "Sir, I swear on the faith of an officer to accompany you wherever you choose to conduct me." The governor was satisfied, and the two sham officers proceeded to "conduct" their friend with the utmost possible despatch to the French coast. Another English officer who had escaped — Captain Wright — joined Sidney Smith outside Rouen, and the problem was how to get through the barriers without a passport. Smith sent Wright on first, and he was duly challenged for his passport by the sentinel; whereupon Sidney Smith, with a majestic air of official authority, marched up and said in faultless Parisian French, "I answer for this citizen, I know him;" whereupon the deluded sentinel saluted and allowed them both to pass!

Sidney Smith's escape from the Temple made him a popular hero in England. He was known to have great influence with the Turkish authorities, and he was sent to the East in the double office of envoy-extraordinary to the Porte, and commander of the squadron at Alexandria. By one of the curious coincidences which marked Sidney Smith's career, he became acquainted while in the Temple with a French Royalist officer named Philippeaux, an engineer of signal ability, and who had been a schoolfellow and a close chum of Napoleon himself at Brienne. Smith took his French friend with him to the East, and he played a great part in the defence of Acre. Napoleon had swept north through the desert to Syria, had captured Gaza and Jaffa, and was about to attack Acre, which lay between him and his ultimate goal, Constantinople. Here Sidney Smith resolved to bar his way, and in his flagship the *Tigre*, with the *Theseus*, under Captain Miller, and two gunboats, he sailed to Acre to assist in its defence. Philippeaux took charge of the fortifications, and thus, in the breaches of a remote Syrian town, the quondam prisoner of the Temple and the ancient school friend of Napoleon joined hands to wreck that dream of a great Eastern empire which lurked in the cells of Napoleon's masterful intellect.

Acre represents a blunted arrow-head jutting out from a point in the Syrian coast. Napoleon could only attack, so to speak, the *neck* of the arrow, which was protected by a ditch and a weak wall, and flanked by towers; but Sidney Smith, having command of the sea, could sweep the four faces of the town with the fire of his guns, as well as command all the sea-roads in its vicinity. He guessed, from the delay of the French in opening fire, that they were waiting for their siege-train to arrive by sea. He kept vigilant watch, pounced on the French flotilla as it rounded the promontory of Mount Carmel, captured nine of the vessels, carried them with their guns and warlike material to Acre, and mounted his thirty-four captured pieces on the batteries of the town. Thus the disgusted French saw the very guns which were intended to batter down the defences of Acre—and which were glorious with the memories of a dozen victories in Italy—frowning at them, loaded with English powder and shot, and manned by English sailors.

It is needless to say that a siege directed by Napoleon —the siege of what he looked upon as a contemptible and almost defenceless town, the single barrier betwixt his ambition and its goal—was urged with amazing fire and vehemence. The wall was battered day and night, a breach fifty feet wide made, and more than twelve assaults delivered, with all the fire and daring of which French soldiers, gallantly led, are capable. So sustained was the fighting, that on one occasion the combat raged in the ditch and on the breach for *twenty-five* successive hours. So close and fierce was it that one half-ruined tower was held by *both* besiegers and besieged for twelve hours in succession, and neither would yield. At the breach, again, the two lines of desperately fighting men on repeated occasions clashed bayonets together, and wrestled and stabbed and died, till the survivors were parted by the barrier of the dead which grew beneath their feet.

Sidney Smith, however, fought like a sailor, and with all the cool ingenuity and resourcefulness of a sailor. His ships, drawn up on two faces of the town, smote the French stormers on either flank till they learned to build up a dreadful screen, made up partly of stones plucked from the breach, and partly of the dead bodies of their comrades. Smith, too, perched guns in all sorts of unexpected positions—a 24-pounder in the lighthouse, under the command of an exultant middy; two 68-pounders under the charge of "old Bray," the carpenter of the *Tigre*, and, as Sidney Smith himself reports, "one of the bravest and most intelligent men I ever served with"; and yet a third gun, a French brass 18-pounder, in one of the ravelins, under a master's mate. Bray dropped his shells with the nicest accuracy in the centre of the French columns as they swept up the breach, and the middy perched aloft, and the master's mate from the ravelin, smote them on either flank with case-shot, while the *Theseus* and the *Tigre* added to the tumult the thunder of their broadsides, and the captured French gunboats contributed the yelp of their lighter pieces.

The great feature of the siege, however, was the fierceness and the number of the sorties. Sidney Smith's sorties actually exceeded in number and vehemence Napoleon's assaults. He broke the strength of Napoleon's attacks, that is, by anticipating them. A crowd of Turkish irregulars, with a few naval officers leading them, and a solid mass of Jack-tars in the centre, would break from a sally-port, or rush vehemently down through the gap in the wall, and scour the French trenches, overturn the gabions, spike the guns, and slay the guards. The French reserves hurried fiercely up, always scourged, however, by the flank fire of the ships, and drove back the sortie. But the process was renewed the same night or the next day with unlessened fire and daring. The French engineers, despairing of success on the surface, betook themselves to mining; whereupon the besieged made a desperate sortie and reached the mouth of the mine. Lieutenant Wright, who led them, and who had already received two shots in his sword-arm, leaped down the mine followed by his sailors, slew the miners, destroyed their work, and safely regained the town.

The British sustained one startling disaster. Captain Miller of the *Theseus*, whose ammunition ran short, carefully collected such French shells as fell into the town without exploding, and duly returned them, alight, and supplied with better fuses, to their original senders. He had collected some seventy shells on the *Theseus*, and was preparing them for use against the French. The carpenter of the ship was endeavouring to get the fuses out of the loaded shells with an auger, and a middy undertook to assist him, in characteristic middy fashion, with a mallet and a spike-nail. A huge shell under his treatment suddenly exploded on the quarter-deck of the *Theseus*, and the other sixty-nine shells followed suit. The too ingenious middy disappeared into space; forty seamen, with Captain Miller himself, were killed; and forty-seven, including the two lieutenants of the ship, the chaplain, and the surgeon, were seriously wounded. The whole of the poop was blown to pieces, and the ship was left a wreck with fire breaking out at half-a-dozen points. The fire was subdued, and the *Theseus* survived in a half-gutted condition, but the disaster was a severe blow to Sir Sidney's resources.

As evening fell on May 7, the white sails of a fleet became visible over the sea rim, and all firing ceased while besiegers and besieged watched the approaching ships. Was it a French fleet or a Turkish? Did it bring succour to the besieged or a triumph to the besiegers? The approaching ships flew the crescent. It was the Turkish fleet from Rhodes bringing reinforcements. But the wind was sinking, and Napoleon, who had watched the approach of the hostile ships with feelings which may be guessed, calculated that there remained six hours before they could cast anchor in the bay. Eleven assaults had been already made, in which eight French generals and the best officers in every branch of the service had perished. There remained time for a twelfth assault. He might yet pluck victory from the very edge of defeat. At ten o'clock that night the French artillery was brought up close to the counterscarp to batter down the curtain, and a new breach was made. Lannes led his division against the shot-wrecked tower, and General Rimbaud took his grenadiers with a resistless rush through the new breach. All night the combat raged, the men fighting desperately hand to hand. When the rays of the level morning sun broke through the pall of smoke which hung sullenly over the combatants, the tricolour flew on the outer angle of the tower, and still the ships bringing reinforcements had not reached the harbour! Sidney Smith, at this crisis, landed every man from the English ships, and led them, pike in hand, to the breach, and the shouting and madness of the conflict awoke once more. To use Sidney Smith's own words, "the muzzles of the muskets touched each other—the spear-heads were locked together." But Sidney Smith's sailors, with the brave Turks who rallied to their help, were not to be denied.

Lannes' grenadiers were tumbled headlong from the tower, Lannes himself being wounded, while Rimbaud's brave men, who were actually past the breach, were swept into ruin, their general killed, and the French soldiers within the breach all captured or slain.

One of the dramatic incidents of the siege was the assault made by Kleber's troops. They had not taken part in the siege hitherto, but had won a brilliant victory over the Arabs at Mount Tabor. On reaching the camp, flushed with their triumph, and seeing how slight were the apparent defences of the town, they demanded clamorously to be led to the assault. Napoleon consented. Kleber, who was of gigantic stature, with a head of hair worthy of a German musicmaster or of a Soudan dervish, led his grenadiers to the edge of the breach and stood there, while with gesture and voice—a voice audible even above the fierce and sustained crackle of the musketry—he urged his men on. Napoleon, standing on a gun in the nearest French battery, watched the sight with eager eyes—the French grenadiers running furiously up the breach, the grim line of levelled muskets that barred it, the sudden roar of the English guns as from every side they smote the staggering French column. Vainly single officers struggled out of the torn mass, ran gesticulating up the breach, and died at the muzzles of the British muskets. The men could not follow, or only died as they leaped forward. The French grenadiers, still fighting, swearing, and screaming, were swept back past the point where Kleber stood, hoarse with shouting, black with gunpowder, furious with rage. The last assault on Acre had failed. The French sick, field artillery, and baggage silently defiled that night to the rear. The heavy guns were buried in the sand, and after sixty days of open trenches

Napoleon, for the first time in his life, though not for the last, ordered a retreat.

Napoleon buried in the breaches of Acre not merely 3000 of his bravest troops, but the golden dream of his life. "In that miserable fort," as he said, "lay the fate of the East." Napoleon expected to find in it the pasha's treasures, and arms for 300,000 men. "When I have captured it," he said to Bourrienne, "I shall march upon Damascus and Aleppo. I shall arm the tribes; I shall reach Constantinople; I shall overturn the Turkish Empire; I shall found in the East a new and grand empire. Perhaps I shall return to Paris by Adrianople and Vienna!" Napoleon was cheerfully willing to pay the price of what religion he had to accomplish this dream. He was willing, that is, to turn Turk. Henri IV. said "Paris was worth a mass," and was not the East, said Napoleon, "worth a turban and a pair of trousers?" In his conversation at St. Helena with Las Cases he seriously defended this policy. His army, he added, would have shared his "conversion," and have taken their new creed with a Parisian laugh. "Had I but captured Acre," Napoleon added, "I would have reached Constantinople and the Indies; I would have changed the face of the world. But that man made me miss my destiny."

Las Cases dwells upon the curious correspondence which existed between Philippeaux, who engineered the defences of Acre, and Napoleon, who attacked it. "They were," he says, "of the same nation, of the same age, of the same rank, of the same corps, and of the same school." But if Philippeaux was in a sense the brains of the defence, Sidney Smith was the sword.

There was, perhaps, it may be regretfully confessed, a streak of the charlatan in him. He shocked the judgment of more sober men. Wellington's stern, sober sense was affronted by him, and he described him as "a mere vaporiser." "Of all the men whom I ever knew who have any reputation," Wellington told Croker, "the man who least deserved it is Sir Sidney Smith." Wellington's temperament made it impossible for him to understand Sidney Smith's erratic and dazzling genius. Napoleon's phrase is the best epitaph of the man who defended Acre. It is true Napoleon himself describes Sidney Smith afterwards as "a young fool," who was "capable of invading France with 800 men." But such "young fools" are often the makers of history.

GREAT SEA-DUELS

"The captain stood on the carronade : 'First Lieutenant,' says he,
'Send all my merry men after here, for they must list to me.
I haven't the gift of the gab, my sons, because I'm bred to the sea.
That ship there is a Frenchman, who means to fight with we.
And odds, bobs, hammer and tongs, long as I've been to sea,
I've fought 'gainst every odds—but I've gained the victory!

. . . .

That ship there is a Frenchman, and if we don't take she,
'Tis a thousand bullets to one, that she will capture we.
I haven't the gift of the gab, my boys ; so each man to his gun ;
If she's not mine in half-an-hour, I'll flog each mother's son.
For odds, bobs, hammer and tongs, long as I've been to sea,
I've fought 'gainst every odds—and I've gained the victory!'"
—MARRYAT.

BRITISH naval history is rich in the records of what may be called great sea-duels—combats, that is, of single ship against single ship, waged often with extraordinary fierceness and daring. They resemble the combat of knight against knight, with flash of cannon instead of thrust of lance, and the floor of the lonely sea for the trampled lists.

He must have a very slow-beating imagination who cannot realise the picturesqueness of these ancient sea-duels. Two frigates cruising for prey catch the far-off gleam of each other's topsails over the rim of the horizon. They approach each other warily, two high-sniffing sea-mastiffs. A glimpse of fluttering colour—the red flag and the *drapeau blanc*, or the Union Jack and the tricolour—reveals to each ship its foe. The men stand grimly at quarters; the captain, with perhaps a solitary lieutenant, and a middy as aide-de-camp, is on his quarter-deck. There is the manœuvring for the weather-gage, the thunder of the sudden broadside, the hurtle and crash of the shot, the stern, quick word of command as the clumsy guns are run in to be reloaded and fired again and again with furious haste. The ships drift into closer wrestle. Masts and yards come tumbling on to the blood-splashed decks. There is the grinding shock of the great wooden hulls as they meet, the wild leap of the boarders, the clash of cutlass on cutlass, the shout of victory, the sight of the fluttering flag as it sinks reluctantly from the mizzen of the beaten ship. Then the smoke drifts away, and on the tossing sea-floor lie, little better than dismantled wrecks, victor and vanquished.

No great issue, perhaps, ever hung upon these lonely sea-combats; but as object-lessons in the qualities by which the empire has been won, and by which it must be maintained, these ancient sea-fights have real and permanent value. What better examples of cool hardihood, of chivalrous loyalty to the flag, of self-reliant energy, need be imagined or desired? The generation that carries the heavy burden of the empire to-day cannot afford to forget the tale of such exploits.

One of the most famous frigate fights in British history is that between the *Arethusa* and *La Belle Poule*, fought off Brest on June 17, 1778. Who is not familiar with the name and fame of "the saucy *Arethusa*"? Yet there is a curious absence of detail as to the fight. The combat, indeed, owes its enduring fame to two somewhat irrelevant circumstances—first, that it was fought when France and England were not actually at war, but were trembling on the verge of it. The sound of the *Arethusa's* guns, indeed, was the signal of war between the two nations. The other fact is that an ingenious rhymester — scarcely a poet — crystallised the fight into a set of verses in which there is something of the true smack of the sea, and an echo, if not of the cannon's roar, yet of the rough-voiced mirth of the forecastle; and the sea-fight lies embalmed, so to speak, and made immortal in the sea-song.

The *Arethusa* was a stumpy little frigate, scanty in crew, light in guns, attached to the fleet of Admiral Keppel, then cruising off Brest. Keppel had as perplexed and delicate a charge as was ever entrusted to a British admiral. Great Britain was at war with her American colonies, and there was every sign that France intended to add herself to the fight. No fewer than thirty-two sail of the line and twelve frigates were gathered in Brest roads, and another fleet of almost equal strength in Toulon. Spain, too, was slowly collecting a mighty armament. What would happen to England if the Toulon and Brest fleets united, were joined by a third fleet from Spain, and the mighty array of ships thus collected swept up the British Channel? On June 13, 1778, Keppel, with twenty-one ships of the line and three frigates, was despatched to keep watch over the Brest fleet. War had not been proclaimed, but Keppel was to prevent a junction of the Brest and Toulon fleets, by persuasion if he could, but by gunpowder in the last resort.

Keppel's force was much inferior to that of the Brest fleet, and as soon as the topsails of the British ships were visible from the French coast, two French frigates, the *Licorne* and *La Belle Poule*, with two lighter craft, bore down upon them to reconnoitre. But Keppel could not afford to let the French admiral know his exact force, and signalled to his own outlying ships to bring the French frigates under his lee.

At nine o'clock at night the *Licorne* was overtaken by the *Milford*, and with some rough sailorly persuasion, and a hint of broadsides, her head was turned towards the British fleet. The next morning, in the grey dawn, the Frenchman, having meditated on affairs during the night, made a wild dash for freedom. The *America*, an English 64—double, that is, the *Licorne's* size—overtook her, and fired a shot across her bow to bring her to. Longford, the captain of the *America*, stood on the gunwale of his own ship politely urging the captain of the *Licorne* to return with him. With a burst of Celtic passion the French captain fired his whole broadside into the big Englishman, and then instantly hauled down his flag so as to escape any answering broadside!

Meanwhile the *Arethusa* was in eager pursuit of the *Belle Poule;* a fox-terrier chasing a mastiff! The *Belle Poule* was a splendid ship, with heavy metal, and a crew more than twice as numerous as that of the tiny *Arethusa*. But Marshall, its captain, was a singularly gallant sailor, and not the man to count odds. The song tells the story of the fight in an amusing fashion:—

"Come all ye jolly sailors bold,
Whose hearts are cast in honour's mould,
While England's glory I unfold.
Huzza to the *Arethusa!*

> She is a frigate tight and brave
> As ever stemmed the dashing wave;
>   Her men are staunch
>   To their fav'rite launch,
> And when the foe shall meet our fire,
> Sooner than strike we'll all expire
>   On board the *Arethusa*.
>
> On deck five hundred men did dance,
> The stoutest they could find in France;
> We, with two hundred, did advance
>   On board the *Arethusa*.
> Our captain hailed the Frenchman, 'Ho!'
> The Frenchman then cried out, 'Hallo!'
>   'Bear down, d'ye see,
>   To our Admiral's lee.'
> 'No, no,' says the Frenchman, 'that can't be.'
> 'Then I must lug you along with me,'
>   Says the saucy *Arethusa!*"

As a matter of fact Marshall hung doggedly on the Frenchman's quarter for two long hours, fighting a ship twice as big as his own. The *Belle Poule* was eager to escape; Marshall was resolute that it should not escape, and, try as he might, the Frenchman, during that fierce two hours' wrestle, failed to shake off his tiny but dogged antagonist. The *Arethusa's* masts were shot away, its jib-boom hung a tangled wreck over its bows, its bulwarks were shattered, its decks were splashed red with blood, half its guns were dismounted, and nearly every third man in its crew struck down. But still it hung, with quenchless and obstinate courage, on the *Belle Poule's* quarter, and by its perfect seamanship and the quickness and the deadly precision with which its lighter guns worked, reduced its towering foe to a condition of wreck almost as complete as its own. The terrier, in fact, was proving too much for the mastiff.

Suddenly the wind fell. With topmasts hanging over the side, and canvas torn to ribbons, the *Arethusa* lay shattered and moveless on the sea. The shot-torn but loftier sails of the *Belle Poule*, however, yet held wind enough to drift her out of the reach of the *Arethusa's* fire. Both ships were close under the French cliffs; but the *Belle Poule*, like a broken-winged bird, struggled into a tiny cove in the rocks, and nothing remained for the *Arethusa* but to cut away her wreckage, hoist what sail she could, and drag herself sullenly back under jury-masts to the British fleet. But the story of that two hours' heroic fight maintained against such odds sent a thrill of grim exultation through Great Britain. Menaced by the combination of so many mighty states, while her sea-dogs were of this fighting temper, what had Great Britain to fear? In the streets of many a British seaport, and in many a British forecastle, the story of how the *Arethusa* fought was sung in deep-throated chorus:—

> "The fight was off the Frenchman's land;
> We forced them back upon their strand;
> For we fought till not a stick would stand
>   Of the gallant *Arethusa*!"

A fight even more dramatic in its character is that fought on August 10, 1805, between the *Phœnix* and the *Didon*. The *Didon* was one of the finest and fastest French frigates afloat, armed with guns of special calibre, and manned by a crew which formed, perhaps, the very élite of the French navy. The men had been specially picked to form the crew of the only French ship which was commanded by a Bonaparte, the *Pomone*, selected for the command of Captain Jerome Bonaparte. Captain Jerome Bonaparte, however, was not just now afloat, and the *Didon* had been selected, on account of its great speed and heavy armament, for a service of great importance. She was manned by the crew chosen for the *Pomone*, placed under an officer of special skill and daring—Captain Milias—and despatched with orders for carrying out one more of those naval "combinations" which Napoleon often attempted, but never quite accomplished. The *Didon*, in a word, was to bring up the Rochefort squadron to join the Franco-Spanish fleet under Villeneuve.

On that fatal August 10, however, it seemed to Captain Milias that fortune had thrust into his hands a golden opportunity of snapping up a British sloop of war, and carrying her as a trophy into Rochefort. An American merchantman fell in with him, and its master reported that he had been brought-to on the previous day by a British man-of-war, and compelled to produce his papers. The American told the French captain that he had been allowed to go round the Englishman's decks and count his guns—omitting, no doubt, to add that he was half-drunk while doing it. Contemplated through an American's prejudices, inflamed with grog, the British ship seemed a very poor thing indeed. She carried, the American told the captain of the *Didon*, only twenty guns of light calibre, and her captain and officers were "so cocky" that if they had a chance they would probably lay themselves alongside even the *Didon* and become an easy prey. The American pointed out to the eagerly listening Frenchmen the topgallant sails of the ship he was describing showing above the sky-line to windward. Captain Milias thought he saw glory and cheap victory beckoning him, and he put his helm down, and stood under easy sail towards the fast-rising topsails of the Englishman.

Now, the *Phœnix* was, perhaps, the smallest frigate in the British navy; a stocky little craft, scarcely above the rating of a sloop; and its captain, Baker, a man with something of Dundonald's gift for ruse, had disguised his ship so as to look as much as possible like a sloop. Baker, too, who believed that light guns quickly handled were capable of more effective mischief than the slow fire of heavier guns, had changed his heavier metal for 18-pounders. The two ships, therefore, were very unequal in fighting force. The broadside of the *Didon* was nearly fifty per cent. heavier than that of the *Phœnix*; her crew was nearly fifty per cent. more numerous, and she was splendidly equipped at every point.

The yellow sides and royal yards rigged aloft told the "cocky" *Phœnix* that the big ship to leeward was a Frenchman, and, with all sails spread, she bore down in the chase. Baker was eager to engage his enemy to leeward, that she might not escape, and he held his fire till he could reach the desired position. The *Didon*, however, a quick and weatherly ship, was able to keep ahead of the *Phœnix*, and thrice poured in a heavy broadside upon the grimly silent British ship without receiving a shot in reply. Baker's men were falling fast at their quarters, and, impatient at being both foiled and raked, he at last ran fiercely at his enemy to windward. The heads of both ships swung parallel, and at

F

pistol-distance broadside furiously answered broadside. In order to come up with her opponent, however, the *Phœnix* had all sail spread, and she gradually forged ahead. As soon as the two ships were clear, the *Didon*, by a fine stroke of seamanship, hauled up, crossed the stern of the *Phœnix*, and raked her, and then repeated the pleasant operation. The rigging of the *Phœnix* was so shattered that for a few minutes she was out of hand. Baker, however, was a fine seaman, and his crew were in a high state of discipline; and when the *Didon* once more bore up to rake her antagonist, the British ship, with her sails thrown aback, evaded the Frenchman's fire. But the stem of the *Didon* smote with a crash on the starboard quarter of the *Phœnix*; the ships were lying parallel; the broadside of neither could be brought to bear. The Frenchmen, immensely superior in numbers, made an impetuous rush across their forecastle, and leaped on the quarter-deck of the *Phœnix*. The marines of that ship, however, drawn up in a steady line across the deck, resisted the whole rush of the French boarders; and the British sailors, turning up from their guns, cutlass and boarding-pike in hand, and wroth with the audacity of the "Frenchmen" round in daring to board the "cocky little *Phœnix*," cutting, no crash, pushed fiercely home, swept the Frenchmen back to their own vessel.

On the French forecastle was a brass 36-pounder carronade; this commanding indeed most destructive of the British ship, and with it the French of the *Didon* could not bring fire. The British ship, as had a chance, however, had a single gun to bear in reply, side even that of his ship fitted the cabin window on the American exactly such a to serve as a port, in preparation contingency as this; and the aftermost main-deck gun was dragged into the cabin, the improvised port thrown open, and Baker himself, with a cluster of officers and men, was eagerly employed in fitting tackles to enable the gun to be worked. As the sides of the two ships were actually grinding together the Frenchmen saw the preparations being made; a double squad of marines was brought up at a run to the larboard gangway, and opened a swift and deadly fire into the cabin, crowded with English sailors busy rigging their gun. The men dropped in clusters; the floor of the cabin was covered with the slain, its walls were splashed with blood. But Baker and the few men not yet struck down kept coolly to their task. The gun was loaded under the actual flash of the French muskets, its muzzle was thrust through the port, and it was fired! Its charge of langrage swept the French ship from her larboard bow to her starboard quarter, and struck down in an instant twenty-four men. The deadly fire was renewed again and again, the British marines on the quarter-deck meanwhile keeping down with their musketry the fire of the great French carronade.

That fierce and bloody wrestle lasted for nearly thirty minutes, then the *Didon* began to fore-reach. Her great bowsprit ground slowly along the side of the *Phœnix*. It crossed the line of the second aftermost gun on the British main-deck. Its flames on the instant smote the Frenchman's head-rails to splinters, and destroyed the gammoning of her bowsprit. Gun after gun of the two ships was brought in succession to bear; but in this close and deadly contest the *Phœnix* had the advantage. Her guns were lighter, her men better drilled, and their fierce energy overbore the Frenchmen. Presently the *Didon*, with her foremast tottering, her maintopmast gone, her decks a blood-stained wreck, passed out of gunshot ahead.

In the tangle between the two ships the fly of the British white ensign at the gaff end dropped on the *Didon's* forecastle. The Frenchmen tore it off, and, as the ships moved apart, they waved it triumphantly from the *Didon's* stern. All the colours of the *Phœnix*, indeed, in one way or another had vanished, and the only response the exasperated British tars could make to the insult of the *Didon* was to immediately lash a boat's ensign to the larboard, and the Union Jack to the starboard end of their cross jack yard-arm.

The wind had dropped; both ships were now lying in a semi-wrecked condition out of gunshot of each other, and it became a question of which could soonest repair damages and get into fighting condition again. Both ships, as it happened, had begun the fight with nearly all canvas spread, and from their splintered masts the sails now hung one wild network of rags. In each ship a desperate race to effect repairs began. On the Frenchman's decks arose a babel of sounds, the shouts of officers, the tumult of the men's voices. The British, on the other hand, worked in grim and orderly silence, with no sound but the cool, stern orders of the officers. In such a race the British were sure to win, and fortune aided them. The two ships were rolling heavily in the windless swell, and a little before noon the British saw the wounded foremast of their enemy suddenly snap and tumble, with all its canvas, upon the unfortunate *Didon's* decks. This gave new and exultant vigour to the British. Shot-holes were plugged, dismounted guns refitted, fresh braces rove, the torn rigging spliced, new canvas spread. The wind blew softly again, and a little after noon the *Phœnix*, sorely battered indeed, but in fighting trim, with guns loaded, and the survivors of her crew at quarters, bore down on the *Didon*, and took her position on that ship's weather bow. Just when the word "Fire!" was about to be given, the *Didon's* flag fluttered reluctantly down; she had struck!

The toils of the *Phœnix*, however, were not even yet ended. The ship she had captured was practically a wreck, its mainmast tottering to its fall, while the prisoners greatly exceeded in numbers their captors. The little *Phœnix* courageously took her big prize in tow, and laid her course for Plymouth. Once the pair of crippled frigates were chased by the whole of Villeneuve's fleet; once, by a few chance words overheard, a plot amongst the French prisoners for seizing the *Phœnix* and then retaking the *Didon* was detected—almost too late—and thwarted. The *Phœnix*, and her prize too, reached Gibraltar when a thick fog lay on the straits, a fog which, as the sorely damaged ships crept through it, was full of the sound of signal guns and the ringing of bells. The Franco-Spanish fleet, in a word, a procession of giants, went slowly past the crippled ships in the fog, and never saw them!

On September 3, however, the *Phœnix* safely brought her hard-won and stubborn-guarded prize safely into Plymouth Sound.

The fight between the two ships was marked by many heroic incidents. During the action the very invalids in the sick-bay of the *Phœnix* crept from their cots and tried to take some feeble part in the fight. The purser is not usually part of the fighting staff of a ship, but the acting purser of the *Phœnix*, while her captain was in the smoke-filled cabin below, trying to rig up a gun to bear on the *Didon*, took charge of the quarter-deck, kept his post right opposite the brazen mouth of the great carronade we have described, and, with a few marines, kept down the fire. A little middy had the distinction of saving his captain's life. The *Didon's* bowsprit was thrust, like the shaft of a gigantic lance, over the quarter of the *Phœnix*, and a Frenchman, lying along it, levelled his musket at Captain Baker, not six paces distant, and took deliberate aim. A middy named Phillips, armed with a musket as big as himself, saw the levelled piece of the Frenchman; he gave his captain an unceremonious jostle aside just as the Frenchman's musket flashed, and with almost the same movement discharged his own piece at the enemy. The French bullet tore off the rim of Captain Baker's hat, but the body of the man who fired it fell with a splash betwixt the two ships into the water. Here was a story, indeed, for a middy to tell, to the admiration of all the gun-rooms in the fleet.

The middy of the period, however, was half imp, half hero. Another youthful Nelson, ætat. sixteen, at the hottest stage of the fight—probably at the moment the acting-purser was in command on the quarter-deck —found an opportunity of getting at the purser's stores. With jaws widely distended, he was in the act of sucking—in the fashion so delightful to boys—a huge orange, when a musket ball, after passing through the head of a seaman, went clean through both the youth's distended cheeks, and this without touching a single tooth. Whether this affected the flavour of the orange is not told, but the historian gravely records that "when the wound in each cheek healed, a pair of not unseemly dimples remained." Happy middy! He would scarcely envy Nelson his peerage.

THE BLOOD-STAINED HILL OF BUSACO

"Who would not fight for England?
  Who would not fling a life
I' the ring, to meet a tyrant's gage,
  And glory in the strife?
. . . . .
Now, fair befall our England,
  On her proud and perilous road;
And woe and wail to those who make
  Her footprints red with blood!
Up with our red-cross banner—roll
  A thunder-peal of drums!
Fight on there, every valiant soul,
  And, courage! England comes!
Now, fair befall our England,
  On her proud and perilous road;
And woe and wail to those who make
  Her footprints red with blood!

Now, victory to our England!
  And where'er she lifts her hand
In Freedom's fight, to rescue Right,
  God bless the dear old land!
And when the storm has passed away,
  In glory and in calm
May she sit down i' the green o' the day,
  And sing her peaceful psalm!
Now, victory to our England!
  And where'er she lifts her hand
In Freedom's fight, to rescue Right,
  God bless the dear old land!"
—GERALD MASSEY.

BUSACO is, perhaps, the most picturesque of Peninsular battles. In the wild nature of the ground over which it raged, the dramatic incidents which marked its progress, the furious daring of the assault, and the stern valour of the defence, it is almost without a rival. The French had every advantage in the fight, save one. They were 65,000 strong, an army of veterans, many of them the men of Austerlitz and Marengo. Massena led; Ney was second in command; both facts being pledges of daring generalship. The English were falling sullenly back in the long retreat which ended at Torres Vedras, and the French were in exultant pursuit. Massena had announced that he was going to "drive the leopard into the sea"; and French soldiers, it may be added, are never so dangerous as when on fire with the *élan* of success.

Wellington's army was inferior to its foe in numbers, and of mixed nationality, and it is probable that retreat had loosened the fibre of even British discipline, if not of British courage. Two days before Busaco, for example, the light division, the very flower of the English army, was encamped in a pine-wood about which a peasant had warned them that it was "haunted." During the night, without signal or visible cause, officers and men, as though suddenly smitten with frenzy, started from their sleep and dispersed in all directions. Nor could the mysterious panic be stayed until some officer, shrewder than the rest, shouted the order, "Prepare to receive cavalry," when the instinct of discipline asserted itself, the men rushed into rallying squares, and, with huge shouts of laughter, recovered themselves from their panic.

But battle is to the British soldier a tonic, and when Wellington drew up his lines in challenge of battle to his pursuer, on the great hill of Bnsaco, his red-coated soldiery were at least full of a grim satisfaction. One of the combatants has described the diverse aspects of the two hosts on the night before the fight. "The French were all bustle and gaiety; but along the whole English line the soldiers, in stern silence, examined their flints, cleaned their locks and barrels, and then stretched themselves on the ground to rest, each with his firelock within his grasp." The single advantage of the British lay in their position. Busaco is a great hill, one of the loftiest and most rugged in Portugal, eight miles in breadth, and barring the road by which Massena was moving on Lisbon. "There are certainly," said Wellington, "many bad roads in Portugal, but the enemy has taken decidedly the worst in the whole kingdom."

The great ridge, with its gloomy tree-clad heights and cloven crest, round which the mists hung in sullen vapour, was an ideal position for defence. In its front was a valley forming a natural ditch so deep that the eye could scarcely pierce its depths. The ravine at one point was so narrow that the English and French guns waged duel across it, but on the British side the chasm was almost perpendicular.

From their eyrie perch on September 27, 1810, the English watched Massena's great host coming on. Every eminence sparkled with their bayonets, every road was crowded with their waggons; it seemed not so much the march of an army as the movement of a nation. The vision of "grim Busaco's iron ridge," glittering with bayonets, arrested the march of the French. But Ney, whose military glance was keen and sure, saw that the English arrangements were not yet complete; an unfilled gap, three miles wide, parted the right wing from the left, and he was eager for an immediate attack. Massena, however, was ten miles in the rear. According to Marbot, who has left a spirited account of Busaco, Massena put off the attack till the next day, and thus threw away a great opportunity. In the gloomy depths of the ravines, however, a war of skirmishers broke out, and the muskets rang loudly through the echoing valleys, while the puffs of eddying white smoke rose through the black pines. But night fell, and the mountain heights above were crowned with the bivouac fires of 100,000 warriors, over whom the serene sky glittered. Presently a bitter wind broke on the mountain summits, and all through the night the soldiers shivered under its keen blast.

Massena's plan of attack was simple and daring. Ney was to climb the steep front on the English left, and assail the light division under Craufurd; Regnier, with a *corps d'élite*, was to attack the English left, held by Picton's division. Regnier formed his attack into five columns while the stars were yet glittering coldly in the morning sky. They had first to plunge into the savage depths of the ravine, and then climb the steep slope leading to the English position. The vigour of the attack was magnificent. General Merle, who had won fame at Austerlitz, personally led the charge. At a run the columns went down the ravine; at a run, scarcely less swift, they swept up the hostile slope. The guns smote the columns from end to end, and the attack left behind it a broad crimson trail of the dead and dying. But it never paused: A wave of steel and fire and martial tumult, it swept up the hill, broke over the crest in a spray of flame, brushed aside a Portuguese regiment in its path like a wisp of straw, and broke on the lines of the third division.

The pressure was too great for even the solid English line to sustain; it, too, yielded to the impetuous French, part of whom seized the rocks at the highest point of the hill, while another part wheeled to the right, intending to sweep the summit of the sierra. It was an astonishing feat. Only French soldiers, magnificently led and in a mood of victory, could have done it; and only British soldiers, it may be added, whom defeat hardens, could have restored such a reverse.

Picton was in command, and he sent at the French a wing of the 88th, the famous Connaught Rangers, led by Colonel Wallace, an officer in whom Wellington reposed great confidence. Wallace's address was brief and pertinent. "Press them to the muzzle, Connaught Rangers; press on to the rascals." There is no better fighting material in the world than an Irish regiment well led and in a high state of discipline, and this matchless regiment, with levelled bayonets, ran in on the French with a grim and silent fury there was no denying. Vain was resistance. Marbot says of the Rangers that "their first volley, delivered at fifteen paces, stretched more than 500 men on the ground"; and the threatening gleam of the bayonet followed fiercely on the flame of the musket.

The French were borne, shouting, struggling, and fighting desperately, over the crest and down the deep slope to the ravine below. In a whirlwind of dust and fire and clamour went the whole body of furious soldiery into the valley, leaving a broad track of broken arms and dying men. According to the regimental records of the 88th, "Twenty minutes sufficed to teach the heroes of Marengo and Austerlitz that they must yield to the Rangers of Connaught!" As the breathless Rangers re-formed triumphantly on the ridge, Wellington galloped up and declared he had never witnessed a more gallant charge.

But a wing of Regnier's attack had formed at right angles across the ridge. It was pressing forward with stern resolution; it swept before it the light companies of the 74th and 88th regiments, and unless this attack could be arrested the position and the battle were lost. Picton rallied his broken lines within *sixty yards* of the French muskets, a feat not the least marvellous in a marvellous fight, and then sent them furiously at the exulting French, who held a strong position amongst the rocks. It is always difficult to disentangle the confusion which marks a great fight. Napier says that it was Cameron who formed line with the 38th under a violent fire, and, without returning a shot, ran in upon the French grenadiers with the bayonet and hurled them triumphantly over the crest. Picton, on the other hand, declares that it was the light companies of the 74th and the 88th, under Major Smith, an officer of great daring—who fell in the moment of victory —that flung the last French down over the cliff. Who can decide when such experts, and actors in the actual scene, differ?

The result, however, as seen from the French side, is clear. The French, Marbot records, "found themselves driven in a heap down the deep descent up which they had climbed, and the English lines followed them half-way down firing murderous volleys. At this point we lost a general, 2 colonels, 80 officers, and 700 or 800 men." "The English," he adds in explanation of this dreadful loss of life, "were the best marksmen in Europe, the only troops who were perfectly practised in the use of small arms, whence their firing was far more accurate than that of any other infantry."

A gleam of humour at this point crosses the grim visage of battle. Picton, on lying down in his bivouac the night before the battle, had adorned his head with a picturesque and highly coloured nightcap. The sudden attack of the French woke him; he clapped on cloak and cocked hat, and rode to the fighting line, when he personally led the attack which flung the last of Regnier's troops down the slope. At the moment of the charge he took off his cocked hat to wave the troops onward; this revealed the domestic head-dress he unconsciously wore, and the astonished soldiers beheld their general on flame with warlike fury gesticulating martially in a nightcap! A great shout of laughter went up from the men as they stopped for a moment to realise the spectacle; then with a tempest of mingled laughter and cheers they flung themselves on the enemy.

Meanwhile Ney had formed his attack on the English left, held by Craufurd and the famous light division. Marbot praises the characteristic tactics of the British in such fights. "After having, as we do," he says, "garnished their front with skirmishers, they post their principal forces out of sight, holding them all the time sufficiently near to the key of the position to be able to attack the enemy the instant they reach it; and this attack, made unexpectedly on assailants who have lost heavily, and think the victory already theirs, succeeds almost invariably." "We had," he adds, "a melancholy experience of this art at Busaco." Craufurd, a soldier of fine skill, made exactly such a disposition of his men. Some rocks at the edge of the ravine formed natural embrasures for the English guns under Ross; below them the Rifles were flung out as skirmishers; behind them the German infantry were the only visible troops; but in a fold of the hill, unseen, Craufurd held the 43rd and 52nd regiments drawn up in line.

Ney's attack, as might be expected, was sudden and furious. The English, in the grey dawn, looking down the ravine, saw three huge masses start from the French lines and swarm up the slope. To climb an ascent so steep, vexed by skirmishers on either flank, and scourged by the guns which flashed from the summit, was a great and most daring feat—yet the French did it. Busaco, indeed, is memorable as showing the French fighting quality at its highest point. General Simon led Loison's attack right up to the lips of the English guns, and in the dreadful charge its order was never disturbed nor its speed arrested. "Ross's guns," says Napier, "were worked with incredible quickness, yet their range was palpably contracted every round; the enemy's shot came singing up in a sharper key; the English skirmishers, breathless and begrimed with powder, rushed over the edge of the ascent; the artillery drew back"—and over the edge of the hill came the bear-skins and the gleaming bayonets of the French! General Simon led the attack so fiercely home that he was the first to leap across the English entrenchments, when an infantry soldier, lingering stubbornly after his comrades had fallen back, shot him point-blank. through the face. The unfortunate general, when the fight was over, was found lying in the redoubt amongst the dying and the dead, with scarcely a human feature left. He recovered, was sent as a prisoner to England, and was afterwards exchanged, but his horrible wound made it impossible for him to serve again.

Craufurd had been watching meanwhile with grim coolness the onward rush of the French. They came storming and exultant, a wave of martial figures, edged with a spray of fire and a tossing fringe of bayonets, over the summit of the hill; when suddenly Craufurd, in a shrill tone, called on his reserves to attack. In an instant there rose, as if out of the ground, before the eyes of the astonished French, the serried lines of the 43rd and 52nd, and what a moment before was empty space was now filled with the frowning visage of battle. The British lines broke into one stern and deep-toned shout, and 1800 bayonets, in one long line of gleaming points, came swiftly down upon the French. To stand against that moving hedge of deadly and level steel was impossible; yet each man in the leading section of the French raised his musket and fired, and two officers and ten soldiers fell before them. Not a Frenchman had missed his mark! They could do no more. "The head of their column," to quote Napier, "was violently thrown back upon the rear, both flanks were overlapped at the same moment by the English wings, and three terrible discharges at five yards' distance shattered the wavering mass." Before those darting points of flame the pride of the French shrivelled. Shining victory was converted, in almost the passage of an instant, into bloody defeat; and a shattered mass, with ranks broken, and colours abandoned, and discipline forgotten, the French were swept into the depths of the ravine out of which they had climbed.

One of the dramatic episodes of the fight at this juncture is that of Captain Jones—known in his regiment as "Jack Jones" of the 52nd. Jones was a fiery Welshman, and led his company in the rush on General Simon's column. The French were desperately trying to deploy, a *chef-de-bataillon* giving the necessary orders with great vehemence. Jones ran ahead of his charging men, outstripping them by speed of foot, challenged the French officer with a warlike gesture to single combat, and slew him with one fierce thrust before his own troops, and the 52nd, as they came on at the run, saw the duel and its result, were lifted by it to a mood of victory, and raised a sudden shout of exultation, which broke the French as by a blast of musketry fire.

For hours the battle spluttered and smouldered amongst the skirmishers in the ravines, and some gallant episodes followed. Towards evening, for example, a French company, with signal audacity, and apparently on its own private impulse, seized a cluster of houses only half a musket shot from the light division, and held it while Craufurd scourged them with the fire of twelve guns. They were only turned out at the point of the bayonet by the 43rd. But the battle was practically over, and the English had beaten, by sheer hard fighting, the best troops and the best marshals of France.

In the fierceness of actual fighting, Busaco has never been surpassed, and seldom did the wounded and dying lie thicker on a battlefield than where the hostile lines struggled together on that fatal September 27. The *mêlée* at some points was too close for even the bayonet to be used, and the men fought with fists or with the butt-end of their muskets. From the rush which swept Regnier's men down the slope the Connaught Rangers came back with faces and hands and weapons literally splashed red with blood. The firing was so fierce that Wellington, with his whole staff, dismounted. Napier, however—one of the famous fighting trio of that name, who afterwards conquered Scinde—fiercely refused to dismount, or even cover his red uniform with a cloak. "This is the uniform of my regiment," he said, "and in it I will show, or fall this day." He had scarcely uttered the words when a bullet smashed through his face and shattered his jaw to pieces. As he was carried past Lord Wellington he waved his hand and whispered through his torn mouth, "I could not die at a better moment!" Of such stuff were the men who fought under Wellington in the Peninsula.

NELSON

After a painting by L. F. ABBOTT *in the National Portrait Gallery*

OF NELSON AND THE NILE

" Britannia needs no bulwarks,
   No towers along the steep;
Her march is o'er the mountain waves,
   Her home is on the deep.
With thunders from her native oak,
   She quells the floods below,
As they roar on the shore
   When the stormy winds do blow;
When the battle rages loud and long,
   And the stormy winds do blow.

The meteor flag of England
   Shall yet terrific burn,
Till danger's troubled night depart,
   And the star of peace return.
Then, then, ye ocean warriors,
   Our song and feast shall flow
To the fame of your name,
   When the storm has ceased to blow;
When the fiery fight is heard no more,
   And the storm has ceased to blow."

—CAMPBELL.

ABOUKIR BAY resembles nothing so much as a piece bitten out of the Egyptian pancake. A crescent-shaped bay, patchy with shoals, stretching from the Rosetta mouth of the Nile to Aboukir, or, as it is now called, Nelson Island, that island being simply the outer point of a sandbank that projects from the western horn of the bay. Flat shores, grey-blue Mediterranean waters, two horns of land six miles apart, that to the north projecting farthest and forming a low island—

this, ninety-eight years ago, was the scene of what might almost be described as the greatest sea-fight in history.

On the evening of August 1, 1798, thirteen great battleships lay drawn up in a single line parallel with the shore, and as close to it as the sandbanks permitted. The head ship was almost stem on to the shoal which, running out at right angles to the shore, forms Aboukir Island. The nose of each succeeding ship was exactly 160 yards from the stern of the ship before it, and, allowing for one or two gaps, each ship was bound by a great cable to its neighbour. It was a thread of beads, only each "bead" was a battleship, whose decks swarmed with brave men, and from whose sides gaped the iron lips of more than a thousand heavy guns. The line was not exactly straight; it formed a very obtuse angle, the projecting point at the centre being formed by the *Orient*, the biggest warship at that moment afloat, a giant of 120 guns.

Next to her came the *Franklin*, of 80 guns, a vessel which, if not the biggest, was perhaps the finest sample of naval architecture in existence. The line of ships was more than one mile and a half long, and consisted of the gigantic flagship, three ships of the line of 80 guns, and nine of 74 guns. In addition, it had a fringe of gunboats and frigates, while a battery of mortars on the island guarded, as with a sword of fire, the gap betwixt the headmost ship and the island. This great fleet had convoyed Napoleon, with 36,000 troops crowded into 400 transports, from France, had captured Malta on the voyage, and three weeks before had safely landed Napoleon and his soldiers in Egypt.

The French admiral, Bruéys, knew that Nelson was coming furiously in his track, and after a consultation with all his captains he had drawn up his ships in the order which we have described, a position he believed to be unassailable. And at three o'clock on the afternoon of August 1, 1798, his look-outs were eagerly watching the white topsails showing above the lee line, the van of Nelson's fleet.

Napoleon had kept the secret of his Egyptian expedition well, and the great Toulon fleet, with its swarm of transports, had vanished round the coast of Corsica and gone off into mere space, as far as a bewildered British Admiralty knew. A fleet of thirteen 74-gun ships and one of 50 guns was placed under Nelson's flag. He was ordered to pursue and destroy the vanished French fleet, and with characteristic energy he set out on one of the most dramatic sea-chases known to history. With the instinct of genius he guessed that Napoleon's destination was Egypt; but while the French fleet coasted Sardinia and went to the west of Sicily, Nelson ran down the Italian coast to Naples, called there for information, found none, and, carrying all sail, swept through the straits of Messina.

On the night of June 22 the two fleets actually crossed each other's tracks. The French fleet, including the transports, numbered 572 vessels, and their lights, it might be imagined, would have lit up many leagues of sea. Yet, through this forest of hostile masts the English fleet, with keen eyes watching at every masthead, swept and saw nothing. Nelson, for one thing, had no frigates to serve as eyes and ears for him; his fleet in sailor-like fashion formed a compact body, three parallel lines of phantom-like pyramids of canvas sweeping in the darkness across the floor of the sea. Above all a haze filled the night; and it is not too much to say that the drifting grey vapour which hid the French ships from Nelson's lookout men changed the face of history.

Nelson used to explain that his ideal of perfect enjoyment would be to have the chance of "trying Bonaparte on a wind"; and if he had caught sound of bell or gleam of lantern from the great French fleet, and brought it to action in the darkness of that foggy night, can any one doubt what the result would have been? Nelson would have done off the coast of Sicily on June 22, 1798, what Wellington did on June 18, 1815; and in that case there would have been no Marengo or Austerlitz, no retreat from Moscow, no Peninsular war, and no Waterloo. For so much, in distracted human affairs, may a patch of drifting vapour count!

Nelson, in a word, overran his prey. He reached Alexandria to find the coast empty; doubled back to Sicily, zigzagging on his way by Cyprus and Candia; and twelve hours after he had left Alexandria the topsails of the French fleet hove in sight from that port. Napoleon's troops were safely landed, and the French admiral had some four weeks in which to prepare for Nelson's return, and at 3 P.M. on August 1 the gliding topsails of the *Swiftsure* above Aboukir Island showed that the tireless Englishman had, after nearly three months of pursuit, overtaken his enemy.

The French, if frigates be included, counted seventeen

ships to fourteen, and ship for ship they had the advantage over the British alike in crew, tonnage, and weight of fire. In size the English ships scarcely averaged 1500 tons; the French ships exceeded 2000 tons. Nelson had only seventy-fours, his heaviest gun being a 32-pounder. The average French 80-gun ship in every detail of fighting strength exceeded an English ninety-eight, and Bruéys had three such ships in his fleet; while his own flagship, the *Orient*, was fully equal to two English seventy-fours. Its weight of ball on the lower deck alone exceeded that from the whole broadside of the *Bellerophon*, the ship that engaged it. The French, in brief, had an advantage in guns of about twenty per cent., and in men of over thirty per cent. Bruéys, moreover, was lying in a carefully chosen position in a dangerous bay, of which his enemies possessed no chart, and the head of his line was protected by a powerful shore battery.

Nothing in this great fight is more dramatic than the swiftness and vehemence of Nelson's attack. He simply leaped upon his enemy at sight. Four of his ships were miles off in the offing, but Nelson did not wait for them. In the long pursuit he had assembled his captains repeatedly in his cabin, and discussed every possible manner of attacking the French fleet. If he found the fleet as he guessed, drawn up in battle-line close in-shore and anchored, his plan was to place one of his ships on the bows, another on the quarter, of each French ship in succession.

It has been debated who actually evolved the idea of rounding the head of the French line and attacking on both faces. One version is that Foley, in the *Goliath*, who led the British line, owed the suggestion to a keen-eyed middy who pointed out that the anchor buoy of the headmost French ship was at such a distance from the ship itself as to prove there was room to pass. But the weight of evidence seems to prove that Nelson himself, as he rounded Aboukir Island, and scanned with fierce and questioning vision Bruéys' formation, with that swiftness of glance in which he almost rivalled Napoleon, saw his chance in the gap between the leading French ship and the shore. "Where a French ship can swing," he held, "an English ship can either sail or anchor." And he determined to double on the French line and attack on both faces at once. He explained his plan to Berry, his captain, who in his delight exclaimed, "If we succeed, what will the world say?" "There is no 'if' in the case," said Nelson; "that we shall succeed is certain; who will live to tell the story is a very different question."

Bruéys had calculated that the English fleet must come down perpendicularly to his centre, and each ship in the process be raked by a line of fire a mile and a half long; but the moment the English ships rounded the island they tacked, hugged the shore, and swept through the gap between the leading vessel and the land. The British ships were so close to each other that Nelson, speaking from his own quarter-deck, was able to ask Hood in the *Zealous*, if he thought they had water enough to round the French line. Hood replied that he had no chart, but would lead and take soundings as he went.

So the British line came on, the men on the yards taking in canvas, the leadsmen in the chains coolly calling the soundings. The battery roared from the island, the leading French ships broke into smoke and flame, but the steady British line glided on. The *Goliath* by this time led; and at half-past five the shadow of its tall masts cast by the westering sun fell over the decks of the *Guerrier*, and as Foley, its captain, swept past the Frenchman's bows, he poured in a furious broadside, bore swiftly up, and dropped—as Nelson, with that minute attention to detail which marks a great commander, had ordered all his captains—an anchor from the stern, so that, without having to "swing," he was instantly in a fighting position on his enemy's quarter. Foley, however, dropped his anchor a moment too late, and drifted on to the second ship in the line; but Hood, in the *Zealous*, coming swiftly after, also raked the *Guerrier*, and, anchoring from the stern at the exact moment, took the place on its quarter Foley should have taken.

The *Orion* came into battle next, blasted the unfortunate *Guerrier*, whose foremast had already gone, with a third broadside, and swept outside the *Zealous* and *Goliath* down to the third ship on the French line. A French frigate, the *Sérieuse*, of thirty-six guns, anchored inside the French line, ventured to fire on the *Orion* as it swept past, whereupon Saumarez, its commander, discharged his starboard broadside into that frigate. The *Sérieuse* reeled under the shock of the British guns, its masts disappeared like chips, and the unfortunate Frenchman went down like a stone; while Saumarez, laying himself on the larboard bow of the *Franklin* and the quarter of the *Peuple Sovrain*, broke upon them in thunder. The *Theseus*

106 DEEDS THAT WON THE EMPIRE

followed hard in the track of the *Orion,* raked the unhappy *Guerrier* in the familiar fashion while crossing its bows, then swept through the narrow water-lane betwixt the *Goliath* and *Zealous* and their French

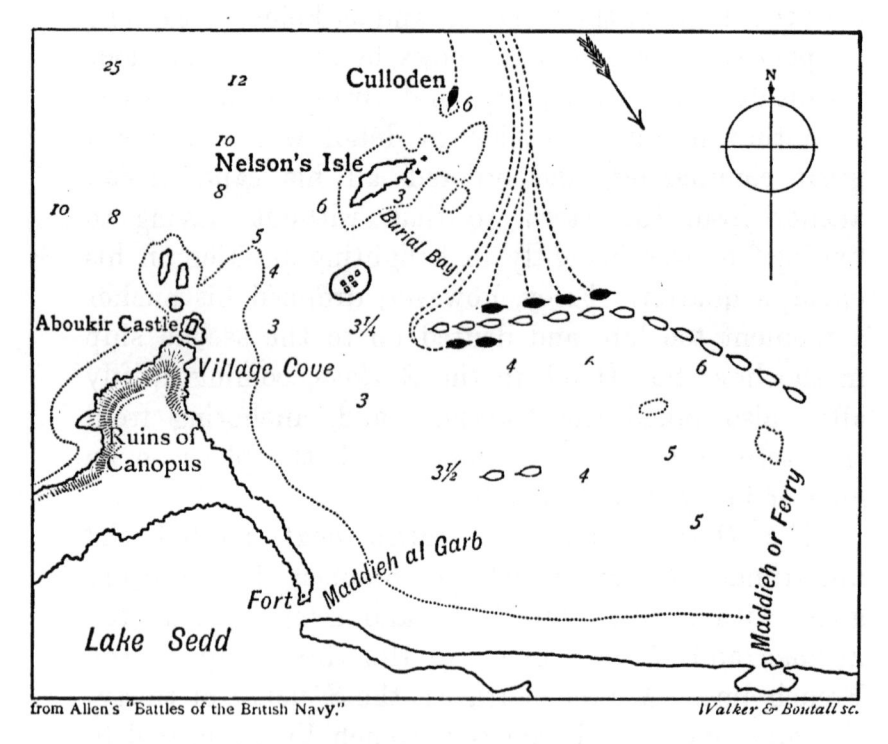

THE BATTLE OF THE NILE.
Doubling on the French Line.

antagonists, poured a smashing broadside into each French ship as it passed, then shot outside the *Orion,* and anchored with mathematical nicety off the quarter of the *Spartiate.* The water-lane was not a pistol-shot wide, and this feat of seamanship was marvellous.

Miller, who commanded the *Theseus*, in a letter to his wife described the fight. "In running along the enemy's line in the wake of the *Zealous* and *Goliath*, I observed," he says, "their shot sweep just over us, and knowing well that at such a moment Frenchmen would not have coolness enough to change their elevation, I closed them suddenly, and, running under the arch of their shot, reserved my fire, every gun being loaded with two, and some with three round shot, until I had the *Guerrier's* masts in a line, and her jib-boom about six feet clear of our rigging. We then opened with such effect that a second breath could not be drawn before her main and mizzen-mast were also gone. This was precisely at sunset, or forty-four minutes past six."

The *Audacious*, meanwhile, was too impatient to tack round the head of the French line; it broke through the gap betwixt the first and second ships of the enemy, delivered itself, in a comfortable manner, of a raking broadside into both as it passed, took its position on the larboard bow of the *Conquerant*, and gave itself up to the joy of battle. Within thirty minutes from the beginning of the fight, that is, five British line-of-battle ships were inside the French line, comfortably established on the bows or quarters of the leading ships. Nelson himself, in the *Vanguard*, anchored on the outside of the French line, within eighty yards of the *Spartiate's* starboard beam; the *Minotaur*, the *Bellerophon*, and the *Majestic*, coming up in swift succession, and at less than five minutes' interval from each other, flung themselves on the next ships.

How the thunder of the battle deepened, and how

the quick flashes of the guns grew brighter as the night gathered rapidly over sea, must be imagined. But Nelson's swift and brilliant strategy was triumphant. Each ship in the French van resembled nothing so much as a walnut in the jaws of a nut-cracker. They were being "cracked" in succession, and the rear of the line could only look on with agitated feelings and watch the operation.

The fire of the British ships for fury and precision was overwhelming. The head of the *Guerrier* was simply shot away; the anchors hanging from her bows were cut in two; her main-deck ports, from the bowsprit to the gangway, were driven into one; her masts, fallen inboard, lay with their tangle of rigging on the unhappy crew; while some of her main-deck beams— all supports being torn away—fell on the guns. Hood, in the *Zealous*, who was pounding the unfortunate *Guerrier*, says, "At last, being tired of killing men in that way, I sent a lieutenant on board, who was allowed, as I had instructed him, to hoist a light, and haul it down as a sign of submission." But all the damage was not on the side of the French. The great French flagship, the *Orient*, by this time had added her mighty voice to the tumult, and the *Bellerophon*, who was engaged with her, had a bad time of it. It was the story of Tom Sayers and Heenan over again—a dwarf fighting a giant. Her mizzen-mast and mainmast were shot away, and after maintaining the dreadful duel for more than an hour, and having 200 of her crew struck down, at 8.20 P.M. the *Bellerophon* cut her cable and drifted, a disabled wreck, out of the fire.

Meanwhile the four ships Nelson had left in the

offing were beating furiously up to add themselves to the fight. Night had fallen by the time Troubridge, in the *Culloden*, came round the island; and then, in full sight of the great battle, the *Culloden* ran hopelessly ashore! She was, perhaps, the finest ship of the British fleet, and the emotions of its crew and commander as they listened to the tumult, and watched through the darkness the darting fires of the Titanic combat they could not share, may be imagined. "Our army," according to well-known authorities, "swore terribly in Flanders." The expletives discharged that night along the decks and in the forecastle of the *Culloden* would probably have made even a Flanders veteran open his eyes in astonishment.

The *Swiftsure* and the *Alexander*, taking warning by the *Culloden's* fate, swept round her and bore safely up to the fight. The *Swiftsure*, bearing down through the darkness to the combat, came across a vessel drifting, dismasted and lightless, a mere wreck. Holliwell, the captain of the *Swiftsure*, was about to fire, thinking it was an enemy, but on second thoughts hailed instead, and got for an answer the words, "*Bellerophon;* going out of action, disabled." The *Swiftsure* passed on, and five minutes after the *Bellerophon* had drifted from the bows of the *Orient*, the *Swiftsure*, coming mysteriously up out of the darkness, took her place, and broke into a tempest of fire.

At nine o'clock the great French flagship burst into flame. The painters had been at work upon her on the morning of that day, and had left oil and combustibles about. The nearest English ships concentrated their fire, both of musketry and of cannon, on the burning patch, and made the task of extinguishing it hopeless. Bruéys, the French admiral, had already been cut in two by a cannon shot, and Casabianca, his commodore, was wounded. The fire spread, the flames leaped up the masts and crept athwart the decks of the great ship. The moon had just risen, and the whole scene was perhaps the strangest ever witnessed—the great burning ship, the white light of the moon above, the darting points of red flame from the iron lips of hundreds of guns below, the drifting battle-smoke, the cries of ten thousand combatants—all crowded into an area of a few hundred square yards!

The British ships, hanging like hounds on the flanks of the *Orient*, knew that the explosion might come at any moment, and they made every preparation for it, closing their hatchways, and gathering their firemen at quarters. But they would not withdraw their ships a single yard! At ten o'clock the great French ship blew up with a flame that for a moment lit shore and sea, and a sound that hushed into stillness the whole tumult of the battle. Out of a crew of over a thousand men only seventy were saved! For ten minutes after that dreadful sight the warring fleets seemed stupefied. Not a shout was heard, not a shot fired. Then the French ship next the missing flagship broke into wrathful fire, and the battle awoke in full passion once more.

The fighting raged with partial intermissions all through the night, and when morning broke Bruéys' curved line of mighty battleships, a mile and a half long, had vanished. Of the French ships, one had been blown up, one was sunk, one was ashore, four had fled, the rest were prizes. It was the most complete and dramatic victory in naval history. The French fought on the whole with magnificent courage; but, though stronger in the mass, Nelson's strategy and the seamanship of his captains made the British stronger at every point of actual battle. The rear of the French line did not fire a shot or lose a man. The wonder is that when Nelson's strategy was developed, and its fatal character understood, Villeneuve, who commanded the French rear, and was a man of undoubted courage, did not cut his cables, make sail, and come to the help of his comrades. A few hundred yards would· have carried him to the heart of the fight. Can any one doubt whether, if the positions had been reversed, Nelson would have watched the destruction of half his fleet as a mere spectator? If nothing better had offered, he would have pulled in a wash-tub into the fight!

Villeneuve afterwards offered three explanations of his own inertness—(1) he "could not spare any of his anchors"; (2) "he had no instructions"! (3) "on board the ships in the rear the idea of weighing and going to the help of the ships engaged occurred to no one"! In justice to the French, however, it may be admitted that nothing could surpass the fierceness and valour with which, say, the *Tonnant* was fought. Its captain, Du Petit-Thouars, fought his ship magnificently, had first both his arms and then one of his legs shot away, and died entreating his officers not to strike. Of the ten French ships engaged, the captains of eight were killed or wounded. Nelson took the seven wounded captains on board the *Vanguard*, and, as they recovered, they dined regularly with him. One of the captains had lost his nose, another an eye, another most of his teeth, with musket-shots, &c. Nelson, who himself had been wounded, and was still half-blind as a result, at one of his dinners offered by mischance a case of toothpicks to the captain on his left, who had lost all his teeth. He discovered his error, and in his confusion handed his snuff-box to the captain on his right, who had lost his nose!

What was the secret of the British victory? Nelson's brilliant strategy was only possible by virtue of the magnificent seamanship of his captains, and the new fashion of close and desperate fighting, which Hood and Jarvis and Nelson himself had created. It is a French writer, Captain Gravière, who says that the French naval habit of evading battle where they could, and of accepting action from an enemy rather than forcing it upon him, had ruined the *morale* of the French navy. The long blockades had made Nelson's captains perfect seamen, and he taught them that close fighting at pistol-shot distance was the secret of victory. "No English captain," he said, "can do wrong who, in fight, lays a ship alongside an enemy." It was a captain of Nelson's school—a Scotchman—who at Camperdown, unable, just as the action began, to read some complicated signal from his chief, flung his signal-book on the deck, and in broad Scotch exclaimed, "D—— me! up with the hellem an' gang in the middle o't." That trick of "ganging into the middle o't" was irresistible.

The battle of the Nile destroyed the naval prestige of France, made England supreme in the Mediterranean, saved India, left Napoleon and his army practically prisoners in Egypt, and united Austria, Russia, and Turkey in league against France. The night battle in Aboukir Bay, in a word, changed the face of history.

THE FUSILEERS AT ALBUERA

" And nearer, fast and nearer,
    Doth the red whirlwind come;
And louder still, and still more loud,
From underneath that rolling cloud,
Is heard the trumpet's war-note proud,
    The trampling and the hum.
And plainly, and more plainly,
    Now through the gloom appears,
Far to left and far to right,
In broken gleams of dark-blue light,
The long array of helmets bright,
    The long array of spears."
              —MACAULAY.

ALBUERA is the fiercest, bloodiest, and most amazing fight in the mighty drama of the Peninsular war. On May 11, 1811, the English guns were thundering sullenly over Badajos. Wellington was beyond the Guadiana, pressing Marmont; and Beresford, with much pluck but little skill, was besieging the great frontier fortress. Soult, however, a master of war, was swooping down from Seville to raise the siege. On the 14th he reached Villafranca, only thirty miles distant, and fired salvos from his heaviest guns all through the night to warn the garrison of approaching succour. Beresford could not both maintain the siege and fight Soult; and on the night of the 13th he abandoned his trenches, burnt his gabions and fascines, and marched to meet Soult at Albuera,

LORD BERESFORD

After a painting by Sir W. Beechey, R.A.

a low ridge, with a shallow river in front, which barred the road to Badajos. As the morning of May 16, 1811, broke, heavy with clouds, and wild with gusty rain-storms, the two armies grimly gazed at each in stern pause, ere they joined in the wrestle of actual battle.

All the advantages, save one, were on the side of the French. Soult was the ablest of the French marshals. If he had not Ney's *élan* in attack, or Massena's stubborn resource in retreat, yet he had a military genius, since Lannes was dead, second only to that of Napoleon himself. He had under his command 20,000 war-hardened infantry, 40 guns, and 4000 magnificent cavalry, commanded by Latour Maubourg, one of the most brilliant of French cavalry generals. Beresford, the British commander, had the dogged fighting courage, half Dutch and half English, of his name and blood; but as a commander he was scarcely third-rate. Of his army of 30,000, 15,000 were Spanish, half drilled, and more than half starved —they had lived for days on horse-flesh—under Blake, a general who had lost all the good qualities of Irish character, and acquired all the bad ones peculiar to Spanish temper. Of Beresford's remaining troop 8000 were Portuguese; he had only 7000 British soldiers.

Beresford ought not to have fought. He had abandoned the siege at Badajos, and no reason for giving battle remained. The condition of Blake's men, no doubt, made retreat difficult. They had reached the point at which they must either halt or lie down and die. The real force driving Beresford to battle, however, was the fighting effervescence in his own blood and the warlike impatience of his

English troops. They had taken no part in the late great battles under Wellington; Busaco had been fought and Fuentes de Onoro gained without them; and they were in the mood, both officers and men, of fierce determination to fight *somebody*! This was intimated somewhat roughly to Beresford, and he had not that iron ascendency over his troops Wellington possessed. As a matter of fact, he was himself as stubbornly eager to fight as any private in the ranks.

The superiority of Soult's warlike genius was shown before a shot was fired. Beresford regarded the bridge that crossed the Albuera and the village that clustered at the bridge-head as the key of his position. He occupied the village with Alten's German brigade, covered the bridge with the fire of powerful batteries, and held in reserve above it his best British brigade, the fusileers, under Cole, the very regiments who, four hours later, on the extreme right of Beresford's position, were actually to win the battle. Soult's sure vision, however, as he surveyed his enemies on the evening of the 15th, saw that Beresford's right was his weak point. It was a rough, broken table-land, curving till it looked into the rear of Beresford's line. It was weakly held by Blake and his Spaniards. Immediately in its front was a low wooded hill, behind which, as a screen, an attacking force could be gathered.

In the night Soult placed behind this hill the fifth corps, under Gerard, the whole of his cavalry, under Latour Maubourg, and the strength of his artillery. When the morning broke, Soult had 15,000 men and 30 guns within ten minutes' march of Beresford's right wing, and nobody suspected it. No gleam of colour, no murmur of packed battalions, no ring of steel, no sound of marching feet warned the deluded English general of the battle-storm about to break on his right wing. A commander with such an unexpected tempest ready to burst on the weakest point of his line was by all the rules of war pre-doomed.

At nine o'clock Soult launched an attack at the bridge, the point where Beresford expected him, but it was only a feint. Beresford, however, with all his faults, had the soldierly brain to which the actual thunder of the cannon gave clearness. He noticed that the French battalions supporting the attack on the bridge did not press on closely. As a matter of fact, as soon as the smoke of artillery from the battle raging at the bridge swept over the field, they swung smartly to the left, and at the double hastened to add themselves to the thunderbolt which Soult was launching at Beresford's right. But Beresford, meanwhile, had guessed Soult's secret, and he sent officer after officer ordering and entreating Blake to change front so as to meet Soult's attack on his flank, and he finally rode thither himself to enforce his commands. Blake, however, was immovable through pride, and his men through sheer physical weakness. They could die, but they could not march or deploy. Blake at last tried to change front, but as he did so the French attack smote him. Pressing up the gentle rise, Gerard's men scourged poor Blake's flank with their fire; the French artillery, coming swiftly on, halted every fifty yards to thunder on the unhappy Spaniards; while Latour Maubourg's lancers and hus-

BATTLE OF ALBUERA
16th. May, 1811.

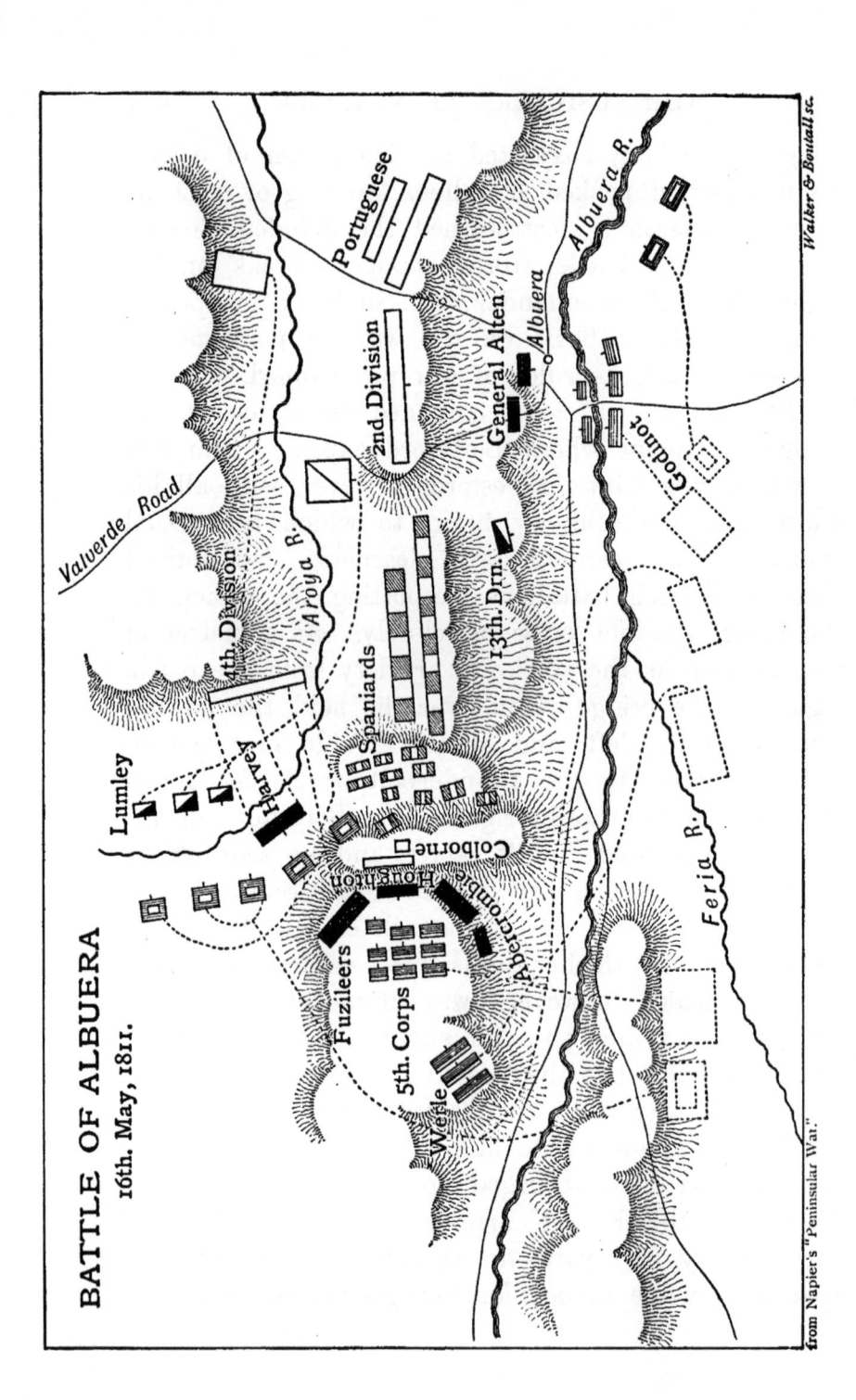

from Napier's "Peninsular War."   Walker & Boutall sc.

sars, galloping in a wider sweep, gathered momentum for a wild ride on Blake's actual rear.

Beresford tried to persuade the Spaniards to charge as the French were thus circling round them. Shouts and gesticulations were in vain. He was a man of giant height and strength, and he actually seized a Spanish ensign in his iron grip, and carried him bodily, flag and all, at a run for fifty yards towards the moving French lines, and planted him there. When released, however, the bewildered Spaniard simply took to his heels and ran back to his friends, as a terrified sheep might run back to the flock. In half-an-hour Beresford's battle had grown desperate. Two-thirds of the French, in compact order of battle, were perpendicular to his right; the Spaniards were falling into disorder. Soult saw the victory in his grasp, and eagerly pushed forward his reserves. Over the whole hill, mingled with furious blasts of rain, rolled the tumult of a disorderly and broken fight. Ten minutes more would have enabled Soult to fling Beresford's right, a shattered and routed mass, on the only possible line of retreat, and with the French superiority in cavalry his army would have been blotted out.

The share of the British in the fight consisted of three great attacks delivered by way of counter-stroke to Soult's overwhelming rush on the hill held by Blake. The first attack was delivered by the second division, under Colborne, led by General Stewart in person. Stewart was a sort of British version of Ney, a man of vehement spirit, with a daring that grew even more flame-like in the eddying tumult and tempest of actual battle. He saw Soult's attack crumpling up Blake's helpless battalions, while the flash of the French artillery every moment grew closer. It was the crisis of the fight, and Stewart brought on Colborne's men at a run. Colborne himself, a fine soldier with cool judgment, wished to halt and form his men in order of battle before plunging into the confused vortex of the fight above; but Stewart, full of breathless ardour, hurried the brigade up the hill in column of companies, reached the Spanish right, and began to form line by succession of battalions as they arrived.

At this moment a wild tempest of rain was sweeping over the British as, at the double, they came up the hill; the eddying fog, thick and slab with the smoke of powder, hid everything twenty yards from the panting soldiers. Suddenly the wall of changing fog to their right sparkled into swiftly moving spots of red; it shone the next instant with the gleam of a thousand steel points; above the thunder of the cannon, the shouts of contending men, rose the awful sound of a tempest of galloping hoofs. The French lancers and hussars caught the English in open order, and in five fierce and bloody minutes almost trampled them out of existence! Two-thirds of the brigade went down. The 31st Regiment flung itself promptly into square, and stood fast—a tiny island, edged with steel and flame, amid the mad tumult; but the French lancers, drunk with excitement, mad with battle fury, swept over the whole slope of the hill. They captured six guns, and might have done yet more fatal mischief but that they occupied themselves in galloping to and fro across the line of their original charge, spearing the wounded.

One lancer charged Beresford as he sat, solitary and

THE FUSILEERS AT ALBUERA

huge, on his horse amid the broken English regiments. But Beresford was at least a magnificent trooper; he put the lance aside with one hand, and caught the Frenchman by the throat, lifted him clean from his saddle, and dashed him senseless on the ground! The ensign who carried the colours of the 3rd Buffs covered them with his body till he was slain by a dozen lance-thrusts; the ensign who carried the other colours of the same regiment tore the flag from its staff and thrust it into his breast, and it was found there, stiff with his blood, after the fight. The Spaniards, meanwhile, were firing incessantly but on general principles merely, and into space or into the ranks of their own allies as might happen; and the 29th, advancing to the help of Colborne's broken men, finding the Spaniards in their path and firing into their lines, broke sternly into volleys on them in turn. Seldom has a battlefield witnessed a tumult so distracted and wild.

The first English counter-stroke had failed, but the second followed swiftly. The furious rain and fog which had proved so fatal to Colborne's men for a moment, was in favour of Beresford. Soult, though eagerly watching the conflict, could not see the ruin into which the British had fallen, and hesitated to launch his reserves into the fight. The 31st still sternly held its own against the French cavalry, and this gave time for Stewart to bring up Houghton's brigade. But this time Stewart, though he brought up his men with as much vehemence as before, brought them up in order of battle. The 29th, the 48th, and the 57th swept up the hill in line, led by Houghton, hat in hand. He fell, pierced by three bullets; but over his dead body, eager to close, the British line still swept. They reached the crest. A deep and narrow ravine arrested their bayonet charge; but with stubborn valour they held the ground they had gained, scourged with musketry fire at pistol-shot distance, and by artillery at fifty yards' range, while a French column smote them with its musketry on their flank. The men fell fast, but fought as they fell. Stewart was twice wounded; Colonel Dutworth, of the 48th, slain; of the 57th, out of 570 men, 430, with their colonel, Inglis, fell. The men, after the battle, were found lying dead in ranks exactly as they fought. "Die hard! my men, die hard!" said Inglis when the bullet struck him; and the 57th have borne the name of "Die hards" ever since. At Inkerman, indeed, more than fifty years afterwards, the "Die hard!" of Inglis served to harden the valour of the 57th in a fight as stern as Albuera itself.

But ammunition began to fail. Houghton's men would not yield, but it was plain that in a few more minutes there would be none of them left, save the dead and the wounded. And at this dreadful moment Beresford, distracted with the tumult and horror of the fight, wavered! He called up Alten's men from the bridge to cover his retreat, and prepared to yield the fatal hill. At this juncture, however, a mind more masterful and daring than his own launched a third British attack against the victorious French and won the dreadful day.

Colonel Hardinge, afterwards famous in Indian battles, acted as quartermaster-general of the Portuguese army; on his own responsibility he organised the third English attack. Cole had just come up the road from Badajos with two brigades, and Hardinge urged him to lead his men straight up the hill; then riding to Abercrombie's brigade, he ordered him to sweep round the flank of the hill. Beresford, on learning of this movement, accepted it, and sent back Alten's men to retake the bridge which they had abandoned.

Abercrombie's men swept to the left of the hill, and Cole, a gallant and able soldier, using the Portuguese regiments in his brigade as a guard against a flank attack of the French cavalry, led his two fusileer regiments, the 7th and 23rd, straight to the crest.

At this moment the French reserves were coming on, the fragments of Houghton's brigade were falling back, the field was heaped with carcases, the lancers were riding furiously about the captured artillery, and with a storm of exultant shouts the French were sweeping on to assured victory. It was the dramatic moment of the fight. Suddenly through the fog, coming rapidly on with stern faces and flashing volleys, appeared the long line of Cole's fusileers on the right of Houghton's staggering groups, while at the same exact moment Abercrombie's line broke through the mist on their left. As these grim and threatening lines became visible, the French shouts suddenly died down. It was the old contest of the British line— the "thin red line"— against the favourite French attack in column, and the story can only be told in Napier's resonant prose. The passage which describes the attack of the fusileers is one of the classic passages of English battle literature, and in its syllables can still almost be heard the tread of marching feet, the shrill clangour of smitten steel, and the thunder of the musketry volleys:—

"Such a gallant line," says Napier, "arising from amid the smoke, and rapidly separating itself from the confused and broken multitude, startled the enemy's masses, which were increasing and pressing forward as to assured victory; they wavered, hesitated, and then, vomiting forth a storm of fire, hastily endeavoured to enlarge their front, while the fearful discharge of grape from all their artillery whistled through the British ranks. Myert was killed, Cole and the three colonels —Ellis, Blackeney, and Hawkshawe—fell wounded, and the fusileer battalions, struck by the iron tempest, reeled and staggered like sinking ships. Suddenly and sternly recovering, they closed on their terrible enemies, and then was seen with what a strength and majesty the British soldier fights. In vain did Soult, by voice and gesture, animate his Frenchmen; in vain did the hardiest veterans break from the crowded columns and sacrifice their lives to gain time for the mass to open on such a fair field; in vain did the mass itself bear up, and, fiercely striving, fire indiscriminately on friends and foes, while the horsemen, hovering on the flanks, threatened to charge the advancing line.

"Nothing could stop that astonishing infantry. No sudden burst of undisciplined valour, no nervous enthusiasm weakened the stability of their order; their flashing eyes were bent on the dark columns in front, their measured tread shook the ground, their dreadful volleys swept away the head of every formation, their deafening shouts overpowered the dissonant cries that broke from all parts of the tumultuous crowd as slowly and with a horrid carnage it was driven by the incessant vigour of the attack to the farthest edge of the hill. In vain did the French reserves mix with the struggling multitude to sustain the fight; their efforts only increased the irremediable confusion, and the mighty mass, breaking off like a loosened cliff, went headlong down the ascent. The rain flowed after in streams discoloured with blood, and 1800 unwounded men, the remnant of 6000 unconquerable British soldiers, stood triumphant on the fatal hill."

The battle of Albuera lasted four hours; its slaughter was dreadful. Within the space of a few hundred feet square were strewn some 7000 bodies, and over this Aceldama the artillery had galloped, the cavalry had charged! The 3rd Buffs went into the fight with 24 officers and 750 rank and file; at the roll-call next morning there were only 5 officers and 35 men. One company of the Royal Fusileers came out of the fight commanded by a corporal; every officer and sergeant had been killed. Albuera is essentially a soldier's fight. The bayonet of the private, not the brain of the general, won it; and never was the fighting quality of our race more brilliantly shown. Soult summed up the battle in words that deserve to be memorable. "There is no beating those troops," he wrote, "*in spite of their generals!*" "I always thought them bad soldiers," he added, with a Frenchman's love of paradox; "now I am sure of it. For I turned their right, pierced their centre, they were everywhere broken, the day was mine, and yet *they did not know it*, and would not run!"

THE "SHANNON" AND THE "CHESAPEAKE"

" The signal to engage shall be
   A whistle and a hollo;
Be one and all but firm, like me,
   And conquest soon will follow!
You, Gunnel, keep the helm in hand—
   Thus, thus, boys! steady, steady,
Till right ahead you see the land—
   Then soon as you are ready,
The signal to engage shall be
   A whistle and a hollo;
Be one and all but firm, like me,
   And conquest soon will follow ! "
                        —C. DIBDIN.

ON the early morning of June 1, 1813, a solitary British frigate, H.M.S. *Shannon*, was cruising within sight of Boston lighthouse. She was a ship of about 1000 tons, and bore every mark of long and hard service. No gleam of colour sparkled about her. Her sides were rusty, her sails weather-stained; a solitary flag flew from her mizzen-peak, and even its blue had been bleached by sun and rain and wind to a dingy grey. A less romantic and more severely practical ship did not float, and her captain was of the same type as the ship.

Captain Philip Bowes Vere Broke was an Englishman *pur sang*, and of a type happily not uncommon.

SIR PHILIP BOWES VERE BROKE

After a painting by LANE

His fame will live as long as the British flag flies, yet a more sober and prosaic figure can hardly be imagined. He was not, like Nelson, a quarter-deck Napoleon; he had no gleam of Dundonald's matchless *ruse de guerre*. He was as deeply religious as Havelock or one of Cromwell's major-generals; he had the frugality of a Scotchman, and the heavy-footed common-sense of a Hollander. He was as nautical as a web-footed bird, and had no more "nerves" than a fish. A domestic Englishman, whose heart was always with the little girls at Brokehall, in Suffolk, but for whom the service of his country was a piety, and who might have competed with Lawrence for his self-chosen epitaph, "Here lies one who tried to do his duty."

A sober-suited, half-melancholy common-sense was Broke's characteristic, and he had applied it to the working of his ship, till he had made the vessel, perhaps, the most formidable fighting machine of her size afloat. He drilled his gunners until, from the swaying platform of their decks, they shot with a deadly coolness and accuracy nothing floating could resist. Broke, as a matter of fact, owed his famous victory over the *Chesapeake* to one of his matter-of-fact precautions. The first broadside fired by the *Chesapeake* sent a 32-pound shot through one of the gun-room cabins into the magazine passage of the *Shannon*, where it might easily have ignited some grains of loose powder and blown the ship up, if Broke had not taken the precaution of elaborately *damping* that passage before the action began. The prosaic side of Broke's character is very amusing. In his diary he records his world-famous victory thus :—

"June 1st.—Off Boston. Moderate."

" N.W.—W(rote) Laurence."

" P.M.—Took *Chesapeake*."

Was ever a shining victory packed into fewer or duller words? Broke's scorn of the histrionic is shown by his reply to one of his own men who, when the *Chesapeake*, one blaze of fluttering colours, was bearing down upon her drab-coloured opponent, said to his commander, eyeing the bleached and solitary flag at the *Shannon's* peak, "Mayn't we have three ensigns, sir, like she has?" "No," said Broke, "we have always been an *unassuming* ship!"

And yet, this unromantic English sailor had a gleam of Don Quixote in him. On this pleasant summer morning he was waiting alone, under easy sail, outside a hostile port, strongly fortified and full of armed vessels, waiting for an enemy's ship bigger than himself to come out and fight him. He had sent in the previous day, by way of challenge, a letter that recalls the days of chivalry. "As the *Chesapeake*," he wrote to Laurence, its captain, "appears now ready for sea, I request that you will do me the favour to meet the *Shannon* with her, ship to ship." He proceeds to explain the exact armament of the *Shannon*, the number of her crew, the interesting circumstance that he is short of provisions and water, and that he has sent away his consort so that the terms of the duel may be fair. "If you will favour me," he says, "with any plan of signals or telegraph, I will warn you should any of my friends be too nigh, while you are in sight, until I can detach them out of the way. Or," he suggests coaxingly, "I would sail under a flag of truce to any place you think safest from our cruisers, hauling it down when fair, to begin hostilities. . . . Choose your terms," he concludes, "but let us meet." Having sent in this amazing letter, this middle-aged, unromantic, but hard-fighting captain climbs at daybreak to his own maintop, and sits there till half-past eleven, watching the challenged ship, to see if her foretopsail is unloosed and she is coming out to fight.

It is easy to understand the causes which kindled a British sailor of even Broke's unimaginative temperament into flame. On June 18, 1812, the United States, with magnificent audacity, declared war against Great Britain. England at that moment had 621 efficient cruisers at sea, 102 being line-of-battle ships. The American navy consisted of 8 frigates and 12 corvettes. It is true that England was at war at the same moment with half the civilised world; but what reasonable chance had the tiny naval power of the United States against the mighty fleets of England, commanded by men trained in the school of Nelson, and rich with the traditions of the Nile and Trafalgar? As a matter of fact, in the war which followed, the commerce of the United States was swept out of existence. But the Americans were of the same fighting stock as the English; to the Viking blood, indeed, they added Yankee ingenuity and resource, making a very formidable combination; and up to the June morning when the *Shannon* was waiting outside Boston Harbour for the *Chesapeake*, the naval honours of the war belonged to the Americans. The Americans had no fleet, and the campaign was one of single ship against single ship, but in these combats the Americans had scored more successes in twelve months than French seamen had gained in twelve years. The *Guerrière*, the *Java*, and the *Macedonian* had each been captured in single combat, and every British post-captain betwixt Portsmouth and Halifax was swearing with mere fury.

The Americans were shrewd enough to invent a new type of frigate which, in strength of frame, weight of metal, and general fighting power, was to a British frigate of the same class almost what an ironclad would be to a wooden ship. The *Constitution*, for example, was in size to the average British frigate as 15.3 to 10.9; in weight of metal as 76 to 51; and in crew as 46 to 25. Broke, however, had a well-founded belief in his ship and his men, and he proposed, in his sober fashion, to restore the tarnished honour of his flag by capturing single-handed the best American frigate afloat.

The *Chesapeake* was a fine ship, perfectly equipped, under a daring and popular commander. Laurence was a man of brilliant ingenuity and courage, and had won fame four months before by capturing in the *Hornet*, after a hard fight, the British brig-of-war *Peacock*. For this feat he had been promoted to the *Chesapeake*, and in his brief speech from the quarter-deck just before the fight with the *Shannon* began, he called up the memory of the fight which made him a popular hero by exhorting his crew to "*Peacock* her, my lads! *Peacock* her!" The *Chesapeake* was larger than the *Shannon*, its crew was nearly a hundred men stronger, its weight of fire 598 lbs. as against the *Shannon's* 538 lbs. Her guns fired double-headed shot, and bars of wrought iron connected by links and loosely tied by a few rope yarns, which, when discharged from

CAPTAIN LAURENCE
From an engraving by WILLIAMSON

the gun, spread out and formed a flying iron chain six feet long. Its canister shot contained jagged pieces of iron, broken bolts, and nails. As the British had a reputation for boarding, a large barrel of unslacked lime was provided to fling in the faces of the boarders. An early shot from the *Shannon*, by the way, struck this cask of lime and scattered its contents in the faces of the Americans themselves. Part of the equipment of the *Chesapeake* consisted of several hundred pairs of handcuffs, intended for the wrists of English prisoners. Boston citizens prepared a banquet in honour of the victors for the same evening, and a small fleet of pleasure-boats followed the *Chesapeake* as she came gallantly out to the fight.

Never was a braver, shorter, or more murderous fight. Laurence, the most gallant of men, bore steadily down, without firing a shot, to the starboard quarter of the *Shannon*. When within fifty yards he luffed; his men sprang into the shrouds and gave three cheers. Broke fought with characteristic silence and composure. He forbade his men to cheer, enforced the sternest silence along his deck, and ordered the captain of each gun to fire as his piece bore on the enemy. "Fire into her quarters," he said, "main-deck into main-deck, quarter-deck into quarter-deck. Kill the men, and the ship is yours."

The sails of the *Chesapeake* swept betwixt the slanting rays of the evening sun and the *Shannon*, the drifting shadow darkened the English main-deck ports, the rush of the enemy's cut-water could be heard through the grim silence of the *Shannon's* decks. Suddenly there broke out the first gun from the

Shannon; then her whole side leaped into flame. Never was a more fatal broadside discharged. A tempest of shot, splinters, torn hammocks, cut rigging, and wreck of every kind was hurled like a cloud across the deck of the *Chesapeake,* and of one hundred and fifty men at stations there, more than a hundred were killed or wounded. A more fatal loss to the Americans instantly followed, as Captain Laurence, the fiery soul of his ship, was shot through the abdomen by an English marine, and fell mortally wounded.

The answering thunder of the *Chesapeake's* guns, of course, rolled out, and then, following quick, the overwhelming blast of the *Shannon's* broadside once more. Each ship, indeed, fired two full broadsides, and, as the guns fell quickly out of range, part of another broadside. The firing of the *Chesapeake* was furious and deadly enough to have disabled an ordinary ship. It is computed that forty effective shots would be enough to disable a frigate; the *Shannon* during the six minutes of the firing was struck by no less than 158 shot, a fact which proves the steadiness and power of the American fire. But the fire of the *Shannon* was overwhelming. In those same six fatal minutes she smote the *Chesapeake* with no less than 362 shots, an average of 60 shots of all sizes every minute, as against the *Chesapeake's* 28 shots. The *Chesapeake* was fir-built, and the British shot riddled her. One *Shannon* broadside partly raked the *Chesapeake* and literally smashed the stern cabins and battery to mere splinters, as completely as though a procession of aerolites had torn through it.

The swift, deadly, concentrated fire of the British

in two quick-following broadsides practically decided the combat. The partially disabled vessels drifted together, and the *Chesapeake* fell on board the *Shannon*, her quarter striking the starboard main-chains. Broke, as the ships ground together, looked over the blood-splashed decks of the American and saw the men deserting the quarter-deck guns, under the terror of another broadside at so short a distance. "Follow me who can," he shouted, and with characteristic coolness "stepped"—in his own phrase—across the *Chesapeake's* bulwark. He was followed by some 32 seamen and 18 marines—50 British boarders leaping upon a ship with a crew of 400 men, a force which, even after the dreadful broadsides of the *Shannon*, still numbered 270 unwounded men in its ranks.

It is absurd to deny to the Americans courage of the very finest quality, but the amazing and unexpected severity of the *Shannon's* fire had destroyed for the moment their morale, and the British were in a mood of victory. The boatswain of the *Shannon*, an old *Rodney* man, lashed the two ships together, and in the act had his left arm literally hacked off by repeated strokes of a cutlass and was killed. One British midshipman, followed by five topmen, crept along the *Shannon's* foreyard and stormed the *Chesapeake's* foretop, killing the men stationed there, and then swarmed down by a back-stay to join the fighting on the deck. Another middy tried to attack the *Chesapeake's* mizzentop from the starboard mainyard arm, but being hindered by the foot of the topsail, stretched himself out on the mainyard arm, and from that post shot three of the enemy in succession.

Meanwhile the fight on the deck had been short and sharp; some of the Americans leaped overboard and others rushed below; and Laurence, lying wounded in his steerage, saw the wild reflux of his own men down the after ladders. On asking what it meant, he was told, "The ship is boarded, and those are the *Chesapeake's* men driven from the upper decks by the English." This so exasperated the dying man that he called out repeatedly, "Then blow her up; blow her up."

The fight lasted exactly thirteen minutes — the broadsides occupied six minutes, the boarding seven — and in thirteen minutes after the first shot the British flag was flying over the American ship. The *Shannon* and *Chesapeake* were bearing up, side by side, for Halifax. The spectators in the pleasure-boats were left ruefully staring at the spectacle; those American handcuffs, so thoughtfully provided, were on American wrists; and the Boston citizens had to consume, with what appetite they might, their own banquet. The carnage on the two ships was dreadful. In thirteen minutes 252 men were either killed or wounded, an average of nearly twenty men for every minute the fight lasted. In the combat betwixt these two frigates, in fact, nearly as many men were struck down as in the whole battle of Navarino! The *Shannon* itself lost as many men as any 74-gun ship ever lost in battle.

Judge Haliburton, famous as "Sam Slick," when a youth of seventeen, boarded the *Chesapeake* as the two battered ships sailed into Halifax. "The deck," he wrote, "had not been cleaned, and the coils and folds of rope were steeped in gore as if in a slaughter-house. Pieces of skin with pendent hair were adhering to the sides of the ship; and in one place I noticed portions of fingers protruding, as if thrust through the outer walls of the frigate."

Watts, the first lieutenant of the *Shannon*, was killed by the fire of his own ship in a very remarkable manner. He boarded with his captain, with his own hands pulled down the *Chesapeake's* flag, and hastily bent on the halliards the English ensign, as he thought, *above* the Stars and Stripes, and then rehoisted it. In the hurry he had bent the English flag *under* the Stars and Stripes instead of above it, and the gunners of the *Shannon*, seeing the American stripes going up first, opened fire instantly on the group at the foot of the mizzen-mast, blew the top of their own unfortunate lieutenant's head off with a grape shot, and killed three or four of their own men.

Captain Broke was desperately wounded in a curious fashion. A group of Americans, who had laid down their arms, saw the British captain standing for a moment alone on the break of the forecastle. It seemed a golden chance. They snatched up weapons lying on the deck, and leaped upon him. Warned by the shout of the sentry, Broke turned round to find three of the enemy with uplifted weapons rushing on him. He parried the middle fellow's pike and wounded him in the face, but was instantly struck down with a blow from the butt-end of a musket, which laid bare his skull. He also received a slash from the cutlass of the third man, which clove a portion of skull completely away and left the brain bare. He fell, and was grappled on the deck by the man he had first wounded, a powerful fellow, who got uppermost and raised a bayonet to thrust through Broke. At this moment a British marine came running up, and concluding that the man underneath *must* be an American, also raised his bayonet to give the *coup de grace*. "Pooh, pooh, you fool," said Broke in the most matter-of-fact fashion, "don't you know your captain?" whereupon the marine changed the direction of his thrust and slew the American.

The news reached London on July 7, and was carried straight to the House of Commons, where Lord Cochrane was just concluding a fierce denunciation of the Admiralty on the ground of the disasters suffered from the Americans, and Croker, the Secretary to the Admiralty, was able to tell the story of the fight off Boston to the wildly cheering House, as a complete defence of his department. Broke was at once created a Baronet and a Knight of the Bath. In America, on the other hand, the story of the fight was received with mingled wrath and incredulity. "I remember," says Rush, afterwards U.S. Minister at the Court of St. James, "at the first rumour of it, the universal incredulity. I remember how the post-offices were thronged for successive days with anxious thousands; how collections of citizens rode out for miles on the highway to get the earliest news the mail brought. At last, when the certainty was known, I remember the public gloom, the universal badges of mourning. 'Don't give up the ship,' the dying words of Laurence, were on every tongue."

It was a great fight, the most memorable and dramatic sea-duel in naval history. The combatants were men of the same stock, and fought with equal bravery. Both nations, in fact, may be proud of a fight so frank, so fair, so gallant. The world, we may hope, will never witness another *Shannon* engaged in the fierce wrestle of battle with another *Chesapeake*, for the Union Jack and the Stars and Stripes are knitted together by a bond woven of common blood and speech and political ideals that grows stronger every year.

For years the *Shannon* and the *Chesapeake* lay peacefully side by side in the Medway, and the two famous ships might well have been preserved as trophies. The *Chesapeake* was bought by the Admiralty after the fight for exactly £21,314, 11s. 11¼d., and six years afterwards she was sold as mere old timber for £500, was broken up, and to-day stands as a Hampshire flour-mill, peacefully grinding English corn; but still on the mill-timbers can be seen the marks of the grape and round shot of the *Shannon*.

THE GREAT BREACH OF CIUDAD RODRIGO

"Attend, all ye who list to hear our noble England's praise,
I tell of the thrice famous deeds she wrought in ancient days."
—MACAULAY.

THE three great and memorable sieges of the Peninsular war are those of Ciudad Rodrigo, Badajos, and San Sebastian. The annals of battle record nowhere a more furious daring in assault or a more gallant courage in defence than that which raged in turn round each of these three great fortresses. Of the three sieges that of Badajos was the most picturesque and bloody; that of San Sebastian the most sullen and exasperated; that of Ciudad Rodrigo the swiftest and most brilliant. A great siege tests the fighting quality of any army as nothing else can test it. In the night watches in the trenches, in the dogged toil of the batteries, and the crowded perils of the breach, all the frippery and much of the real discipline of an army dissolves. The soldiers fall back upon what may be called the primitive fighting qualities—the hardihood of the individual soldier, the daring with which the officers will lead, the dogged loyalty with which the men will follow. As an illustration of the warlike qualities in our race by which empire has been achieved, nothing better can be desired than the story of how the breaches were won at Ciudad Rodrigo.

At the end of 1811 the English and the French were watching each other jealously across the Spanish border. The armies of Marmont and of Soult, 67,000 strong, lay within touch of each other, barring Wellington's entrance into Spain. Wellington, with 35,000 men, of whom not more than 10,000 men were British, lay within sight of the Spanish frontier. It was the winter time. Wellington's army was wasted by sickness, his horses were dying of mere starvation, his men had received no pay for three months, and his muleteers none for eight months. He had no siege-train, his regiments were ragged and hungry, and the French generals confidently reckoned the British army as, for the moment at least, *une quantité négligeable*.

And yet at that precise moment, Wellington, subtle and daring, was meditating a leap upon the great frontier fortress of Ciudad Rodrigo, in the Spanish province of Salamanca. Its capture would give him a safe base of operations against Spain; it was the great frontier *place d'armes* for the French; the whole siege-equipage, and stores of the army of Portugal were contained in it. The problem of how, in the depth of winter, without materials for a siege, to snatch a place so strong from under the very eyes of two armies, each stronger than his own, was a problem which might have taxed the warlike genius of a Cæsar. But Wellington accomplished it with a combination of subtlety and audacity simply marvellous.

He kept the secret of his design so perfectly that

his own engineers never suspected it, and his adjutant-general, Murray, went home on leave without dreaming anything was going to happen. Wellington collected artillery ostensibly for the purpose of arming Almeida, but the guns were trans-shipped at sea and brought secretly to the mouth of the Douro. No less than 800 mule-carts were constructed without anybody guessing their purpose. Wellington, while these preparations were on foot, was keenly watching Marmont and Soult, till he saw that they were lulled into a state of mere yawning security, and then, in Napier's expressive phrase, he "instantly jumped with both feet upon Ciudad Rodrigo."

This famous fortress, in shape, roughly resembles a triangle with the angles truncated. The base, looking to the south, is covered by the Agueda, a river given to sudden inundations; the fortifications were strong and formidably armed; as outworks it had to the east the great fortified Convent of San Francisco, to the west a similar building called Santa Cruz; whilst almost parallel with the northern face rose two rocky ridges called the Great and Small Teson, the nearest within 600 yards of the city ramparts, and crowned by a formidable redoubt called Francisco. The siege began on January 8. The soil was rocky and covered with snow, the nights were black, the weather bitter. The men lacked entrenching tools. They had to encamp on the side of the Agueda farthest from the city, and ford that river every time the trenches were relieved. The 1st, 3rd, and light divisions formed the attacking force; each division held the trenches in turn for twenty-four hours. Let the reader imagine what degree of hardihood it took to wade in the grey and bitter winter dawn through a half-frozen river, and without fire or warm food, and under a ceaseless rain of shells from the enemy's guns, to toil in the frozen trenches, or to keep watch, while the icicles hung from eyebrow and beard, over the edge of the battery for twenty-four hours in succession.

Nothing in this great siege is more wonderful than the fierce speed with which Wellington urged his operations. Massena, who had besieged and captured the city the year before in the height of summer, spent a month in bombarding it before he ventured to assault. Wellington broke ground on January 8, under a tempest of mingled hail and rain; he stormed it on the night of the 19th.

He began operations by leaping on the strong work that crowned the Great Teson the very night the siege began. Two companies from each regiment of the light division were detailed by the officer of the day, Colonel Colborne, for the assault. Colborne (afterwards Lord Seaton), a cool and gallant soldier, called his officers together in a group and explained with great minuteness how they were to attack. He then launched his men against the redoubt with a vehemence so swift that, to those who watched the scene under the light of a wintry moon, the column of redcoats, like the thrust of a crimson sword-blade, spanned the ditch, shot up the glacis, and broke through the parapet with a single movement. The accidental explosion of a French shell burst the gate open, and the remainder of the attacking party instantly swept through it. There was fierce musketry fire and a tumult of shouting for a moment or two, but in twenty minutes from Colborne's launching his attack every Frenchman in the redoubt was killed, wounded, or a prisoner.

The fashion in which the gate was blown open was very curious. A French sergeant was in the act of throwing a live shell upon the storming party in the ditch, when he was struck by an English bullet. The lighted shell fell from his hands within the parapet, was kicked away by the nearest French in mere self-preservation; it rolled towards the gate, exploded, burst it open, and instantly the British broke in.

For ten days a desperate artillery duel raged between the besiegers and the besieged. The parallels were resolutely pushed on in spite of rocky soil, broken tools, bitter weather, and the incessant pelting of the French guns. The temper of the British troops is illustrated by an incident which George Napier — the youngest of the three Napiers—relates. The three brothers were gallant and remarkable soldiers. Charles Napier in India and elsewhere made history; William, in his wonderful tale of the Peninsular war, wrote history; and George, if he had not the literary genius of the one nor the strategic skill of the other, was a most gallant soldier. "I was a field-officer of the trenches," he says, "when a 13-inch shell from the town fell in the midst of us. I called to the men to lie down flat, and they instantly obeyed orders, except one of them, an Irishman and an old marine, but a most worthless drunken dog, who trotted up to the shell, the fuse of which was still burning, and striking it with his spade, knocked the fuse out; then taking the immense shell in his hands, brought it to me, saying, 'There she is for you now, yer 'anner. I've knocked the life out of the crater.'"

The besieged brought fifty heavy guns to reply to the thirty light pieces by which they were assailed, and day and night the bellow of eighty pieces boomed sullenly over the doomed city and echoed faintly back from the nearer hills, while the walls crashed to the stroke of the bullet. The English fire made up by fierceness and accuracy for what it lacked in weight; but the sap made no progress, the guns showed signs of being worn out, and although two apparent breaches had been made, the counterscarp was not destroyed. Yet Wellington determined to attack, and, in his characteristic fashion, to attack by night. The siege had lasted ten days, and Marmont, with an army stronger than his own, was lying within four marches. That he had not appeared already on the scene was wonderful.

In a general order issued on the evening of the 19th Wellington wrote, "Ciudad Rodrigo *must* be stormed this evening." The great breach was a sloping gap in the wall at its northern angle, about a hundred feet wide. The French had crowned it with two guns loaded with grape; the slope was strewn with bombs, hand-grenades, and bags of powder; a great mine pierced it beneath; a deep ditch had been cut betwixt the breach and the adjoining ramparts, and these were crowded with riflemen. The third division, under General Mackinnon, was to attack the breach, its forlorn hope being led by Ensign Mackie, its storming party by-General Mackinnon himself. The lesser breach was a tiny gap, scarcely twenty feet wide, to the left of the great breach; this was to be attacked by the light division, under Craufurd, its forlorn hope of twenty-five men being led by Gurwood, and its storming party by George Napier. General Pack, with a Portuguese brigade, was to make a sham attack on the eastern face, while a fourth attack was to be made on the southern front by a company of the 83rd and some Portuguese troops. In the storming party of the 83rd were the Earl of March, afterwards Duke of Richmond; Lord Fitzroy Somerset, afterwards Lord Raglan; and the Prince of Orange—all volunteers without Wellington's knowledge!

At 7 o'clock a curious silence fell suddenly on the battered city and the engirdling trenches. Not a light gleamed from the frowning parapets, not a murmur arose from the blackened trenches. Suddenly a shout broke out on the right of the English attack; it ran, a wave of stormy sound, along the line of the trenches. The men who were to attack the great breach leaped into the open. In a moment the space betwixt the hostile lines was covered with the stormers, and the gloomy half-seen face of the great fortress broke into a tempest of fire.

Nothing could be finer than the vehement courage of the assault, unless it were the cool and steady fortitude of the defence. Swift as was the upward rush of the stormers, the race of the 5th, 77th, and 94th regiments was almost swifter. Scorning to wait for the ladders, they leaped into the great ditch, outpaced even the forlorn hope, and pushed vehemently up the great breach, whilst their red ranks were torn by shell and shot. The fire, too, ran through the tangle of broken stones over which they climbed; the hand-grenades and powder-bags by which it was strewn exploded. The men were walking on fire! Yet the attack could not be denied. The Frenchmen—shooting, stabbing, yelling—were driven behind their entrenchments. There the fire of the houses commanding the breach came to their help, and they made a gallant stand. "None would go back on either side, and yet the British could not get forward, and men and officers falling in heaps choked up the passage, which from minute to minute was raked with grape from two guns flanking the top of the breach at the distance of a few yards. Thus striving, and trampling alike upon the dead and the wounded, these brave men maintained the combat."

It was the attack on the smaller breach which really carried Ciudad Rodrigo; and George Napier, who led it, has left a graphic narrative of the exciting experiences of that dreadful night. The light division was to attack, and Craufurd, with whom Napier was a favourite, gave him command of the storming party. He was to ask for 100 volunteers from each of the three British regiments—the 43rd, 52nd, and the Rifle Corps—in the division. Napier halted these regiments just as they had forded the bitterly cold river on their way to the trenches. "Soldiers," he said, "I want 100 men from each regiment to form the storming party which is to lead the light division to-night. Those who will go with me come forward!" Instantly there was a rush forward of the whole division, and Napier had to take his 300 men out of a tumult of nearly 1500 candidates. He formed them into three companies, under Captains Ferguson, Jones, and Mitchell. Gurwood, of the 52nd, led the forlorn hope, consisting

K

of twenty-five men and two sergeants. Wellington himself came to the trench and showed Napier and Colborne, through the gloom of the early night, the exact position of the breach. A staff-officer looking on, said, "Your men are not loaded. Why don't you make them load?" Napier replied, "If we don't do the business with the bayonet we shall not do it all. I shall not load." "Let him alone," said Wellington; "let him go his own way." Picton had adopted the same grim policy with the third division. As each regiment passed him, filing into the trenches, his injunction was, "No powder! We'll do the thing with the *could* iron."

A party of Portuguese carrying bags filled with grass were to run with the storming party and throw the bags into the ditch, as the leap was too deep for the men. But the Portuguese hesitated, the tumult of the attack on the great breach suddenly broke on the night, and the forlorn hope went running up, leaped into the ditch a depth of eleven feet, and clambered up the steep slope beyond, while Napier with his stormers came with a run behind them. In the dark for a moment the breach was lost, but found again, and up the steep quarry of broken stone the attack swept. About two-thirds of the way up Napier's arm was smashed by a grape-shot, and he fell. His men, checked for a moment, lifted their muskets to the gap above them, whence the French were firing vehemently, and forgetting their pieces were unloaded, snapped them. "Push on with the bayonet, men!" shouted Napier, as he lay bleeding. The officers leaped to the front, the men with a stern shout followed; they were crushed to a front of not more than three or four. They had to climb without firing a shot in reply up to the muzzles of the French muskets.

But nothing could stop the men of the light division. A 24-pounder was placed across the narrow gap in the ramparts; the stormers leaped over it, and the 43rd and 52nd, coming up in sections abreast, followed. The 43rd wheeled to the right towards the great breach, the 52nd to the left, sweeping the ramparts as they went.

Meanwhile the other two attacks had broken into the town; but at the great breach the dreadful fight still raged, until the 43rd, coming swiftly along the ramparts, and brushing all opposition aside, took the defence in the rear. The British there had, as a matter of fact, at that exact moment pierced the French defence. The two guns that scourged the breach had wrought deadly havoc amongst the stormers, and a sergeant and two privates of the 88th—Irishmen all, and whose names deserve to be preserved—Brazel, Kelly, and Swan—laid down their firelocks that they might climb more lightly, and, armed only with their bayonets, forced themselves through the embrasure amongst the French gunners. They were furiously attacked, and Swan's arm was hewed off by a sabre stroke; but they stopped the service of the gun, slew five or six of the French gunners, and held the post until the men of the 5th, climbing behind them, broke into the battery.

So Ciudad Rodrigo was won, and its governor surrendered his sword to the youthful lieutenant leading the forlorn hope of the light division, who, with smoke-

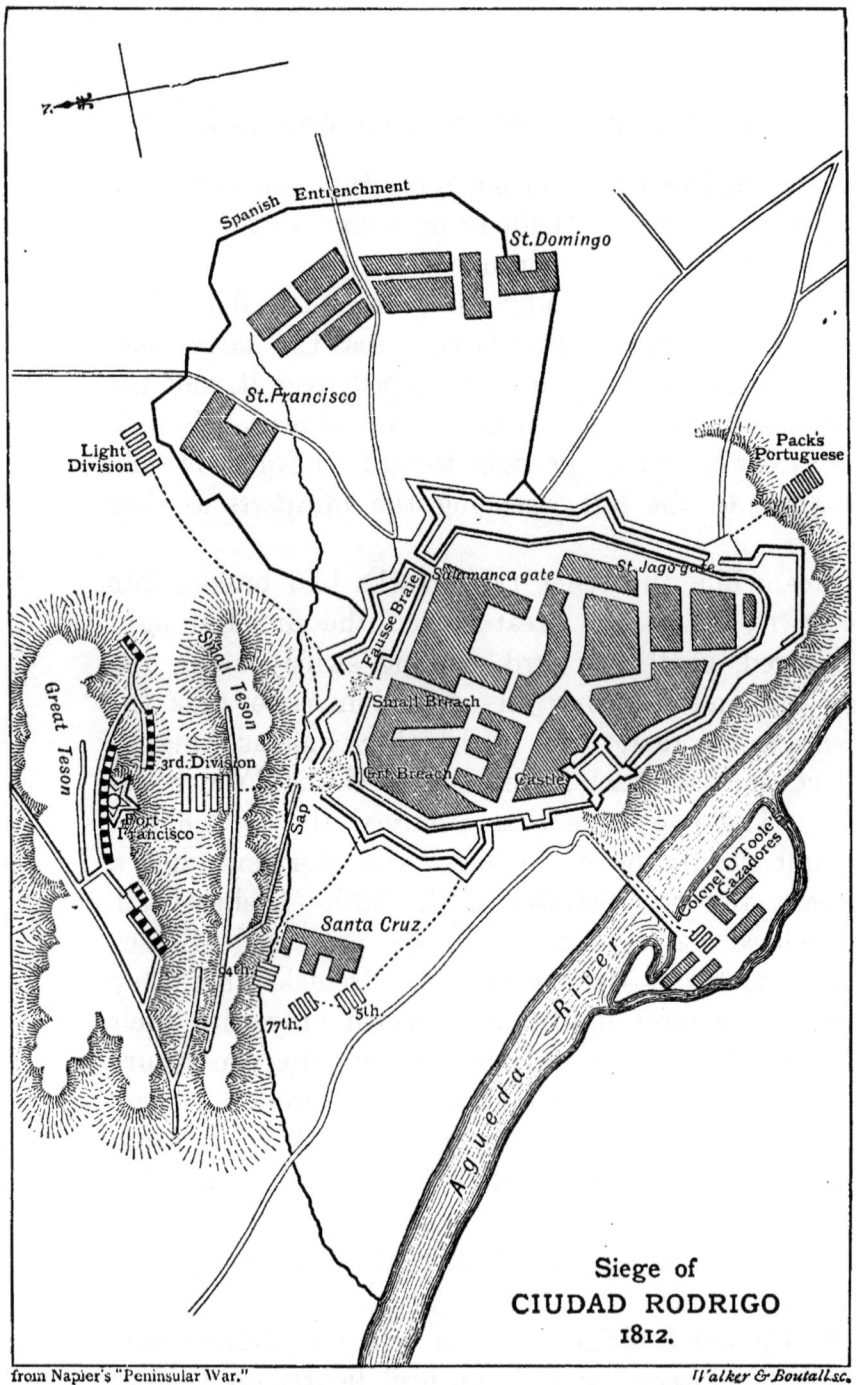

Siege of
CIUDAD RODRIGO
1812.

from Napier's "Peninsular War."

blackened face, torn uniform, and staggering from a dreadful wound, still kept at the head of his men.

In the eleven days of the siege Wellington lost 1300 men and officers, out of whom 650 men and 60 officers were struck down on the slopes of the breaches. Two notable soldiers died in the attack—Craufurd, the famous leader of the light division, as he brought his men up to the lesser breach; and Mackinnon, who commanded a brigade of the third division, at the great breach. Mackinnon was a gallant Highlander, a soldier of great promise, beloved by his men. His "children," as he called them, followed him up the great breach till the bursting of a French mine destroyed all the leading files, including their general. Craufurd was buried in the lesser breach itself, and Mackinnon in the great breach — fitting graves for soldiers so gallant.

Alison says that with the rush of the English stormers up the breaches of Ciudad Rodrigo "began the fall of the French Empire." That siege, so fierce and brilliant, was, as a matter of fact, the first of that swift-following succession of strokes which drove the French in ruin out of Spain, and it coincided in point of time with the turn of the tide against Napoleon in Russia. Apart from all political results, however, it was a splendid feat of arms. The French found themselves almost unable to believe the evidence of their senses. "On the 16th," Marmont wrote to the Emperor, "the English batteries opened their fire at a great distance. On the 19th the place was taken by storm. There is something so *incomprehensible* in this that I allow myself no observations." Napoleon, however, relieved his feelings with some very emphatic observations. "The fall of Ciudad Rodrigo," he wrote to Marmont, "is an affront to you. Why had you not advices from it twice a week? What were you doing with the five divisions of Souham? It is a strange mode of carrying on war," &c. Unhappy Marmont!

HOW THE "HERMIONE" WAS RECAPTURED

> "They cleared the cruiser from end to end,
>   From conning-tower to hold;
> They fought as they fought in Nelson's fleet—
> They were stripped to the waist, they were bare to the feet,
>   As it was in the days of old."
>
> —KIPLING.

THE story of how the *Hermione* was lost is one of the scandals and the tragedies of British naval history; the tale of how it was re-won is one of its glories. The *Hermione* was a 32-gun frigate, cruising off Porto Rico, in the West Indies. On the evening of September 21, 1797, the men were on drill, reefing topsails. The captain, Pigot, was a rough and daring sailor, a type of the brutal school of naval officer long extinct. The traditions of the navy were harsh; the despotic power over the lives and fortunes of his crew which the captain of a man-of-war carried in the palm of his hand, when made the servant of a ferocious temper, easily turned a ship into a floating hell. The terrible mutinies which broke out in British fleets a hundred years ago had some justification, at least, in the cruelties, as well as the hardships, to which the sailors of that period were exposed.

Pigot was rough in speech, vehement in temper, cursed with a semi-lunatic delight in cruelty, and he tormented his men to the verge of desperation. On this fatal night, Pigot, standing at the break of his quarter-deck, stormed at the men aloft, and swore with many oaths he would flog the last man off the mizzen-top yard; and the men knew how well he would keep his word. The most active sailor, as the men lay out on the yard, naturally takes the earing, and is, of course, the last man off, as well as on, the yard. Pigot's method, that is, would punish not the worst sailors, but the best! The two outermost men on the mizzen-top yard of the *Hermione* that night, determined to escape the threatened flogging. They made a desperate spring to get over their comrades crowding into the ratlines, missed their foothold, fell on the quarter-deck beside their furious captain, and were instantly killed. The captain's epitaph on the unfortunate sailors was, "Throw the lubbers overboard!"

All the next day a sullen gloom lay on the ship. Mutiny was breeding. It began, as night fell, in a childish fashion, by the men throwing double-headed shot about the deck. The noise brought down the first lieutenant to restore order. He was knocked down. In the jostle of fierce tempers, murder awoke; knives gleamed. A sailor, as he bent over the fallen officer, saw the naked, undefended throat, and thrust his knife into it. The sight kindled the men's passions to flame. The unfortunate lieutenant was killed with a dozen stabs, and his body thrown overboard. The men had now tasted blood. In the flame of murderous temper suddenly let loose, all the bonds of discipline were in a moment consumed. A wild rush was made for the officers' cabins. The captain tried to break his way out, was wounded, and driven back; the men swept in, and, to quote the realistic official account, "seated in his cabin the captain was stabbed by his own coxswain and three other mutineers, and, forced out of the cabin windows, was heard to speak as he went astern." With mutiny comes anarchy. The men made no distinction between their officers, cruel or gentle; not only the captain, but the three lieutenants, the purser, the surgeon, the lieutenant of marines, the boatswain, the captain's clerk were murdered, and even one of the two midshipmen on board was hunted like a rat through the ship, killed, and thrown overboard. The only officers spared were the master, the gunner, and one midshipman.

Having captured the ship, the mutineers were puzzled how to proceed. Every man-of-war on the station, they knew, would be swiftly on their track. Every British port was sealed to them. They would be pursued by a retribution which would neither loiter nor slumber. On the open sea there was no safety for mutineers. They turned the head of the *Hermione* towards the nearest Spanish port, La Guayra, and, reaching it, surrendered the ship to the Spanish authorities, saying they had turned their officers adrift in the jolly-boat. The Spaniards were not disposed to scrutinise too closely the story. A transaction which put into their hands a fine British frigate was welcomed with rapture. The British admiral in command of the station sent in a flag of truce with the true account of the mutiny, and called upon the Spanish authorities, as a matter of honour, to surrender the *Hermione*, and hand over for punishment the murderers who had carried it off. The appeal, however, was wasted.

The *Hermione*, a handsome ship of 715 tons, when under the British flag, was armed with thirty-two 12-pounders, and had a complement of 220 men. The Spaniards cut new ports in her, increased her broadsides to forty-four guns, and gave her a complement, including a detachment of soldiers and artillerymen, of nearly 400 men. She thus became the most formidable ship carrying the Spanish flag in West Indian waters.

But the *Hermione*, under its new flag, had a very anxious existence. It became a point of honour with every British vessel on the station to look out for the ship which had become the symbol of mutiny, and make a dash at her, no matter what the odds. The brutal murders which attended the mutiny shocked even the forecastle imagination, while the British officers were naturally eager to destroy the ship which represented revolt against discipline. Both fore and aft, too, the fact that what had been a British frigate was now carrying the flag of Spain was resented with a degree of exasperation which assured to the *Hermione*, under its new name and flag, a very warm time if it came under the fire of a British ship. The Spaniards kept the *Hermione* for just two years, but kept her principally in port, as the moment she showed her nose in the open sea some British ship or other, sleeplessly on the watch for her, bore down with disconcerting eagerness.

In September 1799 the *Hermione* was lying in Puerto Cabello, while the *Surprise*, a 28-gun frigate, under Captain Edward Hamilton, was waiting outside, specially detailed by the admiral, Sir Hyde Parker, to attack her the instant she put to sea. The *Surprise* had less than half the complement of the

HOW THE "HERMIONE" WAS RECAPTURED 155

Hermione, and not much more than half her weight of metal. But Hamilton was not only willing to fight the *Hermione* in the open sea against such odds; he told the admiral that if he would give him a barge and twenty men he would undertake to carry the *Hermione* with his boats while lying in harbour. Parker pronounced the scheme too desperate to be entertained, and refused Hamilton the additional boat's crew for which he asked. Yet this was the very plan which Hamilton actually carried out without the reinforcement for which he had asked!

Hamilton, to tempt the *Hermione* out, kept carefully out of sight of Puerto Cabello to leeward, yet in such a position that if the *Hermione* left the harbour her topsails must become visible to the look-outs on the mastheads of the *Surprise;* and he kept that post until his provisions failed. Then, as the *Hermione* would not come out to him, he determined to go into the *Hermione*. Hamilton was a silent, much-meditating man, not apt to share his counsels with anybody. In the cells of his brooding and solitary brain he prepared, down to the minutest details, his plan for a dash at the *Hermione*—a ship, it must be remembered, not only more than double his own in strength, but lying moored head and stern in a strongly fortified port, under the fire of batteries mounting nearly 200 guns, and protected, in addition, by several gunboats. In a boat attack, too, Hamilton could carry only part of his crew with him; he must leave enough hands on board his own ship to work her. As a matter of fact, he put in his boats less than 100 men, and with them, in the blackness of night, rowed off to attack a ship that carried 400 men, and was protected by the fire, including her own broadsides, of nearly 300 guns! The odds were indeed so great that the imagination of even British sailors, if allowed to meditate long upon them, might become chilled. Hamilton therefore breathed not a whisper of his plans, even to his officers, till he was ready to put them into execution, and, when he did announce them, carried them out with cool but unfaltering speed.

On the evening of October 24, Hamilton invited all the officers not on actual duty to dine in his cabin. The scene may be easily pictured. The captain at the head of his table, the merry officers on either side, the jest, the laughter, the toasts; nobody there but the silent, meditative captain dreaming of the daring deed to be that night attempted. When dinner was over, and the officers alone, with a gesture Hamilton arrested the attention of the party, and explained in a few grim sentences his purpose. The little party of brave men about him listened eagerly and with kindling eyes. "We'll stand by you, captain," said one. "We'll all follow you," said another. Hamilton bade his officers follow him at once to the quarter-deck. A roll of the drum called the men instantly to quarters, and, when the officers reported every man at his station, they were all sent aft to where, on the break of the quarter-deck, the captain waited.

It was night, starless and black, but a couple of lanterns shed a few broken rays on the massed seamen with their wondering, upturned faces, and the tall figure of the silent captain. Hamilton explained in a dozen curt sentences that they must run into port for supplies; that if they left their station some more fortunate ship would have the glory of taking the *Hermione*. "Our only chance, lads," he added, " is to cut her out to-night!" As that sentence, with a keen ring on its last word, swept over the attentive sailors, they made the natural response, a sudden growling cheer. "I lead you myself," added Hamilton, whereupon came another cheer; "and here are the orders for the six boats to be employed, with the names of the officers and men." Instantly the crews were mustered, while the officers, standing in a cluster round the captain, heard the details of the expedition. Every seaman was to be dressed in blue, without a patch of white visible; the password was "Britannia," the answer "Ireland"—Hamilton himself being an Irishman.

By half-past seven the boats were actually hoisted out and lowered, the men armed and in their places, and each little crew instructed as to the exact part it was to play in the exciting drama. The orders given were curiously minute. The launch, for example, was to board on the starboard bow, but three of its men, before boarding, were first to cut the bower cable, for which purpose a little platform was rigged up on the launch's quarter, and sharp axes provided. The jolly-boat was to board on the starboard quarter, cut the stern cable, and send two men aloft to loose the mizzen topsail. The gig, under the command of the doctor, was to board on the larboard bow, and instantly send four men aloft to loose the fore topsail. If the *Hermione* was reached without any alarm being given, only the boarders were to leap on board; the ordinary crews of the boats were to take the frigate in tow. Thus, if Hamilton's plans were carried out, the Spaniards would find themselves suddenly boarded at six different points, their cables cut, their topsails dropped, and their ship being towed out—and all this at the same instant of time. "The rendezvous," said Hamilton to his officers, as the little cluster of boats drew away from the *Surprise*, "is the *Hermione's* quarter-deck!"

Hamilton himself led, standing up in his pinnace, with his night-glass fixed on the doomed ship, and the boats followed with stem almost touching stern, and a rope passed from each boat to the one behind. Can a more impressive picture of human daring be imagined than these six boats pulling silently over the black waters and through the black night to fling themselves, under the fire of two hundred guns, on a foe four times more numerous than themselves! The boats had stolen to within less than a mile of the *Hermione*, when a Spanish challenge rang out of the darkness before them. Two Spanish gunboats were on guard within the harbour, and they at once opened fire on the chain of boats gliding mysteriously through the gloom. There was no longer any possibility of surprise, and Hamilton instantly threw off the rope that connected him with the next boat and shouted to his men to pull. The men, with a loud "Hurrah!" dashed their oars into the water, and the boats leaped forward towards the *Hermione*. But Hamilton's boats —two of them commanded by midshipmen—could not find themselves so close to a couple of Spanish gunboats without "going" for them. Two of the six boats swung aside and dashed at the gunboats; only three followed Hamilton at the utmost speed towards the *Hermione*.

That ship, meanwhile, was awake. Lights flashed

from every port; a clamour of voices broke on the quiet of the night; the sound of the drum rolled along the decks, the men ran to quarters. Hamilton, in the pinnace, dashed past the bows of the *Hermione* to reach his station, but a rope, stretched from the *Hermione* to her anchor-buoy, caught the rudder of the pinnace and stopped her in full course, the coxswain reporting the boat "aground." The pinnace had swung round till her starboard oars touched the bend of the *Hermione*, and Hamilton gave the word to "board." Hamilton himself led, and swung himself up till his feet rested on the anchor hanging from the *Hermione's* cat-head. It was covered with mud, having been weighed that day, and his feet slipping off it, Hamilton hung by the lanyard of the *Hermione's* foreshroud. The crew of the pinnace meanwhile climbing with the agility of cats and the eagerness of boys, had tumbled over their own captain's shoulders as well as the bulwarks of the *Hermione*, and were on that vessel's forecastle, where Hamilton in another moment joined them. Here were sixteen men on board a vessel with a hostile crew four hundred strong.

Hamilton ran to the break of the forecastle and looked down, and to his amazement found the whole crew of the *Hermione* at quarters on the main-deck, with battle-lanterns lit, and firing with the utmost energy at the darkness, in which their excited fancy saw the tall masts of at least a squadron of frigates bearing down to attack them. Hamilton, followed by his fifteen men, ran aft to the agreed rendezvous on the *Hermione's* quarter-deck. The doctor, with his crew, had meantime boarded, and forgetting all about the rendezvous, and obeying only the natural fighting impulse in their own blood, charged upon the Spaniards in the gangway.

Hamilton sent his men down to assist in the fight, waiting alone on the quarter-deck till his other boats boarded. Here four Spaniards rushed suddenly upon him; one struck him over the head with a musket with a force that broke the weapon itself, and knocked him semi-senseless upon the combings of the hatchway. Two British sailors, who saw their commander's peril, rescued him, and, with blood streaming down from his battered head upon his uniform, Hamilton flung himself into the fight at the gangway. At this juncture the black cutter, in command of the first lieutenant, with the *Surprise's* marines on board, dashed up to the side of the *Hermione*, and the men came tumbling over the larboard gangway. They had made previously two unsuccessful attempts to board. They came up first by the steps of the larboard gangway, the lieutenant leading. He was incontinently knocked down, and tumbled all his men with him as he fell back into the boat. They then tried the starboard of the *Hermione*, and were again beaten back, and only succeeded on a third attempt.

Three boats' crews of the British were now together on the deck of the *Hermione*. They did not number fifty men in all, but the marines were instantly formed up and a volley was fired down the after hatchway. Then, following the flash of their muskets, with the captain leading, the whole party leaped down upon the main-deck, driving the Spaniards before them. Some sixty Spaniards took refuge in the cabin, and shouted they surrendered, whereupon they were ordered to throw down their arms, and the doors were locked upon them, turning them into prisoners. On the main-deck and under the forecastle, however, the fighting was fierce and deadly; but by this time the other boats had come up, and the cables fore and aft were cut, as had been arranged. The men detailed for that task had raced up the Spaniard's rigging, and while the desperate fight raged below, had cast loose the topsails of the *Hermione*. Three of the boats, too, had taken her in tow. She began to move seaward, and that movement, with the sound of the rippling water along the ship's sides, appalled the Spaniards, and persuaded them the ship was lost.

On the quarter-deck the gunner and two men—all three wounded—stood at the wheel, and flung the head of the *Hermione* seaward. They were fiercely attacked, but while one man clung to the wheel and kept control of the ship, the gunner and his mate kept off the Spaniards. Presently the foretopsail filled with the land breeze, the water rippled louder along the sides of the moving vessel, the ship swayed to the wind. The batteries by this time were thundering from the shore, but though they shot away many ropes, they fired with signal ill-success. Only fifty British sailors and marines, it must be remembered, were actually on the deck of the *Hermione*, and amongst the crowd of sullen and exasperated Spaniards below, who had surrendered, but were still furious with the astonishment of the attack and the passion of the fight, there arose a shout to "blow up the ship." The British had to fire down through the hatchway upon the swaying crowd to enforce order. By two o'clock the struggle was over, the *Hermione* was beyond the fire of the batteries, and the crews of the boats towing her came on board.

There is no more surprising fight in British history. The mere swiftness with which the adventure was carried out is marvellous. It was past six P.M. when Hamilton disclosed his plan to his officers, the *Hermione* at that moment lying some eight miles distant; by two o'clock the captured ship, with the British flag flying from her peak, was clear of the harbour. Only half a hundred men actually got on board the *Hermione*, but what a resolute, hard-smiting, strong-fisted band they were may be judged by the results. Of the Spaniards, 119 were killed, and 97 wounded, most of them dangerously. Hamilton's 50 men, that is, in those few minutes of fierce fighting, cut down four times their own number! Not one of the British, as it happened, was killed, and only 12 wounded, Captain Hamilton himself receiving no less than five serious wounds. The *Hermione* was restored to her place in the British Navy List, but under a new name—the *Retribution*—and the story of that heroic night attack will be for all time one of the most stirring incidents in the long record of brave deeds performed by British seamen.

MARSHAL SOULT

After a portrait by Rouillard

FRENCH AND ENGLISH IN THE PASSES

> "Beating from the wasted vines
> Back to France her banded swarms,
> Back to France with countless blows,
> Till o'er the hills her eagles flew
> Beyond the Pyrenean pines;
> Follow'd up in valley and glen
> With blare of bugle, clamour of men,
> Roll of cannon and clash of arms,
> And England pouring on her foes.
> Such a war had such a close."
> —TENNYSON.

"IN both the passes, and on the heights above them, there was desperate fighting. They fought on the mountain-tops, which could scarcely have witnessed any other combat than that of the Pyrenean eagles; they fought among jagged rocks and over profound abysses; they fought amidst clouds and mists, for those mountain-tops were 5000 feet above the level of the plain of France, and the rains, which had fallen in torrents, were evaporating in the morning and noonday sun, were steaming heavenward and clothing the loftiest peaks with fantastic wreaths." These words describe, with picturesque force, the most brilliant and desperate, and yet, perhaps, the least known chapter in the great drama of the Peninsular war: the furious combats waged between British and French in the gloomy valleys and on the mist-shrouded summits of the Western Pyrenees. The great campaign, which found its climax at Vittoria, lasted six weeks. In that brief period Wellington marched with 100,000 men 600 miles, passed six great rivers, gained one historic and decisive battle, invested two fortresses, and drove 120,000 veteran troops from Spain. There is no more brilliant chapter in military history; and, at its close, to quote Napier's clarion-like sentences, "the English general, emerging from the chaos of the Peninsular struggle, stood on the summit of the Pyrenees a recognised conqueror. From those lofty pinnacles the clangour of his trumpets pealed clear and loud, and the splendour of his genius appeared as a flaming beacon to warring nations."

But the great barrier of the Pyrenees stretched across Wellington's path, a tangle of mountains sixty miles in length; a wild table-land rough with crags, fierce with mountain torrents, shaggy with forests, a labyrinth of savage and snow-clad hills. On either flank a great fortress—San Sebastian and Pampeluna—was held by the French, and Wellington was besieging both at once, and besieging them without battering trains. The echoes of Vittoria had aroused Napoleon, then fighting desperately on the Elbe, and ten days after Vittoria the French Emperor, acting with the lightning-like decision characteristic of his genius, had despatched Soult, the ablest of all his generals, to bar the passes of the Pyrenees against Wellington. Soult travelled day and night to the scene of his new command, gathering reinforcements on every side as he went, and in an incredibly short period he had assembled on the French side of the Pyrenees a great and perfectly equipped force of 75,000 men.

Wellington could not advance and leave San Sebastian and Pampeluna on either flank held by the enemy. Some eight separate passes pierce the giant chain of the Pyrenees. Soult was free to choose any one of them for his advance to the relief of either of the besieged fortresses, but Wellington had to keep guard over the whole eight, and the force holding each pass was almost completely isolated from its comrades. Thus all the advantages of position were with Soult. He could pour his whole force through one or two selected passes, brush aside the relatively scanty force which held it, relieve San Sebastian or Pampeluna, and, with the relieved fortress as his base, fling himself on Wellington's flank while the allied armies were scattered over the slopes of the Pyrenees for sixty miles. And Soult was exactly the general to avail himself of these advantages. He had the swift vision, the resolute will, and the daring of a great commander. "It is on Spanish soil," he said in a proclamation to his troops, "your tents must next be pitched. Let the account of our successes be dated from Vittoria, and let the fête-day of his Imperial Majesty be celebrated in that city." These were brave words, and having uttered them, Soult led his gallant troops, with gallant purpose, into the gloomy passes of the Pyrenees, and for days following the roar of battle sank and swelled over the snow-clad peaks. But when the Imperial fête-day arrived—August 15—Soult's great army was pouring back from those same passes a shattered host, and the allied troops, sternly following them, were threatening French soil!

Soult judged Pampeluna to be in greater peril than San Sebastian, and moved by his left to force the passes of Roncesvalles and Maya. The rain fell furiously, the mountain streams were in flood, gloomy mists shrouded the hill-tops; but by July 24, with more than 60,000 fighting men, and nearly seventy guns, Soult was pouring along the passes he had chosen. It is impossible to do more than pick out a few of the purple patches in the swift succession of heroic combats that followed: fights waged on mountain summits 5000 feet above the sea-level, in shaggy forests, under tempests of rain and snow. D'Erlon, with a force of 20,000 men, took the British by surprise in the pass of Maya. Ross, an eager and hardy soldier, unexpectedly encountering the French advance guard, instantly shouted the order to "Charge!" and with a handful of the 20th flung himself upon the enemy, and actually checked their advance until Cole, who had only 10,000 bayonets to oppose to 30,000, had got into fighting form. A thick fog fell like a pall on the combatants, and checked the fight, and Cole, in the night, fell back. The French columns were in movement at daybreak, but still the fog hid the whole landscape, and the guides of the French feared to lead them up the slippery crags. At Maya, however, the French in force broke upon Stewart's division, holding that pass. The British regiments, as they came running up, not in mass, but by companies, and breathless with the run, were flung with furious haste upon the French. The 34th, the 39th, the 28th in succession crashed into the fight, but were flung back by overpowering numbers. It was a battle of 4000 men against 13,000.

The famous 50th, fiercely advancing, checked the French rush at one point; but Soult's men were full of the *élan* of victory, and swept past the British flanks. The 71st and 92nd were brought into the fight, and the latter especially clung sternly to their position till two men out of every three were shot down, the mound of dead and dying forming a solid barrier between the wasted survivors of the regiment and the shouting edge of the French advance. "The stern valour of the 92nd," says Napier, "principally composed of Irishmen, would have graced Thermopylæ." No one need question the fighting quality of the Irish soldier, but, as a matter of fact, there were 825 Highlanders in the regiment, and 61 Irishmen. The British, however, were steadily pushed back, ammunition failed, and the soldiers were actually defending the highest crag with stones, when Barnes, with a brigade of the seventh division, coming breathlessly up the pass, plunged into the fight, and checked the French. Soult had gained ten of the thirty miles of road toward Pampeluna, but at an ominous cost, and, meanwhile, the plan of his attack was developed, and Wellington was in swift movement to bar his path.

Soult had now swung into the pass of Roncesvalles, and was on the point of attacking Cole, who held the pass with a very inadequate force, when, at that exact moment, Wellington, having despatched his aides in various directions to bring up the troops, galloped alone along the mountain flank to the British line. He was recognised; the nearest troops raised a shout; it ran, gathering volume as it travelled down all the slope, where the British stood waiting for the French

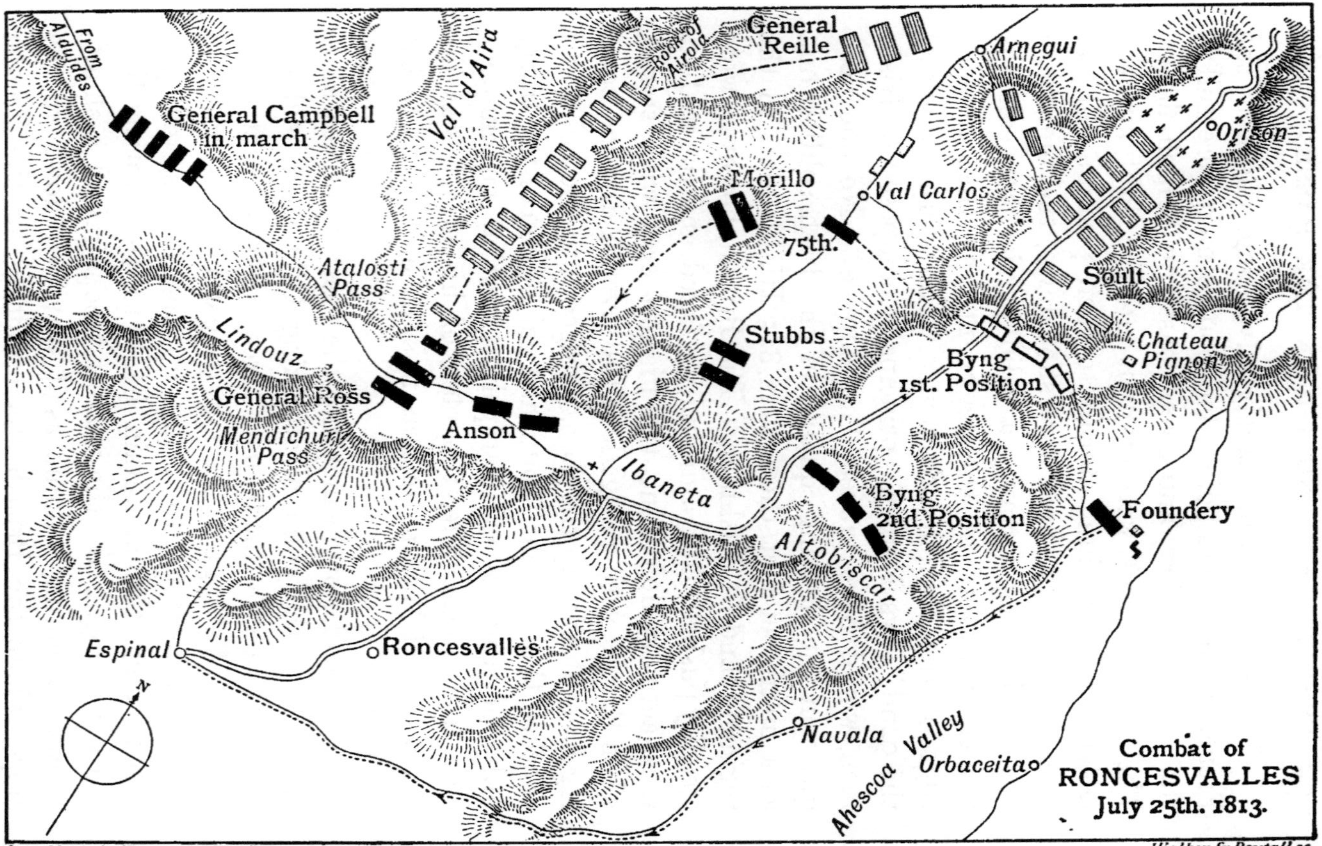

from Napier's "Peninsular War." Walker & Boutall sc.

attack. That sudden shout, stern and exultant, reached the French lines, and they halted. At the same moment, round the shoulder of the hill on the opposite side of the pass, Soult appeared, and the two generals, near enough to see each other's features, eagerly scrutinised one another. "Yonder is a great commander,' said Wellington, as if speaking to himself, "but he is cautious, and will delay his attack to ascertain the cause of these cheers. That will give time for the sixth division to arrive, and I shall beat him." Wellington's forecast of Soult's action was curiously accurate. He made no attack that day. The sixth division came up, and Soult was beaten!

There were two combats of Sauroren, and each was, in Wellington's own phrase, "bludgeon work"—a battle of soldiers rather than of generals, a tangle of fierce charges and counter-charges, of volleys delivered so close that they scorched the very clothes of the opposing lines, and sustained so fiercely that they died down only because the lines of desperately firing men crumbled into ruin and silence. Nothing could be finer than the way in which a French column, swiftly, sternly, and without firing a shot, swept up a craggy steep crowned by rocks like castles, held by some Portuguese battalions, and won the position. Ross's brigade, in return, with equal vehemence recharged the position from its side, and dashed the French out of it; the French in still greater force came back, a shouting mass, and crushed Ross's men. Then Wellington sent forward Byng's brigade at running pace, and hurled the French down the mountain side. At another point in the pass the French renewed their assault four times; in their second assault they gained the summit. The 40th were in reserve at that point; they waited in steady silence till the edge of the French line, a confused mass of tossing bayonets and perspiring faces, came clear over the crest; then, running forward with extraordinary fury, they flung them, a broken, tumultuous mass, down the slope. In the later charges, so fierce and resolute were the French officers that they were seen dragging their tired soldiers up the hill by their belts!

It is idle to attempt the tale of this wild mountain fighting. Soult at last fell back, and Wellington followed, swift and vehement, on his track, and moved Alten's column to intercept the French retreat. The story of Alten's march is a marvellous record of soldierly endurance. His men pressed on with speed for nineteen consecutive hours, and covered forty miles of mountain tracks, wilder than the Otway Ranges, or the paths of the Australian Alps between Bright and Omeo. The weather was close; many men fell and died, convulsed and frothing at the mouth. Still, their officers leading, the regiment kept up its quick step, till, as evening fell, the head of the column reached the edge of the precipice overlooking the bridge across which, in all the confusion of a hurried retreat, the French troops were crowding. "We overlooked the enemy," says Cook in his "Memoirs," "at stone's-throw. The river separated us; but the French were wedged in a narrow road, with inaccessible rocks on one side, and the river on the other." Who can describe the scene that followed! Some of the French fired vertically up at the British; others ran; others shouted for quarter; some pointed with eager gestures to the wounded, which they carried on branches of trees, as if entreating the British not to fire.

In nine days of continual marching, ten desperate actions had been fought, at what cost of life can hardly be reckoned. Napier, after roughly calculating the losses, says: "Let this suffice. It is not needful to sound the stream of blood in all its horrid depths." But the fighting sowed the wild passes of the Pyrenees thick with the graves of brave men.

Soult actually fought his way to within sight of the walls of Pampeluna, and its beleaguered garrison waved frantic welcomes to his columns as, from the flanks of the overshadowing hills, they looked down on the city. Then broken as by the stroke of a thunderbolt, and driven like wild birds caught in a tempest, the French poured back through the passes to French soil again. "I never saw such fighting," was Wellington's comment on the struggle.

For the weeks that followed, Soult could only look on while San Sebastian and Pampeluna fell. Then the allied outposts were advanced to the slopes looking down on France and the distant sea. It is recorded that the Highlanders of Hill's division, like Xenophon's Greeks 2000 years before them, broke into cheers when they caught their first glimpse of the sea, the great, wrinkled, azure-tinted floor, flecked with white sails. It was "the way home!" Bearn and Gascony and Languedoc lay stretched like a map under their feet. But the weather was bitter, the snow lay thick in the passes, sentinels were frozen at the outposts, and a curious stream of desertions began. The warm plains of sunny France tempted the half-frozen troops, and Southey computes, with an arithmetical precision which is half-humorous, that the average weekly proportion of desertions was 25 Spaniards, 15 Irish, 12 English, 6 Scotch, and half a Portuguese! One indignant English colonel drew up his regiment on parade, and told the men that "if any of them wanted to join the French they had better do so at once. He gave them free leave. He wouldn't have men in the regiment who wished to join the enemy!"

Meanwhile Soult was trying to construct on French soil lines of defence as mighty as those of Wellington at Torres Vedras; and on October 7, Wellington pushed his left across the Bidassoa, the stream that marks the boundaries of Spain and France. On the French side the hills rise to a great height. One huge shoulder, called La Rhune, commands the whole stream; another lofty ridge, called the "Boar's Back," offered almost equal facilities for defence. The only road that crossed the hills rose steeply, with sharp zigzags, and for weeks the French had toiled to make the whole position impregnable. The British soldiers had watched while the mountain sides were scarred with trenches, and the road was blocked with abattis, and redoubt rose above redoubt like a gigantic staircase climbing the sky. The Bidassoa at its mouth is wide, and the tides rose sixteen feet.

But on the night of October 7—a night wild with rain and sleet—Wellington's troops marched silently to their assigned posts on the banks of the river. When day broke, at a signal-gun seven columns could be seen moving at once in a line of five miles, and before Soult could detect Wellington's plan the river was crossed, the French entrenched camps on the Bidassoa won! The next morning the heights were attacked. The Rifles carried the Boar's Back with a single effort. The Bayonette Crest, a huge spur guarded by battery above battery, and crowned by a great redoubt, was attacked by Colborne's brigade and some Portuguese. The tale of how the hill was climbed, and the batteries carried in swift succession, cannot be told here. It was a warlike feat of the most splendid quality. Other columns moving along the flanks of the great hill alarmed the French lest they should be cut off, and they abandoned the redoubt on the summit. Colborne, accompanied by only one of his staff and half-a-dozen files of riflemen, came suddenly round a shoulder of the hill on the whole garrison of the redoubt, 300 strong, in retreat. With great presence of mind, he ordered them, in the sharpest tones of authority, to "lay down their arms," and, believing themselves cut off, they obeyed!

A column of Spanish troops moving up the flanks of the great Rhune found their way barred by a strong line of abattis and the fire of two French regiments. The column halted, and their officers vainly strove to get the Spaniards to attack. An officer of the 43rd named Havelock—a name yet more famous in later wars—attached to Alten's staff, was sent to see what caused the stoppage of the column. He found the Spaniards checked by the great abattis, through which flashed, fierce and fast, the fire of the French. Waving his hat, he shouted to the Spaniards to "follow him," and, putting his horse at the abattis, at one leap went headlong amongst the French. There is a swift contagion in valour. He was only a light-haired lad, and the Spaniards with one vehement shout for "el chico blanco"—"the fair lad"—swept over abattis and French together!

FAMOUS CUTTING-OUT EXPEDITIONS

"We have fed our sea for a thousand years,
   And she calls us, still unfed,
Though there's never a wave of all her waves
   But marks our English dead
We have strawed our best to the weed's unrest,
   To the shark and the sheering gull.
If blood be the price of admiralty,
   Lord God, we ha' paid in full!

There's never a flood goes shoreward now
   But lifts a keel we manned;
There's never an ebb goes seaward now
   But drops our dead on the sand.
   .   .   .   .   .
We must feed our sea for a thousand years,
   For that is our doom and pride,
As it was when they sailed with the "Golden Hind,"
   Or the wreck that struck last tide—
Or the wreck that lies on the spouting reef
   Where the ghastly blue lights flare.
If blood be the price of admiralty,
If blood be the price of admiralty,
If blood be the price of admiralty,
   Lord God, we ha' bought it fair!"

                          —Kipling.

AS illustrations of cool daring, of the courage that does not count numbers or depend on noise, nor flinch from flame or steel, few things are more wonderful than the many cutting-out stories to be found in the history of the British navy. The soldier in the forlorn hope, scrambling up the breach swept by grape and barred by a triple line of steadfast bayonets, must be a brave man. But it may be doubted whether he shows a courage so cool and high as that of a boat's crew of sailors in a cutting-out expedition.

The ship to be attacked lies, perhaps, floating in a tropic haze five miles off, and the attacking party must pull slowly, in a sweltering heat, up to the iron lips of her guns. The greedy, restless sea is under them, and a single shot may turn the eager boat's crew at any instant into a cluster of drowning wretches. When the ship is reached, officers and men must clamber over bulwarks and boarding-netting, exposed, almost helplessly, as they climb, to thrust of pike and shot of musket, and then leap down, singly and without order, on to the deck crowded with foes. Or, perhaps, the ship to be cut out lies in a hostile port under the guard of powerful batteries, and the boats must dash in through the darkness, and their crews tumble, at three or four separate points, on to the deck of the foe, cut her cables, let fall her sails, and—while the mad fight still rages on her deck and the great battery booms from the cliff overhead—carry the ship out of the harbour. These, surely, are deeds of which only a sailor's courage is capable! Let a few such stories be taken from faded naval records and told afresh to a new generation.

In July 1800 the 14-gun cutter *Viper*, commanded by acting-Lieutenant Jeremiah Coghlan, was attached to Sir Edward Pellew's squadron off Port Louis. Coghlan, as his name tells, was of Irish blood. He had just emerged from the chrysalis stage of a midshipman, and, flushed with the joy of an independent command, was eager for adventure. The entrance to Port Louis was watched by a number of gunboats constantly on sentry-go, and Coghlan conceived the idea of jumping suddenly on one of these, and carrying her off from under the guns of the enemy's fleet. He persuaded Sir Edward Pellew to lend him the flagship's ten-oared cutter, with twelve volunteers. Having got this reinforcement, and having persuaded the *Amethyst* frigate to lend him a boat and crew, Mr. Jeremiah Coghlan proceeded to carry out another and very different plan from that he had ventured to suggest to his admiral. A French gun-brig, named the *Cerbère*, was lying in the harbour of St. Louis. She mounted three long 24 and four 6-pounders, and was moored, with springs in her cables, within pistol-shot of three batteries. A French seventy-four and two frigates were within gunshot of her. She had a crew of eighty-six men, sixteen of whom were soldiers. It was upon this brig, lying under three powerful batteries, within a hostile and difficult port, that Mr. Jeremiah Coghlan proposed, in the darkness of night, to make a dash. He added the *Viper's* solitary midshipman, with himself and six of his crew, to the twelve volunteers on board the flagship's cutter, raising its crew to twenty men, and, with the *Amethyst's* boat and a small boat from the *Viper*, pulled off in the blackness of the night on this daring adventure.

The ten-oared cutter ran away from the other two boats, reached the *Cerbère*, found her with battle lanterns alight and men at quarters, and its crew at once jumped on board the Frenchman. Coghlan, as was proper, jumped first, landed on a trawl-net hung up to dry, and, while sprawling helpless in its meshes, was thrust through the thigh with a pike, and with his men—several also severely hurt—tumbled back into the boat. The British picked themselves up, hauled their boat a little farther ahead, clambered up the sides of the *Cerbère* once more, and were a second time beaten back with new wounds. They clung to the Frenchman, however, fought their way up to a new point, broke through the French defences, and after killing or wounding twenty-six of the enemy—or more than every fourth man of the *Cerbère's* crew—actually captured her, the other two boats coming up in time to help in towing out the prize under a wrathful fire from the batteries. Coghlan had only one killed and eight wounded, himself being wounded in two places, and his middy in six. Sir Edward Pellew, in his official despatch, grows eloquent over "the courage which, hand to hand, gave victory to a handful of brave fellows over four times their number, and the skill which planned, conducted, and effected so daring an enterprise." Earl St. Vincent, himself the driest and grimmest of admirals, was so delighted with the youthful Irishman's exploit that he presented him with a handsome sword.

In 1811, again, Great Britain was at war with the Dutch—a tiny little episode of the great revolutionary war. A small squadron of British ships was cruising off Batavia. A French squadron, with troops to strengthen the garrison, was expected daily. The only fortified port into which they could run was Marrack, and the commander of the British squadron cruising to intercept the French ships determined to make a dash by night on Marrack, and so secure the only possible landing-place for the French. Marrack was defended by batteries mounting fifty-four heavy guns. The attacking force was to consist of 200 seamen and 250 troops, under the command of Lieutenant Lyons of the *Minden*. Just before the boats pushed off, however, the British commander learned that the Dutch garrison had been heavily reinforced, and deeming an assault too hazardous, the plan was abandoned. A few days afterwards Lyons, with the *Minden's* launch and cutter, was despatched to land nineteen prisoners at Batavia, and pick up intelligence. Lyons, a very daring and gallant officer, learned that the Marrack garrison was in a state of sleepy security, and, with his two boats' crews, counting thirty-five officers and men, he determined to make a midnight dash on the fort, an exploit which 450 men were reckoned too weak a force to attempt.

Lyons crept in at sunset to the shore, and hid his two boats behind a point from which the fort was visible. A little after midnight, just as the moon dipped below the horizon, Lyons stole with muffled oars round the point, and instantly the Dutch sentries gave the alarm. Lyons, however, pushed fiercely on, grounded his boats in a heavy surf under the very embrasures of the lower battery, and, in an instant, thirty-five British sailors were tumbling over the Dutch guns and upon the heavy-breeched and astonished Dutch gunners. The battery was carried. Lyons gathered his thirty-five sailors into a cluster, and, with a rush, captured the upper battery. Still climbing up, they reached the top of the hill, and found the whole Dutch garrison forming in line to receive them. The sailors instantly ran in upon the half-formed line, cutlass in hand; Lyons roared that he "had 400 men, and would give no quarter;" and the Dutch, finding the pace of events too rapid for their nerves, broke and fled. But the victorious British were only thirty-five in number, and were surrounded by powerful forces. They began at once to dismantle the guns and destroy the fort, but two Dutch gunboats in the bay opened fire on them, as did a heavy battery in the rear.

At daybreak a strong Dutch column was formed, and came on at a resolute and laborious trot towards the shattered gate of the fort. Lyons had trained two 24-pounders, loaded to the muzzle with musket balls, on the gate, left invitingly open. He himself stood, with lighted match, by one gun; his second in command, with another lighted match, by the other. They waited coolly by the guns till the Dutch, their officers leading, reached the gate, raising a tumult of angry guttural shouts as they came on. Then, from a distance of little over ten yards, the British fired. The head of the column was instantly smashed, its tail broken up into flying fragments. Lyons finished the destruction of the fort at leisure, sank one of the two gunboats with the last shot fired from the last gun before he spiked it, and marched off, leaving the British flag flying on the staff above the fort, where, in the fury of the attack, it had been hoisted in a most gallant fashion by the solitary middy of the party, a lad named Franks, only fifteen years old. One of the two boats belonging to the British had been bilged by the surf, and the thirty-five seamen—only four of them wounded—packed themselves into the remaining boat and pulled off, carrying with them the captured Dutch colours. Let the reader's imagination illuminate, as the writer's pen cannot, that midnight dash by thirty-five men on a heavily armed fort with a garrison twelve times the strength of the attacking force. Where in stories of warfare, ancient or modern, is such another tale of valour to be found? Lyons, however, was not promoted, as he had "acted without orders."

A tale, with much the same flavour in it, but not so dramatically successful, has for its scene the coast of Spain. In August 1812, the British sloop *Minstrel*, of 24 guns, and the 18-gun brig *Philomel*, were blockading three small French privateers in the port of Biendom, near Alicante. The privateers were protected by a strong fort mounting 24 guns. By way of precaution, two of the ships were hauled on shore, six of their guns being landed, and formed into a battery manned by eighty of their crews. The *Minstrel* and her consort could not pretend to attack a position so strong, but they kept vigilant watch outside, and a boat from one ship or the other rowed guard every night near the shore. On the night of the 12th the *Minstrel's* boat, with seven seamen, was in command of an Irish midshipman named Michael Dwyer. Dwyer had all the fighting courage of his race, with almost more of the gay disregard of odds than is natural to even an Irish midshipman. It occurred to Mr. Michael Dwyer that if he could carry by surprise the 6-gun battery, there would be a chance of destroying the privateers. A little before ten P.M. he pulled silently to the beach, at a point three miles distant from the battery, and, with his seven followers, landed, and was instantly challenged by a French sentry. Dwyer by some accident knew Spanish, and, with ready-witted audacity, replied in that language that "they were peasants." They were allowed to pass, and these seven tars, headed by a youth, set off on the three miles' trudge to attack a fort!

There were eighty men in the battery when Michael and his amazing seven rushed upon it. There was a wild struggle for five minutes, and then the eighty fled before the eight, and the delighted middy found himself in possession of the battery. But the alarm was given, and two companies of French infantry, each one hundred strong, came resolutely up to retake the battery. Eight against eighty seemed desperate odds, but eight against two hundred is a quite hopeless proportion. Yet Mr. Dwyer and his seven held the fort till one of their number was killed, two (including the midshipman) badly wounded, and, worst of all, their ammunition exhausted. When the British had fired their last shot, the French, with levelled bayonets, broke in; but the inextinguishable Dwyer was not subdued till he had been stabbed in seventeen places, and of the whole eight British only one was left unwounded. The French amazement when they discovered that the force which attacked them consisted of seven men and a boy, was too deep for words.

Perhaps the most brilliant cutting-out in British records is the carrying of the *Chevrette* by the boats of three British frigates in Cameret Bay in 1801. A previous and mismanaged attempt had put the *Chevrette* on its guard; it ran a mile and a half farther up the bay, moored itself under some heavy batteries, took on board a powerful detachment of infantry, bringing its number of men up to 339, and then hoisted in defiance a large French ensign over the British flag. Some temporary redoubts were thrown up on the points of land commanding the *Chevrette*, and a heavily armed gunboat was moored at the entrance of the bay as a guard-boat. After all these preparations the *Chevrette's* men felt both safe and jubilant; but the sight of that French flag flying over the British ensign was a challenge not to be refused, and at half-past nine that night the boats of the three frigates—the *Doris*, the *Uranie*, and the *Beaulieu* —fifteen in all, carrying 280 officers and men, were in the water and pulling off to attack the *Chevrette*.

Lieutenant Losack, in command, with his own and five other boats, suddenly swung off in the gloom in chase of what he supposed to be the look-out boat of the enemy, ordering the other nine boats to lie on their oars till he returned. But time stole on; he failed to return; and Lieutenant Maxwell, the next in command, reflecting that the night was going, and the boats had six miles to pull, determined to carry out the expedition, though he had only nine boats and less than 180 men, instead of fifteen boats and 280 men. He summoned his little squadron in the darkness about him, and gave exact instructions. As the boats dashed up, one was to cut the *Chevrette's* cables; when they boarded, the smartest topmen, named man by man, were to fight their way aloft and cut loose the *Chevrette's* sails; one of the finest sailors in the boats, Wallis, the quartermaster of the *Beaulieu*, was to take charge of the *Chevrette's* helm. Thus at one and the same instant the *Chevrette* was to be boarded, cut loose, its sails dropped, and its head swung round towards the harbour mouth.

At half-past twelve the moon sank. The night was windless and black; but the bearing of the *Chevrette* had been taken by compass, and the boats pulled gently on, till, ghost-like in the gloom, the doomed ship was discernible. A soft air from the land began to blow at that moment. Suddenly the *Chevrette* and the batteries overhead broke into flame. The boats were discovered! The officers leaped to their feet in the stern of each boat, and urged the men on. The leading boats crashed against the *Chevrette's* side. The ship was boarded simultaneously on both bows and quarters. The force on board the *Chevrette*, however, was numerous enough to make a triple line of armed men round the whole sweep of its bulwarks; they were armed with pikes, tomahawks, cutlasses, and muskets, and they met the attack most gallantly, even venturing in their turn to board the boats. By this time, however, the nine boats Maxwell was leading had all come up, and although the defence outnumbered the attack by more than two to one, yet the British were not to be denied. They clambered fiercely on board; the topmen raced aloft, found the foot-ropes on the yards all strapped up, but running out, cutlass in hand, they cut loose the *Chevrette's* sails. Wallis, meanwhile, had fought his way to the wheel, slew two of the enemy in the process, was desperately wounded himself, yet stood steadily at the wheel, and kept the *Chevrette* under command, the batteries by this time opening upon the ship a fire of grape and heavy shot.

In less than three minutes after the boats came alongside, although nearly every second man of their crews had been killed or wounded, the three topsails and courses of the *Chevrette* had fallen, the cables had been cut, and the ship was moving out in the darkness. She leaned over to the light breeze, the ripple sounded louder at her stem, and when the French felt the ship under movement, it for the moment paralysed their defence. Some jumped overboard; others threw down their arms and ran below. The fight, though short, had been so fierce that the deck was simply strewn with bodies. Many of the French who had retreated below renewed the fight there; they tried to blow up the quarter-deck with gunpowder in their desperation, and the British had to fight a new battle between decks with half their force while the ship was slowly getting under weigh. The fire of the batteries was furious, but, curiously enough, no important spar was struck, though some of the boats towing alongside were sunk. And while the batteries thundered overhead, and the battle still raged on the decks below, the British seamen managed to set every sail on the ship, and even got topgallant yards across. Slowly the *Chevrette* drew out of the harbour. Just then some boats were discovered pulling furiously up through the darkness; they were taken to be French boats bent on recapture, and Maxwell's almost exhausted seamen were summoned to a new conflict. The approaching boats, however, turned out to be the detachment under Lieutenant Losack, who came up to find the work done and the *Chevrette* captured.

The fight on the deck of the *Chevrette* had been of a singularly deadly character. The British had a total of 11 killed and 57 wounded; the *Chevrette* lost 92 killed and 62 wounded, amongst the slain being the *Chevrette's* captain, her two lieutenants, and three midshipmen. Many stories are told of the daring displayed by British seamen in this attack. The boatswain of the *Beaulieu*, for example, boarded the *Chevrette's* taffrail; he took one glance along the crowded decks, waved his cutlass, shouted "Make a lane there!" and literally carved his way through to the forecastle, which he cleared of the French, and kept clear, in spite of repeated attacks, while he assisted to cast the ship about and make sail with as much coolness as though he had been on board the *Beaulieu*. Wallis, who fought his way to the helm of the *Chevrette*, and, though wounded, kept his post with iron coolness while the fight raged, was accosted by his officer when the fight was over with an expression of sympathy for his wounds. "It is only a prick or two, sir," said Wallis, and he added he "was ready to go out on a similar expedition the next night." A boatswain's mate named Ware had his left arm cut clean off by a furious slash of a French sabre, and fell back into the boat. With the help of a comrade's tarry fingers Ware bound up the bleeding stump with rough but energetic surgery, climbed with his solitary hand on board the *Chevrette*, and played a most gallant part in the fight.

The fight that captured the *Chevrette* is almost without parallel. Here was a ship carried off from an enemy's port, with the combined fleets of France and Spain looking on. The enemy were not taken by surprise; they did not merely defy attack, they invited it. The British had to assail a force three times their number, with every advantage of situation and arms. The British boats were exposed to a heavy fire from the *Chevrette* itself and from the shore batteries before they came alongside. The crews fought their way up the sides of the ship in the face of overwhelming odds; they got the vessel under weigh while the fight still raged, and brought her out of a narrow and difficult roadstead before they had actually captured her. "All this was done," to quote the "Naval Chronicle" for 1802, "in the presence of the grand fleet of the enemy; it was done by nine boats out of fifteen, which originally set out upon the expedition; it was done under the conduct of an officer who, in the absence of the person appointed to command, undertook it upon his own responsibility, and whose intrepidity, judgment, and presence of mind, seconded by the wonderful exertions of the officers and men under his command, succeeded in effecting an enterprise which, by those who reflect upon its peculiar circumstances, will ever be regarded with astonishment."

MOUNTAIN COMBATS

> "At length the freshening western blast
> Aside the shroud of battle cast;
> And first the ridge of mingled spears
> Above the brightening cloud appears;
> And in the smoke the pennons flew,
> As in the storm the white sea-mew.
> Then marked they, dashing broad and far,
> The broken billows of the war,
> And plumèd crests of chieftains brave
> Floating like foam upon the wave,
>   But nought distinct they see."
> —Scott.

THE brilliant and heroic combats on the Nive belong to the later stages of the Pyrenean campaign; and here, as on the Bidassoa, Soult had all the advantages of position. He had a fortified camp and a great fortress as his base; excellent roads linked the whole of his positions together; he held the interior lines, and could reach any point in the zone of operations in less time than his great opponent. Wellington, on the other hand, had almost every possible disadvantage. The weather was bitter; incessant rains fell; he had to operate on both sides of a dangerous river; the roads were mere ribbons of tenacious clay, in which the infantry sank to mid-leg, the guns to their axles, the cavalry sometimes to their saddle-girths. Moreover, Wellington's Spanish troops had the sufferings and outrages of a dozen campaigns to avenge, and when they found themselves on French soil the temptations to plunder and murder were irresistible. Wellington would not maintain war by plunder, and, as he found he could not restrain his Spaniards, he despatched the whole body, 25,000 strong, back to Spain. It was a great deed. It violated all military canons, for by it Wellington divided his army in the presence of the enemy. It involved, too, a rare sacrifice of personal ambition. "If I had 20,000 Spaniards, paid and fed," he wrote to Lord Bathurst, " I should have Bayonne. If I had 40,000 I do not know where I should stop. Now I have both the 20,000 and the 40,000, . . . but if they plunder they will ruin all." Wellington was great enough to sacrifice both military rules and personal ambition to humanity. He was wise enough, too, 'to know that a policy which outrages humanity in the long-run means disaster.

Wellington's supreme advantage lay in the fighting quality of his troops. The campaigns of six years had made them an army of veterans. "Danger," says Napier, "was their sport," and victory, it might also be added, was their habit. They fought with a confidence and fierceness which, added to the cool and stubborn courage native to the British character, made the battalions which broke over the French frontier under Wellington perhaps the most formidable fighting force known in the history of war. To quote Napier once more: "What Alexander's Macedonians were at Arbela, Hannibal's Africans at Cannæ, Cæsar's Romans at Pharsalia, Napoleon's Guards at Austerlitz, such were Wellington's British soldiers at this period."

On November 10, 1813, was fought what is called

the battle of Nivelle, in which Wellington thrust Soult roughly and fiercely from the strong positions he held on the flanks of the great hills under which the Nivelle flows. The morning broke in great splendour; three signal-guns flashed from the heights of one of the British hills, and at once the 43rd leaped out and ran swiftly forward from the flank of the great Rhune to storm the "Hog's Back" ridge of the Petite Rhune, a ridge walled with rocks 200 feet high, except at one point, where it was protected by a marsh. William Napier, who commanded the 43rd, has told the story of the assault. He placed four companies in reserve, and led the other four in person to the attack on the rocks; and he was chiefly anxious not to rush his men—to "keep down the pace," so that they would not arrive spent and breathless at the French works. The men were eager to rush, however; the fighting impulse in them was on flame, and they were held back with difficulty. When they were still nearly 200 yards from the enemy, a youthful aide-de-camp, his blood on fire, came galloping up with a shout, and waving his hat. The 43rd broke out of hand at once with the impulse of the lad's enthusiasm and the stroke of his horse's flying hoofs, and with a sudden rush they launched themselves on the French works still high above them.

Napier had nothing for it but to join the charging mass. "I was the first man but one," he says, "who reached and jumped into the rocks, and I was only second because my strength and speed were unequal to contend with the giant who got before me. He was the tallest and most active man in the regiment, and the day before, being sentenced to corporal punishment, I had pardoned him on the occasion of an approaching action. He now repaid me by striving always to place himself between me and the fire of the enemy. His name was Eccles, an Irishman." The men won the first redoubt, but simply had not breath and strength enough left to reach the one above it, and fell gasping and exhausted in the rocks before it, the French firing fiercely upon them. In a few minutes, however, they had recovered breath; they leaped up with a shout, and tumbled over the wall of the castle; and so, from barrier to barrier, as up some Titanic stairway, the 43rd swept with glittering bayonets. The summit was held by a powerful work called the Donjon; it was so strong that attack upon it seemed madness. But a keen-eyed British officer detected signs of wavering in the French within the fort, and with a shout the 43rd leaped at it, and carried it. It took the 43rd twenty minutes to carry the whole chain of positions; and of the eleven officers of the regiment, six were killed or desperately wounded. The French showed bravery; they fought, in fact, muzzle to muzzle up the whole chain of positions. But the 43rd charged with a daring and fury absolutely resistless.

Another amazing feature in the day's fight was the manner in which Colborne, with the 52nd, carried what was called the Signal Redoubt, a strong work, crowning a steep needle-pointed hill, and overlooking the whole French position. Colborne led his men up an ascent so sharp that his horse with difficulty could climb it. The summit was reached, and the men went in, with a run, at the work, only to find the redoubt girdled by a wide ditch thirty feet deep. The men halted on the edge of the deep cutting, and under the fire of the French they fell fast. Colborne led back his men under the brow of the hill for shelter, and at three separate points brought them over the crest again. In each case, after the men had rested under shelter long enough to recover breath, the word was passed, "Stand up and advance." The men instantly obeyed, and charged up to the edge of the ditch again, many of the leading files jumping into it. But it was impossible to cross, and each time the mass of British infantry stepped coolly back into cover again.

One sergeant named Mayne, who had leaped into the ditch, found he could neither climb the ramparts nor get back to his comrades, and he flung himself on his face. A Frenchman leaned over the rampart, took leisurely aim, and fired at him as he lay. Mayne had stuck the billhook of his section at the back of his knapsack, and the bullet struck it and flattened upon it. Colborne was a man of infinite resource in war, and at this crisis he made a bugler sound a parley, hoisted his white pocket-handkerchief, and coolly walked round to the gate of the redoubt and invited the garrison to surrender. The veteran who commanded it answered indignantly, "What! I with my battalion surrender to you with yours?" "Very well," answered Colborne in French, "the artillery will be up immediately; you cannot hold out, and you will be surrendered to the Spaniards." That threat was sufficient. The French officers remonstrated stormily with their commander, and the work was surrendered. But only one French soldier in the redoubt had fallen, whereas amongst the 52nd "there fell," says Napier, "200 soldiers of a regiment never surpassed in arms since arms were first borne by men." In this fight Soult was driven in a little more than three hours from a mountain position he had been fortifying for more than three months.

Amongst the brave men who died that day on the side of the British were two whose portraits Napier has drawn with something of Plutarch's minuteness:—

"The first, low in rank, for he was but a lieutenant; rich in honour, for he bore many scars; was young of days—he was only nineteen—and had seen more combats and sieges than he could count years. So slight in person and of such surpassing and delicate beauty that the Spaniards often thought him a girl disguised in man's clothing; he was yet so vigorous, so active, so brave, that the most daring and experienced veterans watched his looks on the field of battle, and, implicitly following where he led, would, like children, obey his slightest sign in the most difficult situations. His education was incomplete, yet were his natural powers so happy that the keenest and best-furnished shrank from an encounter of wit; and every thought and aspiration was proud and noble, indicating future greatness if destiny had so willed it. Such was Edward Freer of the 43rd. The night before the battle he had that strange anticipation of coming death so often felt by military men. He was struck by three balls at the first storming of the Rhune rocks, and the sternest soldiers wept, even in the middle of the fight, when they saw him fall."

"On the same day, and at the same hour, was killed Colonel Thomas Lloyd. He likewise had been a long time in the 43rd. Under him Freer had learned the rudiments of his profession; but in the course of the war, promotion placed Lloyd at the head of the 94th, and it was leading that regiment he fell. In him also were combined mental and bodily powers of no ordinary kind. Graceful symmetry, herculean strength, and a countenance frank and majestic, gave the true index of his nature; for his capacity was great and commanding, and his military knowledge extensive, both from experience and study. Of his mirth and wit, well known in the army, it only need be said that he used the latter without offence, yet so as to increase the ascendency over those with whom he held intercourse; for, though gentle, he was ambitious, valiant, and conscious of his fitness for great exploits. And he, like Freer, was prescient of and predicted his own fall, but with no abatement of courage, for when he received the mortal wound, a most painful one, he would not suffer himself to be moved, and remained to watch the battle, making observations upon its changes until death came. It was thus, at the age of thirty, that the good, the brave, the generous Lloyd died. Tributes to his memory have been published by Wellington, and by one of his own poor soldiers, by the highest and by the lowest. To their testimony I add mine. Let those who served on equal terms with him say whether in aught it has exaggerated his deserts."

A pathetic incident may be added, found in Napier's biography, but which he does not give in his History. The night before the battle Napier was stretched on the ground under his cloak, when young Freer came to him and crept under the cover of his cloak, sobbing as if his heart would break. Napier tried to soothe and comfort the boy, and learnt from him that he was fully persuaded he should lose his life in the approaching battle, and his distress was caused by thinking of his mother and sister in England.

On December 9, Wellington, by a daring movement and with some fierce fighting, crossed the Nive. It was a movement which had many advantages, but one drawback—his wings were now separated by the Nive; and Soult at this stage, like the great and daring commander he was, took advantage of his position to attempt a great counter-stroke. It was within his power to fling his whole force on either wing of Wellington, and so confident was he of success that he wrote to the Minister of War telling him to "expect good news" the next day. Wellington himself was on the right bank of the Nive, little dreaming that Soult was about to leap on the extremity of his scattered forces. The country was so broken that Soult's movements were entirely hidden, and the roads so bad that even the cavalry outposts could scarcely move. On the night of the 9th Soult had gathered every available bayonet, and was ready to burst on the position held by Sir John Hope at Arcanques.

In the grey dawn of the 10th the out-pickets of the 43rd noticed that the French infantry were pushing each other about as if in sport; but the crowd seemed to thicken and to eddy nearer and nearer the British line. It was a trick to deceive the vigilance of the British outposts. Presently the apparently sportive crowd made a rush forwards and resolved itself into a spray of swiftly moving skirmishers. The French columns broke from behind a screen of houses, and, at a running pace, and with a tumult of shouts, charged the British position. In a moment the crowd of French soldiers had penetrated betwixt the 43rd and 52nd, and charging eagerly forward, tried to turn the flanks of both. But these were veteran regiments; they fell coolly and swiftly back, firing fiercely as they went. It was at once a race and a combat. The roads were so narrow and so bad that the British could keep no order, and if the French outpaced them and reached the open position at the rear first, the British line would be pierced. The 43rd came through the pass first, apparently a crowd of running fugitives, officers and men jumbled together. The moment they had reached the open ground, however, the men fell, as if by a single impulse, into military form, and became a steadfast red line, from end to end of which ran, and ran again, and yet again, the volleying flame of a sustained musketry fire. The pass was barred!

The troops to the right of the French were not quite so quick or so fortunate, and about 100 of the British —riflemen and men of the 43rd—were intercepted. The French never doubted that they would surrender, for they were but a handful of men cut off by a whole column. An ensign of the 43rd named Campbell, a lad not eighteen years of age, was in the front files of the British when the call to surrender was heard. With a shout the boy-ensign leaped at the French column. Where an officer leads, British soldiers will always follow, and the men followed him with a courage as high as his own. With a rush the column was rent, and though fifty of the British were killed or taken, fifty, including the gallant boy who led them, escaped.

The fighting at other points was of the sharpest,

and was strangely entangled and confused. It was a fight of infantry against infantry, and the whole field of the combat was interlaced by almost impassable hedges. At one point, so strangely broken was the ground, and so obscured the fight with smoke and mist, that a French regiment passed unseen betwixt the British and Portuguese, and was rapidly filing into line on the rear of the 9th, fiercely occupied at that moment against a strong force in front. Cameron, its colonel, left fifty men of his regiment to answer the fire in his front, faced about, and went at a run against the French regiment, which by this time had commenced volley-firing. Cameron's men fell fast— eighty men and officers, in fact, dropped in little more than five minutes—but the rush of the 9th was irresistible. The Frenchmen wavered, broke, and swept, a disorganised mass, past the flank of the Royals, actually carrying off one of its officers in the rush, and disappeared.

The sternest and most bewildering fighting took place round a building known as the "mayor's house," surrounded by a coppice-wood. Coppice and outbuildings were filled with men of all regiments and all nations, swearing, shooting, and charging with the bayonet. The 84th was caught in a hollow road by the French, who lined the banks above, and lost its colonel and a great proportion of its rank and file. Gronow tells an amusing incident of the fight at this stage. An isolated British battalion stationed near the mayor's house was suddenly surrounded by a flood of French. The French general galloped up to the British officer in command and demanded his sword. "Upon this," says Gronow, "without the least hesitation the British officer shouted out, 'This fellow wants us to surrender! Charge! my boys, and show them what stuff we are made of.'" The men answered with a shout, sudden, scornful, and stern, and went with a run at the French. "In a few minutes," adds Gronow, "they had taken prisoners or killed the whole of the infantry regiment opposed to them!"

On the 11th desperate fighting took place on the same ground, but the British were by this time reinforced—the Guards, in particular, coming up after a rapid and exhausting march—and Soult's attack had failed. But on the night of the 12th the rain fell fast and steadily, the Nive was flooded, the bridge of boats which spanned it swept away, and Hill was left at St. Pierre isolated, with less than 14,000 men. Soult saw his opportunity. The interior lines he held made concentration easy, and on the morning of the 13th he was able to pour an attacking force of 35,000 bayonets on Hill's front, while another infantry division, together with the whole of the French cavalry under Pierre Soult, attacked his rear. Then there followed what has been described as "the most desperate battle of the whole Peninsular war."

THE BLOODIEST FIGHT IN THE PENINSULA

> "Then out spoke brave Horatius,
> The captain of the gate:
> 'To every man upon this earth
> Death cometh soon or late;
> And how can man die better
> Than facing fearful odds,
> For the ashes of his fathers
> And the temples of his gods?'"
>
> —MACAULAY.

HILL's front stretched through two miles; his left, a wooded craggy ridge, was held by Pringle's brigade, but was parted from the centre by a marshy valley and a chain of ponds; his centre occupied a crescent-shaped broken ridge; his right, under General Byng, held a ridge parallel with the Adour. The French gathered in great masses on a range of counter-heights, an open plain being between them and Hill's centre. The day was heavy with whirling mist; and as the wind tore it occasionally asunder, the British could see on the parallel roads before them the huge, steadily flowing columns of the French.

Abbé led the attack on the British centre. He was "the fighting general" of Soult's army, famous for the rough energy of his character and the fierceness of his onfall. He pushed his attack with such ardour that he forced his way to the crest of the British ridge.

Battle of ST. PIERRE
December 9th. & 13th. 1813.

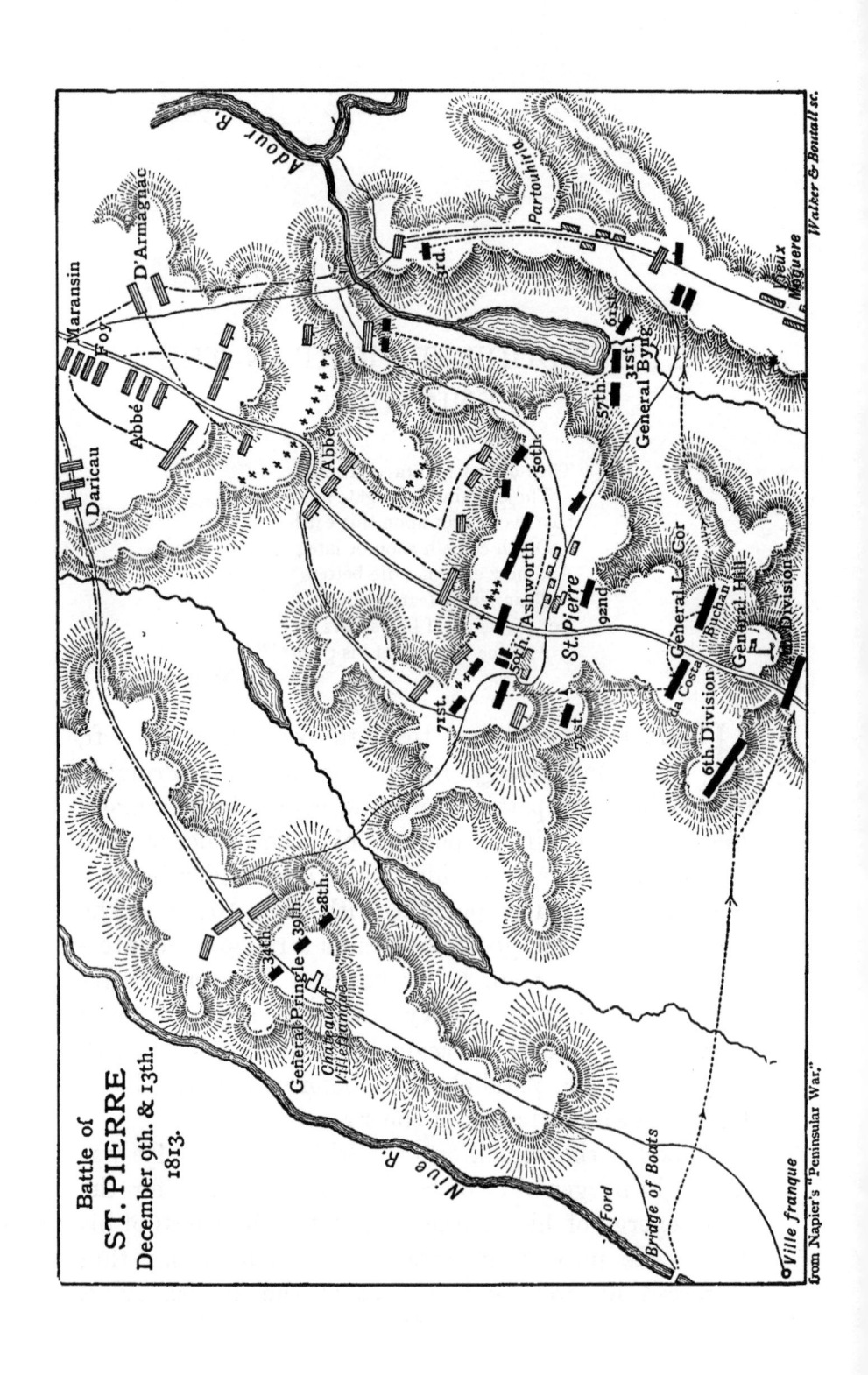

The famous 92nd, held in reserve, was brought forward by way of counter-stroke, and pushed its attack keenly home. The head of Abbé's column was crushed; but the French general replaced the broken battalions by fresh troops, and still forced his way onward, the 92nd falling back.

In the meanwhile on both the right and the left of the British position an almost unique disaster had befallen Hill's troops. Peacock, the colonel of the 71st, through some bewitched failure of nerve or of judgment, withdrew that regiment from the fight. It was a Highland regiment, great in fighting reputation, and full of daring. How black were the looks of the officers, and what loud swearing in Gaelic took place in the ranks, as the gallant regiment—discipline overcoming human nature—obeyed the mysterious order to retire, may be imagined. Almost at the same moment on the right, Bunbury, who commanded the 3rd or Buffs, in the same mysterious fashion abandoned to the French the strong position he held. Both colonels were brave men, and their sudden lapse into unsoldierly conduct has never been explained. Both, it may be added, were compelled to resign their commissions after the fight.

Hill, surveying the spectacle from the post he had taken, commanding the whole field of battle, hastened down, met and halted the Buffs, sent them back to the fight, drew his whole reserves into the fray, and himself turned the 71st and led them to the attack. With what joy the indignant Highlanders of the 71st obeyed the order to "Right about face" may be imagined, and so vehement was their charge that the French column upon which it was flung, though coming on at the double, in all the *élan* of victory, was instantly shattered.

Meanwhile the 92nd was launched again at Abbé's column. Cameron, its colonel, was a soldier of a very gallant type, and, himself a Highlander, he understood the Highland temperament perfectly. He dressed his regiment as if on parade, the colours were uncased, the pipes shrilled fiercely, and in all the pomp of military array, with green tartans and black plumes all wind-blown, and with the wild strains of their native hills and lochs thrilling in their ears, the Highlanders bore down on the French, their officers fiercely leading. On all sides at that moment the British skirmishers were falling back. The 50th was clinging desperately to a small wood that crowned the ridge, but everywhere the French were forcing their way onward. Ashworth's Portuguese were practically destroyed; Barnes, who commanded the centre, was shot through the body. But the fierce charge of the 92nd along the high-road, and of the 71st on the left centre, sent an electric thrill along the whole British front. The skirmishers, instead of falling back, ran forward; the Portuguese rallied. The 92nd found in its immediate front two strong French regiments, and their leading files brought their bayonets to the charge, and seemed eager to meet the 92nd with the actual push of steel. It was the crisis of the fight.

At that moment the French commander's nerve failed him. That steel-edged line of kilted, plume-crested Highlanders, charging with a step so fierce, was too much for him. He suddenly turned his horse, waved his sword; his men promptly faced about, and marched back to their original position. The French on both the right and the left drew back, and the battle for the moment seemed to die down. Hill's right was safe, and he drew the 57th from it to strengthen his sorely battered centre; and just at that moment the sixth division, which had been marching since daybreak, crossed the bridge over the Nive, which the British engineers with rare energy had restored, and appeared on the ridge overlooking the field of battle. Wellington, too, appeared on the scene, with the third and fourth divisions. At two o'clock the allies commenced a forward movement, and Soult fell back; his second counter-stroke had failed.

St. Pierre was, perhaps, the most desperately contested fight in the Peninsular war, a field almost as bloody as Albuera. Hill's ranks were wasted as by fire; three British generals were carried from the field; nearly the whole of the staff was struck down. On a space scarcely one mile square, 5000 men were killed and wounded within three hours. Wellington, as he rode over the field by the side of Hill after the fight was over, declared he had never seen the dead lie so thickly before. It was a great feat for less than 14,000 men with 14 guns to withstand the assault of 35,000 men with 22 guns; and, at least where Abbé led, the fighting of the French was of the most resolute character. The victory was due, in part, to Hill's generalship and the lion-like energy with which he restored his broken centre and flung back the Buffs and the 71st into the fight. But in a quite equal degree the victory was due to the obstinate fighting quality of the British private. The 92nd, for example, broke the French front no less than four times by bayonet charges pushed home with the sternest resolution, and it lost in these charges 13 officers and 171 rank and file.

The French, it might almost be said, lost the field by the momentary failure in nerve of the officer commanding the column upon which the 92nd was rushing in its last and most dramatic charge. His column was massive and unbroken; the men, with bent heads and levelled bayonets, were ready to meet the 92nd with a courage as lofty as that of the Highlanders themselves; and the 92nd, for all its parade of fluttering colours and wind-blown tartans and feathers, was but a single weak battalion. An electrical gesture, a single peremptory call on the part of the leader, even a single daring act by a soldier in the ranks, and the French column would have been hurled on the 92nd, and by its mere weight must have broken it. But the oncoming of the Highlanders proved too great a strain for the nerve of the French general. He wheeled the head of his horse backward, and the fight was lost.

Weeks of the bitterest winter weather suspended all military operations after St. Pierre. The rivers were flooded; the clayey lowlands were one far-stretching quagmire; fogs brooded in the ravines; perpetual tempests shrieked over the frozen summits of the Pyrenees; the iron-bound coast was furious with breakers. But Wellington's hardy veterans—ill-clad, ill-sheltered, and ill-fed—yet kept their watch on the slopes of the Pyrenees. The outposts of the two armies, indeed, fell into almost friendly relations with each other. Barter sprang up between them, a regular code of signals was established, friendly offices were exchanged. Wellington on one occasion desired to reconnoitre Soult's camp from the top of a hill occupied by a French picket, and ordered some English rifles to drive them off. No firing was necessary. An English soldier held up the butt of his rifle and tapped it in a peculiar way. The signal meant, "We must have the hill for a short time," and the French at once retired. A steady traffic in brandy and tobacco sprang up between the pickets of the two armies. A rivulet at one point flowed between the outposts, and an Irish soldier named Patten, on sentry there, placed a canteen with a silver coin in it on a stone by the bank of the rivulet, to be filled with brandy by the French in the usual way. Canteen and coin vanished, but no brandy arrived. Patten, a daring fellow, regarded himself as cheated, and the next day seeing, as he supposed, the same French sentry on duty, he crossed the rivulet, seized the Frenchman's musket, shook the amazed sentry out of his accoutrements as a pea is shaken out of its pod, and carried them off. The French outposts sent in a flag of truce, complained of this treatment, and said the unfortunate sentry's life would be forfeited unless his uniform and gun were restored. Patten, however, insisted that he held these "in pawn for a canteen of brandy," and he got his canteen before the uniform was restored.

On February 12 a white hard frost suddenly fell on the whole field of operations, and turned the viscid mud everywhere to the hardness of stone. The men could march, the artillery move; and Wellington, whose strategy was ripe, was at once in action.

Soult barred his path by a great entrenched camp at Bayonne, to which the Adour served as a Titanic wet ditch. The Adour is a great river, swift and broad—swiftest and broadest through the six miles of its course below the town to its mouth. Its bed is of shifting sand; the spring-tide rises in it fourteen feet, the ebb-tide runs seven miles an hour. Where the swift river and the great rollers of the Bay of Biscay meet is a treacherous bar—in heavy weather a mere tumult of leaping foam. Soult assumed that Wellington would cross the river above the town; the attempt to cross it near the mouth, where it was barred with sand, and beaten with surges, and guarded, too, by a tiny squadron of French gunboats, was never suspected. Yet exactly this was Wellington's plan; and his bridge across the Adour is declared by Napier to be a stupendous undertaking, which must always rank amongst "the prodigies of war." Forty large sailing-boats, of about twenty tons burden each, carrying the materials for the bridge, were to enter the mouth of the Adour at the moment when Hope, with part of Hill's division, made his appearance on the left bank of the river, with materials for rafts, by means of which sufficient troops could be thrown across the Adour to capture a battery which commanded its entrance.

On the night of February 22, Hope, with the first division, was in the assigned position on the banks of the Adour, hidden behind some sandhills. But a furious gale made the bar impassable, and not a boat was in sight. Hope, the most daring of men, never hesitated; he would cross the river without the aid of the fleet. His guns were suddenly uncovered, the tiny French flotilla was sunk or scattered, and a pontoon or raft, carrying sixty men of the Guards, pushed out from the

British bank. A strong French picket held the other shore; but, bewildered and ill led, they made no opposition. A hawser was dragged across the stream, and pontoons, each carrying fifteen men, were in quick succession pulled across. When about a thousand men had in this way reached the French bank, some French battalions, made their appearance. Colonel Stopford, who was in command, allowed the French to come on—their drums beating the *pas de charge*, and their officers waving their swords—to within a distance of twenty yards, and then opened upon them with his rocket brigade. The fiery flight and terrifying sound of these missiles put the French to instant rout. All night the British continued to cross, and on the morning of the 24th the flotilla was off the bar, the boats of the men-of-war leading.

The first boat that plunged into the tumult of breakers, leaping and roaring over the bar, sank instantly. The second shot through and was safe; but the tide was running out furiously, and no boat could follow till it was high water again. When high water came, the troops crowding the sandbanks watched with breathless interest the fight of the boats to enter. They hung and swayed like a flock of gigantic sea-birds on the rough and tumbling sea. Lieutenant Bloye of the *Lyra*, who led the way in his barge, dashed into the broad zone of foam, and was instantly swallowed up with all his crew. The rest of the flotilla bore up to right and left, and hovered on the edge of the tormented waters. Suddenly Lieutenant Cheyne of the *Woodlark* caught a glimpse of the true course and dashed through, and boat after boat came following with reeling decks and dripping crews; but in the whole passage no fewer than eight of the flotilla were destroyed. The bridge was quickly constructed. Thirty-six two-masted vessels were moored head to stern, with an interval between each vessel, across the 800 yards of the Adour; a double line of cables, about ten feet apart, linked the boats together; strong planks were lashed athwart the cables, making a roadway; a double line of masts, forming a series of floating squares, served as a floating boom; and across this swaying, flexible, yet mighty bridge, Wellington was able to pour his left wing, with all its artillery and material, and so draw round Bayonne an iron line of investment.

This movement thrust back Soult's right, but he clung obstinately to the Gave. He held by Napoleon's maxim that the best way to defend is to attack, and Wellington's very success gave him what seemed a golden opportunity. Wellington's left had crossed the Adour, but that very movement separated it from the right.

Soult took up his position on a ridge of hills above Orthez. He commanded the fords by which Picton must cross, and his plan was to crush him while in the act of crossing. The opportunity was clear, but somehow Soult missed it. There failed him at the critical moment the swift-attacking impulse which both Napoleon and Wellington possessed in so high a degree. Picton's two divisions crossed the Gave, and climbed the bank through mere fissures in the rocks, which broke up all military order, and the nearest point which allowed them to fall into line was within cannon-shot of the enemy. Even Picton's iron nerve shook at such a crisis;

but Wellington, to use Napier's phrase, "calm as deepest sea," watched the scene. Soult ought to have attacked; he waited to be attacked, and so missed victory.

By nine o'clock Wellington had formed his plan, and Ross's brigade was thrust through a gorge on Soult's left. The French were admirably posted: they had a narrow front, abundant artillery, and a great battery placed so as to smite on the flank any column forcing its way through the gorge which pierced Soult's left. Ross's men fought magnificently. Five times they broke through the gorge, and five times the fire of the French infantry on the slopes above them, and the grape of the great battery at the head of the gorge, drove the shattered regiments back. On Soult's right, again, Foy flung back with loss an attack by part of Picton's forces. On both the right and left, that is, Soult was victorious, and, as he saw the wasted British lines roll sullenly back, it is said that the French general smote his thigh in exultation, and cried, "At last I have him!"

Almost at that moment, however, the warlike genius of Wellington changed the aspect of the scene. He fed the attacks on Soult's right and left, and the deepening roar of the battle at these two points absorbed the senses of the French general. Soult's front was barred by what was supposed to be an impassable marsh, above which a great hill frowned; and across the marsh, and upon this hill, the centre of Soult's position, Wellington launched the famous 52nd.

Colborne plunged with his men into the marsh; they sank at every step above the knee, sometimes to the middle. The skirmishers shot fiercely at them. But with stern composure the veterans of the light division

—soldiers, as Napier never tires in declaring, who "had never yet met their match in the field"—pressed on. The marsh was crossed, the hill climbed, and with a sudden and deafening shout—the cheer which has a more full and terrible note than any other voice of fighting men, the shout of the British regiment as it charges—the 52nd dashed between Foy and Taupin. A French battalion in their path was scattered as by the stroke of a thunderbolt. The French centre was pierced; both victorious wings halted, and began to ebb back. Hill, meanwhile, had crossed the Gave, and taking a wider circle, threatened Soult's line of retreat. The French fell back, and fell back with ever-quickening steps, but yet fighting sternly; the British, with deafening musketry and cannonade, pressed on them. Hill quickened his pace on the ridge along which he was pressing. It became a race who should reach first the single bridge on the Luy-de-Béarn over which the French must pass. The pace became a run. Many of the French broke from their ranks and raced forward. The British cavalry broke through some covering battalions and sabred the fugitives. A great disaster was imminent; and yet it was avoided, partly by Soult's cool and obstinate defence, and partly by the accident that at that moment Wellington was struck by a spent ball and was disabled, so that his swift and imperious will no longer directed the pursuit.

Orthez may be described as the last and not the least glorious fight in the Peninsular war. Toulouse was fought ten day afterwards, but it scarcely belongs to the Peninsular campaigns, and was actually fought after a general armistice had been signed.

CAPTAIN EDWARD RIOU

After a miniature by SHELLEY

THE BATTLE OF THE BALTIC

" Let us think of them that sleep
Full many a fathom deep
By thy wild and stormy deep,
Elsinore ! "
—CAMPBELL.

" I HAVE been in a hundred and five engagements, but that of to-day is the most terrible of them all." This was how Nelson himself summed up the great fight off Copenhagen, or the battle of the Baltic as it is sometimes called, fought on April 2, 1801. It was a battle betwixt Britons and Danes. The men who fought under the blood-red flag of Great Britain, and under the split flag of Denmark with its white cross, were alike the descendants of the Vikings. The blood of the old sea-rovers ran hot and fierce in their veins. Nelson, with the glories of the Nile still ringing about his name, commanded the British fleet, and the fire of his eager and gallant spirit ran from ship to ship like so many volts of electricity. But the Danes fought in sight of their capital, under the eyes of their wives and children. It is not strange that through the four hours during which the thunder of the great battle rolled over the roofs of Copenhagen and up the narrow waters of the Sound, human valour and endurance in both fleets were at their very highest.

Less than sixty years afterwards " thunders of fort

and fleet" along all the shores of England were welcoming a daughter of the Danish throne as

"Bride of the heir of the kings of the sea."

And Tennyson, speaking for every Briton, assured the Danish girl who was to be their future Queen—

"We are each all Dane in our welcome of thee."

What was it in 1801 which sent a British fleet on an errand of battle to Copenhagen?

It was a tiny episode of the long and stern drama of the Napoleonic wars. Great Britain was supreme on the sea, Napoleon on the land, and, in his own words, Napoleon conceived the idea of "conquering the sea by the land." Paul I. of Russia, a semi-lunatic, became Napoleon's ally and tool. Paul was able to put overwhelming pressure on Sweden, Denmark, and Prussia, and these Powers were federated as the "League of Armed Neutrality," with the avowed purpose of challenging the marine supremacy of Great Britain. Paul seized all British ships in Russian ports; Prussia marched troops into Hanover; every port from the North Cape to Gibraltar was shut against the British flag. Britain stood alone, practically threatened with a naval combination of all the Northern Powers, while behind the combination stood Napoleon, the subtlest brain and most imperious will ever devoted to the service of war. Napoleon's master passion, it should be remembered, was the desire to overthrow Great Britain, and he held in the palm of his hand the whole military strength of the Continent. The fleets of France and Spain were crushed or blockaded; but the three Northern Powers could have put into battle-line a fleet of fifty great ships and twenty-five frigates. With this force they could raise the blockade of the French ports, sweep triumphant through the narrow seas, and land a French army in Kent or in Ulster.

Pitt was Prime Minister, and his masterful intellect controlled British policy. He determined that the fleets of Denmark and of Russia should not become a weapon in the hand of Napoleon against England; and a fleet of eighteen ships of the line, with frigates and bomb-vessels, was despatched to reason, from the iron lips of their guns, with the misguided Danish Government. Sir Hyde Parker, a decent, unenterprising veteran, was commander-in-chief by virtue of seniority; but Nelson, with the nominal rank of second in command, was the brain and soul of the expedition. "Almost all the safety and certainly all the honour of England," he said to his chief, "is more entrusted to you than ever yet fell to the lot of a British officer." And all through the story of the expedition it is amusing to notice the fashion in which Nelson's fiery nature strove to kindle poor Sir Hyde Parker's sluggish temper to its own flame.

The fleet sailed from Yarmouth on March 12, and fought its way through fierce spring gales to the entrance of the Kattegat. The wind was fair; Nelson was eager to sweep down on Copenhagen with the whole fleet, and negotiate with the whole skyline of Copenhagen crowded with British topsails. "While the negotiation is going on," he said, "the Dane should see our flag waving every time he lifts up his head." Time was worth more than gold; it was worth brave men's lives. The Danes were toiling day and night to prepare the defence of their capital. But prim Sir Hyde anchored, and sent up a single frigate with his ultimatum, and it was not until March 30 that the British fleet, a long line of stately vessels, came sailing up the Sound, passed Elsinore, and cast anchor fifteen miles from Copenhagen. Nothing could surpass the gallant energy shown by the Danes in their preparation for defence, and Nature had done much to make the city impregnable from the sea.

The Sound is narrow and shallow, a mere tangle of shoals wrinkled with twisted channels and scoured by the swift tides. King's Channel runs straight up towards the city, but a huge sandbank, like the point of a toe, splits the channel into two just as it reaches the harbour. The western edge runs up, pocket-shaped, into the city, and forms the actual port; the main channel contracts, swings round to the south-east, and forms a narrow passage between the shallows in front of the city and a huge shoal called the Middle Ground. A cluster of grim and heavily armed fortifications called the Three-Crown Batteries guarded the entrance to the harbour, and looked right up King's Channel; a stretch of floating batteries and line-of-battle ships, a mile and a half in extent, ran from the Three-Crown Batteries along the edge of the shoals in front of the city, with some heavy pile batteries at its termination. The direct approach up King's Channel, together with the narrow passage between the city and the Middle Ground, were thus commanded by the fire of over 600 heavy guns. The Danes had removed the buoys that marked all the channels, the British had no charts, and only the most daring and skilful seamanship could bring the great ships of the British fleet through that treacherous tangle

THE BATTLE OF THE BALTIC
April 2nd. 1801.

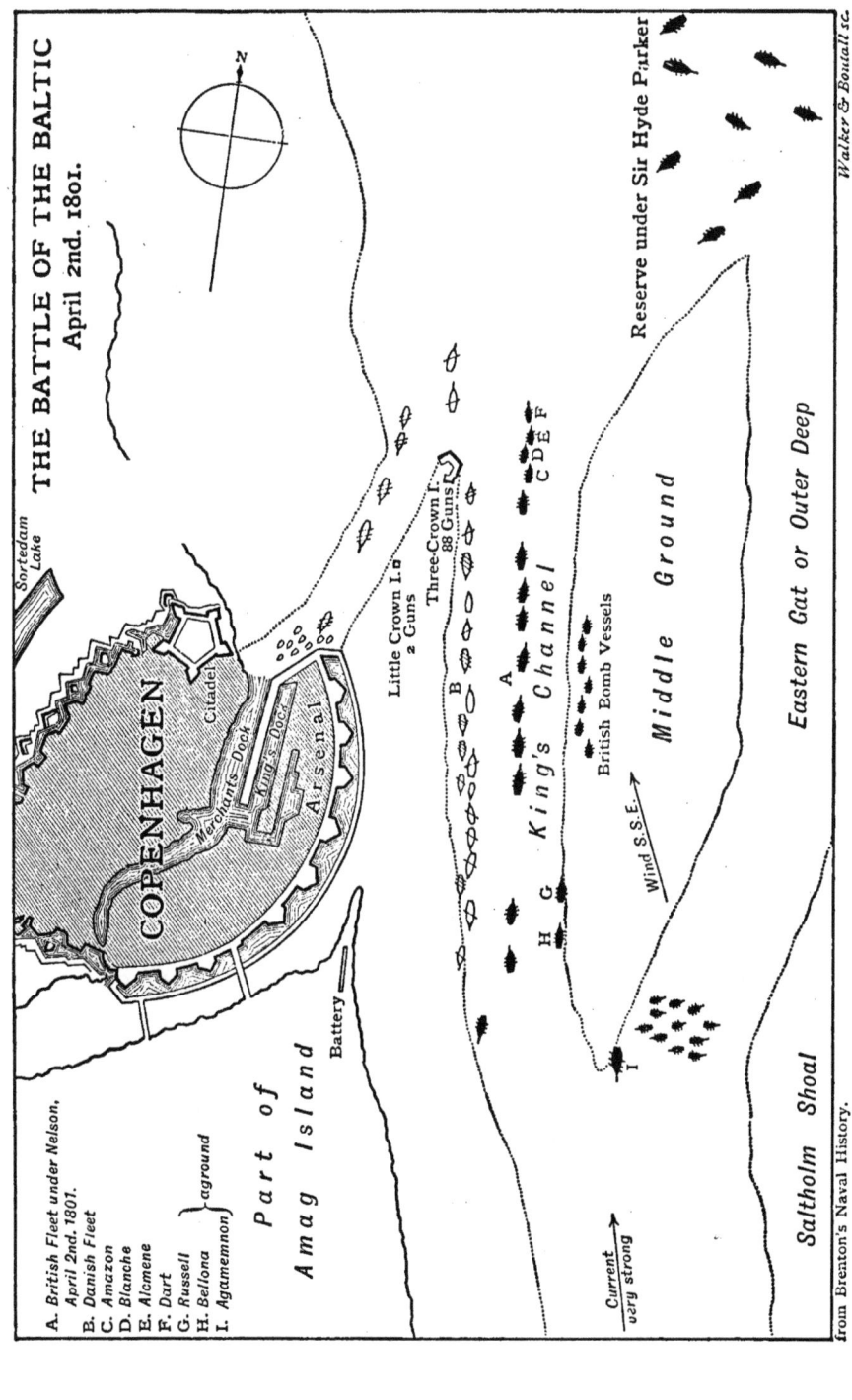

A. British Fleet under Nelson, April 2nd. 1801.
B. Danish Fleet
C. Amazon
D. Blanche
E. Alcmene
F. Dart
G. Russell ⎫
H. Bellona ⎬ aground
I. Agamemnon ⎭

Sortedam Lake

COPENHAGEN
Citadel
Merchants' Dock
King's Dock
Arsenal

Little Crown I. 2 Guns
Three Crown I. 88 Guns

Part of Amag Island

Battery

King's Channel
British Bomb Vessels
Wind S.S.E.

Middle Ground

Reserve under Sir Hyde Parker

Current very strong

Saltholm Shoal

Eastern Gat or Outer Deep

from Brenton's Naval History.

Walker & Boutall sc.

of shoals to the Danish front. As a matter of fact, the heavier ships in the British fleet never attempted to join in the desperate fight which was waged, but hung as mere spectators in the offing.

Meanwhile popular enthusiasm in the Danish capital was at fever-point. Ten thousand disciplined troops manned the batteries; but peasants from the farms, workmen from the factories, merchants from the city, hastened to volunteer, and worked day and night at gun-drill. A thousand students from the university enrolled themselves, and drilled from morning till night. These student-soldiers had probably the best military band ever known; it consisted of the entire orchestra of the Theatre Royal, all volunteers. A Danish officer, sent on some message under a flag of truce to the British fleet, was required to put his message in writing, and was offered a somewhat damaged pen for that purpose. He threw it down with a laugh, saying that "if the British guns were not better pointed than their pens they wouldn't make much impression on Copenhagen." That flash of gallant wit marked the temper of the Danes. They were on flame with confident daring.

Nelson, always keen for a daring policy, had undertaken to attack the Danish defences with a squadron of twelve seventy-fours, and the frigates and bomb-vessels of the fleet. He determined to shun the open way of King's Channel, grope through the uncertain passage called the Dutch Deep, at the back of the Middle Ground, and forcing his way up the narrow channel in front of the shallows, repeat on the anchored batteries and battleships of the Danes the exploit of the Nile. He spent the nights of March 30 and 31 sounding the channel, being himself, in spite of fog and ice, in the boat nearly the whole of these two bitter nights. On April 1 the fleet came slowly up the Dutch Deep, and dropped anchor at night about two miles from the southern extremity of the Danish line. At eleven o'clock that night, Hardy—in whose arms Nelson afterwards died on board the *Victory*—pushed off from the flagship in a small boat and sounded the channel in front of the Danish floating batteries. So daring was he that he actually sounded round the leading ship of the Danish line, using a pole to avoid being detected.

In the morning the wind blew fair for the channel. Nelson's plans had been elaborated to their minutest details, and the pilots of the fleet were summoned at nine o'clock to the flagship to receive their last instructions. But their nerve failed them. They were simply the mates or masters of Baltic traders turned for the moment into naval pilots. They had no charts. They were accustomed to handle ships of 200 or 300 tons burden, and the task of steering the great British seventy-fours through the labyrinths of shallows, with the tide running like a mill-race, appalled them. At last Murray, in the *Edgar*, undertook to lead. The signal was made to weigh in succession, and one great ship after another, with its topsails on the caps, rounded the shoulder of the Middle Ground, and in stately procession, the *Edgar* leading, came up the channel. Campbell in his fine ballad has pictured the scene:—

> "Like leviathans afloat
> Lay their bulwarks on the brine,
> While the sign of battle flew
> On the lofty British line.

> It was ten of April morn by the chime ;
> As they drifted on their path
>   There was silence deep as death,
>   And the boldest held his breath
>   For a time.
> But the might of England flushed
>   To anticipate the scene,
> And her van the fleeter rushed
>   O'er the deadly space between."

The leading Danish ships broke into a tempest of fire as the British ships came within range. The *Agamemnon* failed to weather the shoulder of the Middle Ground, and went ignobly ashore, and the scour of the tide kept her fast there, in spite of the most desperate exertions of her crew. The *Bellona*, a pile of white canvas above, a double line of curving batteries below, hugged the Middle Ground too closely, and grounded too; and the *Russell*, following close after her, went ashore in the same manner, with its jib-boom almost touching the *Bellona's* taffrail. One-fourth of Nelson's force was thus practically out of the fight before a British gun was fired. These were the ships, too, intended to sail past the whole Danish line and engage the Three-Crown Batteries. As they were *hors de combat*, the frigates of the squadron, under Riou—"the gallant, good Riou" of Campbell's noble lines—had to take the place of the seventy-fours.

Meanwhile, Nelson, in the *Elephant*, came following hard on the ill-fated *Russell*. Nelson's orders were that each ship should pass her leader on the starboard side, and had he acted on his own orders, Nelson too would have grounded, with every ship that followed him. The interval betwixt each ship was so narrow that decision had to be instant; and Nelson, judging the water to the larboard of the *Russell* to be deeper, put his helm a-starboard, and so shot past the *Russell* on its larboard beam into the true channel, the whole line following his example. That sudden whirl to starboard of the flagship's helm—a flash of brilliant seamanship—saved the battle.

Ship after ship shot past, and anchored, by a cable astern, in its assigned position. The sullen thunder of the guns rolled from end to end of the long line, the flash of the artillery ran in a dance of flame along the mile and a half of batteries, and some 2000 pieces of artillery, most of them of the heaviest calibre, filled the long Sound with the roar of battle. Nelson loved close fighting, and he anchored within a cable's length of the Danish flagship, the pilots refusing to carry the ship nearer on account of the shallow depth, and the average distance of the hostile lines was less than a hundred fathoms. The cannonade raged, deep-voiced, unbroken, and terrible, for three hours. "Warm work," said Nelson, as it seemed to deepen in fury and volume, "but, mark you, I would not be elsewhere for thousands." The carnage was terrific. Twice the Danish flagship took fire, and out of a crew of 336 no fewer than 270 were dead or wounded. Two of the Danish prams drifted from the line, mere wrecks, with cordage in rags, bulwarks riddled, guns dismounted, and decks veritable shambles.

The battle, it must be remembered, raged within easy sight of the city, and roofs and church towers were crowded with spectators. They could see nothing but a low-lying continent of whirling smoke, shaken with the tumult of battle, and scored perpetually, in crimson bars, with the flame of the guns. Above the drifting smoke towered the tops of the British seventy-fours, stately and threatening. The south-east wind presently drove the smoke over the city, and beneath that inky roof, as under the gloom of an eclipse, the crowds of Copenhagen, white-faced with excitement, watched the Homeric fight, in which their sons, and brothers, and husbands were perishing.

Nothing could surpass the courage of the Danes. Fresh crews marched fiercely to the floating batteries as these threatened to grow silent by mere slaughter, and, on decks crimson and slippery with the blood of their predecessors, took up the fight. Again and again, after a Danish ship had struck from mere exhaustion, it was manned afresh from the shore, and the fight renewed. The very youngest officer in the Danish navy was a lad of seventeen named Villemoes. He commanded a tiny floating battery of six guns, manned by twenty-four men, and he managed to bring it under the very counter of Nelson's flagship, and fired his guns point-blank into its huge wooden sides. He stuck to his work until the British marines shot down every man of his tiny crew except four. After the battle Nelson begged that young Villemoes might be introduced to him, and told the Danish Crown Prince that a boy so gallant ought to be made an admiral. "If I were to make all my brave officers admirals," was the reply, "I should have no captains or lieutenants left."

The terrific nature of the British fire, as well as the stubbornness of Danish courage, may be judged from the fact that most of the prizes taken in the fight were so absolutely riddled with shot as to have to be destroyed. Foley, who led the van at the battle of the Nile, was Nelson's flag-captain in the *Elephant*, and he declared he burned fifty more barrels of powder in the four hours' furious cannonade at Copenhagen than he did during the long night struggle at the Nile! The fire of the Danes, it may be added, was almost as obstinate and deadly. The *Monarch*, for example, had no fewer than 210 of its crew lying dead or wounded on its decks. At one o'clock Sir Hyde Parker, who was watching the struggle with a squadron of eight of his heaviest ships from the offing, hoisted a signal to discontinue the engagement. Then came the incident which every boy remembers.

The signal-lieutenant of the *Elephant* reported that the admiral had thrown out No. 39, the signal to discontinue the fight. Nelson was pacing his quarter-deck fiercely, and took no notice of the report. The signal-officer met him at the next turn, and asked if he should repeat the signal. Nelson's reply was to ask if his own signal for close action was still hoisted. "Yes," said the officer. "Mind you keep it so," said Nelson. Nelson continued to tramp his quarter-deck, the thunder of the battle all about him, his ship reeling to the recoil of its own guns. The stump of his lost arm jerked angrily to and fro, a sure sign of excitement with him. "Leave off action!" he said to his lieutenant; "I'm hanged if I do." "You know, Foley," he said, turning to his captain, "I've only one eye; I've a right to be blind sometimes." And then putting the glass to his blind eye, he exclaimed, "I really do not see the signal!" He dismissed the incident by saying,

"D—— the signal! Keep mine for closer action flying!"

As a matter of fact, Parker had hoisted the signal only to give Nelson the opportunity for withdrawing from the fight if he wished. The signal had one disastrous result—the little cluster of frigates and sloops engaged with the Three-Crown Batteries obeyed it and hauled off. As the *Amazon*, Riou's ship, ceased to fire, the smoke lifted, and the Danish battery got her in full sight, and smote her with deadly effect. Riou himself, heartbroken with having to abandon the fight, had just exclaimed, "What will Nelson think of us!" when a chain-shot cut him in two, and with him a sailor with something of Nelson's own genius for battle perished.

By two o'clock the Danish fire began to slack. One-half the line was a mere chain of wrecks; some of the floating batteries had sunk; the flagship was a mass of flames. Nelson at this point sent his boat ashore with a flag of truce, and a letter to the Prince Regent. The letter was addressed, "To the Danes, the brothers of Englishmen." If the fire continued from the Danish side, Nelson said he would be compelled to set on fire all the floating batteries he had taken, "without being able to save the brave Danes who had defended them." Somebody offered Nelson, when he had written the letter, a wafer with which to close it. "This," said Nelson, "is no time to appear hurried or informal," and he insisted on the letter being carefully sealed with wax. The Crown Prince proposed an armistice. Nelson, with great shrewdness, referred the proposal to his admiral lying four miles off in the *London*, foreseeing that the long pull out and back would give him time to get his own crippled ships clear of the shoals, and past the Three-Crown Batteries into the open channel beyond—the only course the wind made possible; and this was exactly what happened. Nelson, it is clear, was a shrewd diplomatist as well as a great sailor.

The night was coming on black with the threat of tempest; the Danish flagship had just blown up; but the white flag of truce was flying, and the British toiled, as fiercely as they had fought, to float their stranded ships and take possession of their shattered prizes. Of these, only one was found capable of being sufficiently repaired to be taken to Portsmouth. On the 4th Nelson himself landed and visited the Crown Prince, and a four months' truce was agreed upon. News came at that moment of the assassination of Paul I., and the League of Armed Neutrality—the device by which Napoleon hoped to overthrow the naval power of Great Britain—vanished into mere space. The fire of Nelson's guns at Copenhagen wrecked Napoleon's whole naval policy.

It is curious that, familiar as Nelson was with the grim visage of battle, the carnage of that four hours' cannonade was too much for even his steady nerves. He could find no words too generous to declare his admiration of the obstinate courage shown by the Danes. "The French and Spanish fight well," he said, "but they could not have stood for an hour such a fire as the Danes sustained for four hours."

KING-MAKING WATERLOO

> " Last noon beheld them full of lusty life,
> Last eve in Beauty's circle proudly gay,
> The midnight brought the signal-sound of strife,
> The morn the marshalling in arms—the day
> Battle's magnificently stern array !
> The thunder-clouds close o'er it, which when rent
> The earth is cover'd thick with other clay,
> Which her own clay shall cover, heap'd and pent,
> Rider and horse—friend, foe—in one red burial blent !"
> —BYRON.

"I look upon Salamanca, Vittoria, and Waterloo as my three best battles—those which had great and permanent consequences. Salamanca relieved the whole south of Spain, changed all the prospects of the war, and was felt even in Prussia. Vittoria freed the Peninsula altogether, broke off the armistice at Dresden, and thus led to Leipsic and the deliverance of Europe; and Waterloo did more than any other battle I know of towards the true object of all battles—the peace of the world."—WELLINGTON, *Conversation with Croker.*

ON June 18, 1815, the grey light of a Sunday morning was breaking over a shallow valley lying between parallel ridges of low hills some twelve miles to the south of Brussels. All night the rain had fallen furiously, and still the fog hung low, and driving showers swept over plain and hill as from the church spires of half-a-dozen tiny villages the matin bells began to ring. For centuries those bells had called the villagers to prayers; to-day, as the wave of sound stole through the misty air, it was the signal for the awakening of

NAPOLEON

After a portrait by PAUL DELAROCHE

two mighty armies to the greatest battle of modern times.

More ink has, perhaps, been shed about Waterloo than about any other battle known to history, and still the story bristles with conundrums, questions of fact, and problems in strategy, about which the experts still wage, with pen and diagram, strife almost as furious as that which was waged with lance and sword, with bayonet and musket, more than eighty years ago on the actual slopes of Mont St. Jean. It is still, for example, a matter of debate whether, when Wellington first resolved to fight at Waterloo, he had any express promise from Blücher to join him on that field. Did Wellington, for example, ride over alone to Blücher's headquarters on the night before Waterloo, and obtain a pledge of aid, on the strength of which he fought next day? It is not merely possible to quote experts on each side of this question; it is possible to quote the same expert on both sides. Ropes, for example, the latest Waterloo critic, devotes several pages to proving that the interview never took place, and then adds a note to his third edition declaring that he has seen evidence which convinces him it did take place! It is possible even to quote Wellington himself both for the alleged visit and against it. In 1833 he told a circle of guests at Strathfieldsaye, in minute detail, how he got rid of his only aide-de-camp, Lord Fitzroy Somerset, and rode over on " Copenhagen " in the rain and darkness to Wavre, and got from Blücher's own lips the assurance that he would join him next day at Waterloo. In 1838, when directly asked by Baron Gurney whether the story was true, he replied, "No, I did not see Blücher the day before Waterloo." If Homer nodded, it is plain that sometimes the Duke of Wellington forgot!

Clearness on some points, it is true, is slowly emerging. It is admitted, for example, that Napoleon took the allies by surprise when he crossed the Sambre, and, in the very first stage of the campaign, scored a brilliant strategic success over them. Wellington himself, on the night of the famous ball, took the Duke of Richmond into his dressing-room, shut the door, and said, "Napoleon has humbugged me, by —— ; he has gained twenty-four hours' march on me." The Duke went on to explain that he had ordered his troops to concentrate at Quatre Bras; "but," he added, "we shall not stop him there, and I must fight him here," at the same time passing his thumb-nail over the position of Waterloo. That map, with the scratch of the Duke's thumb-nail over the very line where Waterloo was afterwards fought, was long preserved as a relic. Part of the surprise, the Duke complained, was due to Blücher. But, as he himself explained to Napier, "I cannot tell the world that Blücher picked the fattest man in his army (Muffling) to ride with an express to me, and that he took thirty hours to go thirty miles."

The hour at which Waterloo began, though there were 150,000 actors in the great tragedy, was long a matter of dispute. The Duke of Wellington puts it at ten o'clock, General Alava says half-past eleven, Napoleon and Drouet say twelve o'clock, and Ney one o'clock. Lord Hill may be credited with having settled this minute question of fact. He took two watches with

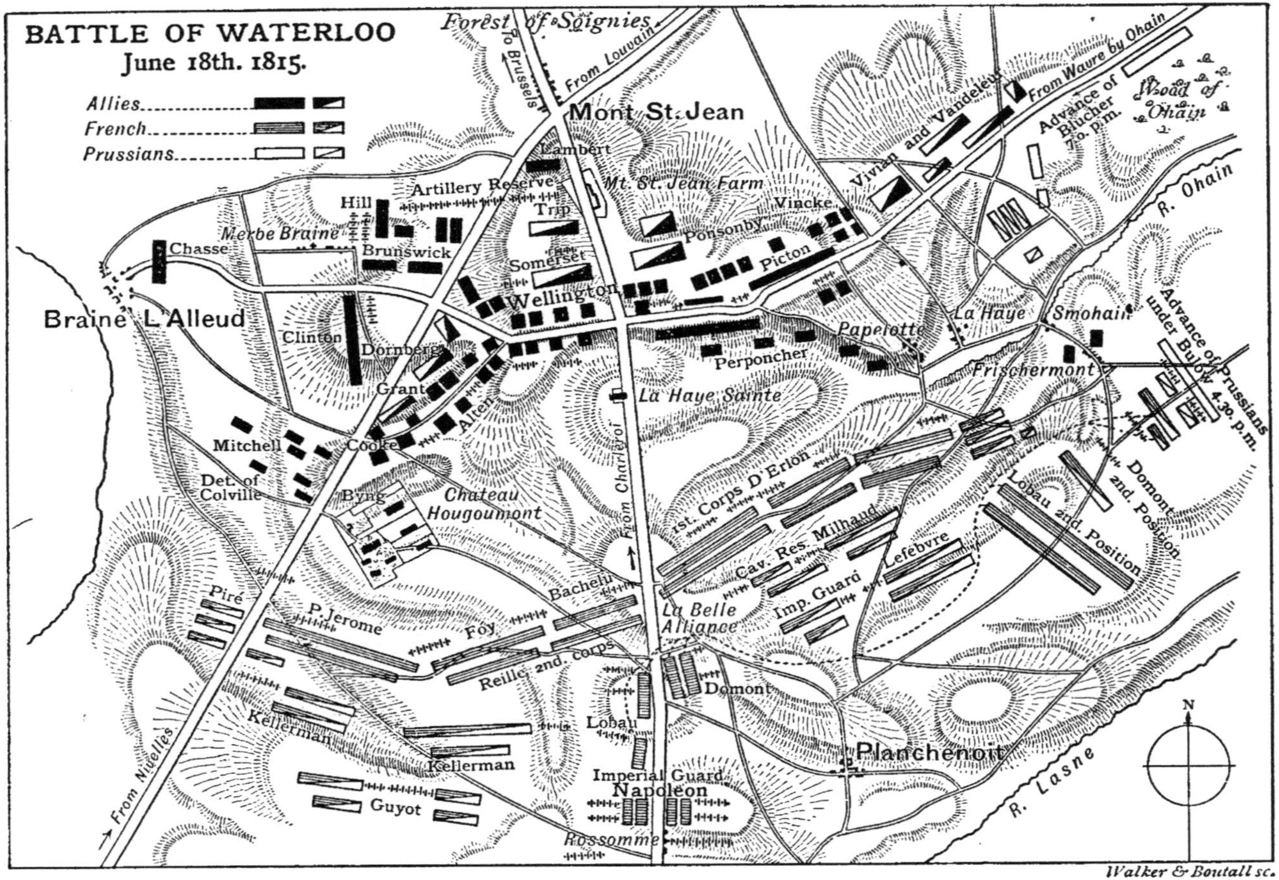

Walker & Boutall sc.

him into the fight, one a stop-watch, and he marked with it the sound of the first shot fired, and this evidence is now accepted as proving that the first flash of red flame which marked the opening of the world-shaking tragedy of Waterloo took place at exactly ten minutes to twelve.

As these sketches are not written for military experts, but only pretend to tell, in plain prose, and for younger Britons, the story of the great deeds which are part of their historical inheritance, all the disputed questions about Waterloo may be at the outset laid aside. It is a great tale, and it seems all the greater when it is simply told. The campaign of Waterloo, in a sense, lasted exactly four days, yet into that brief space of time there is compressed so much of human daring and suffering, of genius and of folly, of shining triumph and of blackest ruin, that the story must always be one of the most exciting records in human history.

I. THE RIVAL HOSTS

" Hark ! I hear the tramp of thousands,
 And of armèd men the hum ;
Lo ! a nation's hosts have gathered
 Round the quick alarming drum,—
  Saying, 'Come,
  Freeman, come,
Ere your heritage be wasted,' said the quick alarming drum.

. . . .

' Let me of my heart take counsel :
 War is not of life the sum ;
Who shall stay and reap the harvest
 When the autumn days shall come ? '
  But the drum
  Echoed, ' Come !
Death shall reap the braver harvest,' said the solemn-sounding drum.

' What if, 'mid the cannons' thunder,
 Whistling shot and bursting bomb,
When my brothers fall around me,
 Should my heart grow cold and numb ? '
  But the drum
  Answered, ' Come !
Better there in death united, than in life a recreant,—Come ! ' "

—Bret Harte.

FOR weeks the British and Prussian armies, scattered over a district 100 miles by 40, had been keeping guard over the French frontier. Mighty hosts of Russians and Austrians were creeping slowly across Europe to join them. Napoleon, skilfully shrouding his movements in impenetrable secrecy, was about to leap across the Sambre, and both Blücher and Wellington had to guess what would be his point of attack; and they, as it happened, guessed wrongly. Napoleon's strategy was determined partly by his knowledge of the personal characters of the two generals, and partly by the fact that the bases of the allied armies lay at widely separate points—the English base at Antwerp, the Prussian on the Rhine. Blücher was essentially "a hussar general"; the fighting impulse ran riot in his blood. If attacked, he would certainly fight where he stood; if defeated, and driven back on his base, he must move in diverging lines from Wellington. That Blücher would abandon his base to keep touch with Wellington—as actually happened—Napoleon never guessed. Wellington, cooler and more methodical than his Prussian fellow-commander, would not fight, it was certain, till his troops were called in on every side and he was ready. Blücher was nearer the French frontier. Napoleon calculated that he could leap upon him, bar Wellington from coming to his help by planting Ney at Quatre Bras, win a great battle before Wellington could join hands with his ally, and then in turn crush Wellington. It was splendid strategy, splendidly begun, but left fatally incomplete.

Napoleon fought and defeated Blücher at Ligny on June 16, attacking Quatre Bras at the same time, so as to occupy the English. Wellington visited Blücher's lines before the fight began, and said to him, "Every general knows his own men, but if my lines were drawn up in this fashion I should expect to get beaten;" and as he cantered back to his own army he said to those about him, "If Bonaparte be what I suppose he is, the Prussians will get a —— good licking to-day." Captain Bowles was standing beside the Duke at Quatre Bras on the morning of the 17th, when a Prussian staff-officer, his horse covered with sweat, galloped up and whispered an agitated message in the Duke's ear. The Duke, without a change of countenance, dismissed him, and, turning to Bowles, said, "Old Blücher has had a —— good licking, and gone back to Wavre, eighteen miles. As he has gone back, we must go too. I suppose in England they will say we have been licked. I can't help it! As they have gone back, we must go too." And in five minutes, without stirring from the spot, he had given complete orders for a retreat to Waterloo.

The low ridge on which the Duke took up his position runs east and west. The road from Brussels to the south, just before it crosses the crest of the ridge, divides like the upper part of the letter Y into two roads, that on the right, or westward, running to Nivelles, that on the left, or eastward, to Charleroi. A country road, in parts only a couple of feet deep, in parts sunk from twelve to fifteen feet, traverses the crest of the ridge, and intersects the two roads just named before they unite to form the main Brussels road. Two farmhouses— La Haye Sainte, on the Charleroi road, and Hougoumont, on that to Nivelles—stand out some 250 yards in advance of the ridge. Thus the cross-road served as a ditch to Wellington's front; the two farmhouses were, so to speak, horn-works guarding his right centre and left centre; while in the little valley on the reverse side of the crest Wellington was able to act on his favourite tactics of keeping his men out of sight till the moment for action arrived. The ridge, in fact, to the French generals who surveyed it from La Belle Alliance, seemed almost bare, showing nothing but batteries at intervals along the crest, and a spray of skirmishers on the slopes below.

Looked at from the British ridge, the plain over which the great fight raged is a picture of pastoral simplicity and peace. The crops that Sunday morning were high upon it, the dark green of wheat and clover chequered with the lighter green of rye and oats. No fences intersect the plain; a few farmhouses, each with a leafy girdle of trees, and the brown roofs of one or two distant villages, alone break the level floor of green. The present writer has twice visited Waterloo, and the image of verdurous and leafy peace conveyed by the landscape is still most vivid. Only Hougoumont, where the orchard walls are still pierced by the loop-holes through which the Guards fired that long June Sunday, helps one to realise the fierce strife which once raged and echoed over this rich valley with its grassy carpet of vivid green. Waterloo is a battlefield of singularly small dimensions. The British front did not extend for more than two miles; the gap betwixt Hougoumont and La Haye Sainte, through which Ney poured his living tide of cavalry, 15,000 strong, is only 900 yards wide, a distance equal, say, to a couple of city blocks. The ridge on which Napoleon drew up his army is less than 2000 yards distant from that on which the British stood. It sloped steadily upward, and, as a consequence, Napoleon's whole force was disclosed at a glance, and every combination of troops made in preparation for an attack on the British line was clearly visible, a fact which greatly assisted Wellington in his arrangements for meeting it.

The opposing armies differed rather in quality than

in numbers. Wellington had, roughly, 50,000 infantry, 12,000 cavalry, a little less than 6000 artillerymen; a total of 67,000 men and 156 guns. Napoleon had 49,000 infantry, nearly 16,000 cavalry, over 7000 artillery; a total of, say, 72,000 men, with 246 guns. In infantry the two armies were about equal, in cavalry the French were superior, and in guns their superiority was enormous. But the French were war-hardened veterans, the men of Austerlitz and of Wagram, of one blood and speech and military type, a homogeneous mass, on flame with warlike enthusiasm. Of Wellington's troops, only 30,000 were British and German; many even of these had never seen a shot fired in battle, and were raw drafts from the militia, still wearing the militia uniform. Only 12,000 were old Peninsula troops. Less than 7000 of Wellington's cavalry were British, and took any part in the actual battle. Wellington himself somewhat ungratefully described his force as an "infamous army"; "the worst army ever brought together!" Nearly 18,000 were Dutch-Belgians, whose courage was doubtful, and whose loyalty was still more vehemently suspected. Wellington had placed some battalions of these as part of the force holding Hougoumont; but when, an hour before the battle actually began, Napoleon rode through his troops, and their tumultuous shouts echoed in a tempest of sound across to the British lines, the effect on the Dutch-Belgians in Hougoumont was so instant and visible that Wellington at once withdrew them. "The mere name of Napoleon," he said, "had beaten them before they fired a shot!" The French themselves did justice to the native fighting quality of the British.

"The English infantry," as Foy told the Emperor on the morning of Waterloo, "are the very d—— to fight;" and Napoleon, five years after, at St. Helena, said, "One might as well try to charge through a wall." Soult, again, told Napoleon, "Sire, I know these English. They will die on the ground on which they stand before they lose it." That this was true, even of the raw lads from the militia, Waterloo proved. But it is idle to deny that of the two armies the French, tried by abstract military tests, was far the stronger.

The very aspect of the two armies reflected their different characteristics. A grim silence brooded over the British position. Nothing was visible except the scattered clusters of guns and the outposts. The French army, on the other side, was a magnificent spectacle, gay with flags, and as many-coloured as a rainbow. Eleven columns deployed simultaneously, and formed three huge lines of serried infantry. They were flanked by mail-clad cuirassiers, with glittering helmets and breast-plates; lines of scarlet-clad lancers; and hussars, with bearskin caps and jackets glittering with gold lace. The black and menacing masses of the Old Guard and of the Young Guard, with their huge bearskin caps, formed the reserve. As Napoleon, with a glittering staff, swept through his army, the bands of 114 battalions and 112 squadrons poured upon the peaceful air of that June Sunday the martial cadences of the Marseillaise, and the "Vive l'Empereur!" which broke from the crowded host was heard distinctly by the grimly listening ranks of the British. "As far as the eye could reach," says one who describes the fight from the French ranks, "nothing was to be seen but cuirasses, helmets, busbies, sabres and lances, and glittering lines of bayonets."

As for the British, there was no tumult of enthusiasm visible among them. Flat on the ground, in double files, on the reverse side of the hill, the men lay, and jested in rough fashion with each other, while the officers in little groups stood on the ridge and watched the French movements. Let it be remembered that many of the troops had fought desperately on the 16th, and retreated on the 17th from Quatre Bras to Waterloo under furious rain, and the whole army was soddened and chilled with sleeping unsheltered on the soaked ground. Many of the men, as they rose hungry and shivering from their sleeping-place in the mud, were so stiff and cramped that they could not stand upright.

II. HOUGOUMONT

> " The trumpets sound, the banners fly,
>   The glittering spears are rankèd ready,
>   The shouts o' war are heard afar,
>   The battle closes thick and bloody."
> 											—Burns.

THE ground was heavy with the rains of the night, and Napoleon lingered till nearly noon before he launched his attack on the British lines. At ten minutes to twelve the first heavy gun rang sullenly from the French ridge, and from the French left Reille's corps, 6000 strong, flung itself on Hougoumont. The French are magnificent skirmishers, and as the great mass moved down the slope, a dense spray of tirailleurs ran swiftly before it, reached the hedge, and broke into the wood, which, in a moment, was full of white smoke and the red flashes of musketry. In a solid mass the main body followed; but the moment it came within range, the British guns keeping guard over Hougoumont smote it with a heavy fire. The French batteries answered fiercely, while in the garden and orchard below the Guards and the French fought almost literally muzzle to muzzle.

Hougoumont was a strong post. The fire from the windows in the main building commanded the orchard, that from the orchard commanded the wood, that from the wood swept the ridge. The French had crossed the ridge, cleared the wood, and were driving the Guards, fighting vehemently, out of the orchard into the hollow road between the house and the British ridge. But they could do no more. The light companies of the Foot Guards, under Lieut.-Colonel Macdonnell, held the buildings and orchard, Lord Saltoun being in command of the latter. Muffling, the Prussian commissioner on Wellington's staff, doubted whether Hougoumont could be held against the enemy; but Wellington had great confidence in Macdonnell, a Highlander of gigantic strength and coolest daring, and nobly did this brave Scotsman fulfil his trust. All day long the attack thundered round Hougoumont. The French masses moved again and again to the assault upon it; it was scourged with musketry and set on fire with shells. But steadfastly under the roar of the guns and the fierce crackle of small-arms, and even while the roofs were in flames above their heads, the gallant Guardsmen held their post. Once the main gateway was burst open, and the French broke in. They were instantly bayoneted, and Macdonnell, with a cluster of officers and a sergeant named Graham, by sheer force shut the gate again in the face of the desperate French. In the fire which partially consumed the building, some of the British wounded were burned to death, and Mercer, who visited the spot the morning after the fight, declared that in the orchard and around the walls of the farmhouse the dead lay as thick as on the breach of Badajos.

More than 2000 killed and wounded fell in the long seven hours' fight which raged round this Belgian farmhouse. More than 12,000 infantry were flung into the attack; the defence, including the Dutch and Belgians in the wood, never exceeded 2000 men. But when, in the tumult of the victorious advance of the British at nightfall, Wellington found himself for a moment beside

Muffling, with a flash of exultation rare in a man so self-controlled, he shouted, " Well, you see Macdonnell held Hougoumont after all!" Towards evening, at the close of the fight, Lord Saltoun, with the wreck of the light companies of the Guards, joined the main body of their division on the ridge. As they came up to the lines, a scanty group with torn uniforms and smoke-blackened faces, the sole survivors of the gallant hundreds who had fought continuously for seven hours, General Maitland rode out to meet them and cried, " Your defence has saved the army! Every man of you deserves promotion." Long afterwards a patriotic Briton bequeathed £500 to the bravest soldier at Waterloo, the Duke of Wellington to be the judge. The Duke named Macdonnell, who handed the money to the sergeant who was his comrade in the struggle at the gate of Hougoumont.

III. PICTON AND D'ERLON

> " But on the British heart were lost
> The terrors of the charging host ;
> For not an eye the storm that view'd
> Changed its proud glance of fortitude.
> Nor was one forward footstep staid,
> As dropp'd the dying and the dead."
>
> —Scott.

MEANTIME a furious artillery duel raged between the opposing ridges. Wellington had ordered his gunners not to fire at the French batteries, but only at the French columns, while the French, in the main, concentrated their fire on the British guns. French practice under these conditions was naturally very beautiful, for no hostile bullets disturbed their aim, and the British gunners fell fast; yet their fire on the French masses was most deadly. At two o'clock Napoleon launched his great infantry attack, led by D'Erlon, against La Haye Sainte and the British left. It was an attack of terrific strength. Four divisions, numbering 16,000 men, moved forward in echelon, with intervals between them of 400 paces; seventy-two guns swept as with a besom of fire the path along which these huge masses advanced with shouts to the attack, while thirty light guns moved in the intervals between them; and a cavalry division, consisting of lancers and cuirassiers, rode on their flank ready to charge the broken masses of the British infantry. The British line at this point consisted of Picton's division, formed of the shattered remains of Kempt's and Pack's brigades, who had suffered heavily at Quatre Bras. They formed a mere thread of scarlet, a slender two-deep line of about 3000 men. As the great mass of the enemy came slowly on, the British line was "dressed," the men ceased to talk, except in monosyllables, the skirmishers lying flat on the trampled corn prepared to fire. The grape of the French guns smote Picton's red lines with fury, and the men fell fast, yet they closed up at the word of command with the most perfect coolness. The French skirmishers, too, running forward with great speed and daring, drove in the British skirmishers, who came running back to the main line smoke-begrimed and breathless.

As the French masses began to ascend the British slope, the French guns had to cease their fire for fear of striking their own forces. The British infantry, too, being drawn slightly back from the crest, were out of sight, and the leading French files saw nothing before them but a cluster of British batteries and a thin line of quickly retreating skirmishers. A Dutch-Belgian brigade had, somehow, been placed on the exterior slope of the hill, and when D'Erlon's huge battalions came on, almost shaking the earth with their steady tread, the Dutch-Belgians simply took to their heels and ran. They swept, a crowd of fugitives, through the intervals of the British lines, and were received with groans and hootings, the men with difficulty being restrained from firing upon them.

A sand-pit lay in the track of the French columns on the left. This was held by some companies of the 95th Rifles, and these opened a fire so sudden and close and deadly that the huge mass of the French swung almost involuntarily to the right, off its true track; then with fierce roll of drums and shouts of "En avant!" the Frenchmen reached the crest. Suddenly there rose before them Picton's steady lines, along which there ran, in one red flame from end to end, a dreadful volley. Again the fierce musketry crackled, and yet again. The Frenchmen tried to deploy, and Picton, seizing the moment, ordered his lines to charge. "Charge! charge!" he cried. "Hurrah!"

It is yet a matter keenly disputed as to whether or not D'Erlon's men actually pierced the British line. It is alleged that the Highlanders were thrown into confusion, and it is certain that Picton's last words to his aide-de-camp, Captain Seymour, were, "Rally the Highlanders!" Pack, too, appealed to the 92nd. "You must charge," he said; "all in front have given way." However this may be, the British regiments charged, and the swift and resolute advance of Picton's lines—though it was a charge of 3000 men on a body four times their number—was irresistible. The leading ranks of the French opened a hurried fire, under which Picton himself fell shot through the head; then as the British line came on at the double—the men with bent heads, the level bayonets one steady edge of steel, the fierce light which gleams along the fighting line playing on them—the leading battalions of the French halted irresolute, shrunk back, swayed to and fro, and fell into a shapeless receding mass.

There were, of course, many individual instances of great gallantry amongst them. Thus a French mounted officer had his horse shot, and when he struggled from beneath his fallen charger he found himself almost under the bayonets of the 32nd. But just in front of the British line was an officer carrying the colours of the regiment, and the brave Frenchman instantly leaped upon him. He would capture the flag! There was a momentary struggle, and the British officer at the head of the wing shouted, "Save the brave fellow!" but almost at the same moment the gallant Frenchman was bayoneted by the colour-sergeant, and shot by a British infantryman.

The head of the French column was falling to pieces, but the main body was yet steady, and the cuirassiers covering its flank were coming swiftly on. But at this moment there broke upon them the terrific counter-stroke, not of Wellington, but of Lord Uxbridge, into whose hands Wellington, with a degree of confidence quite unusual for him, had given the absolute control of his cavalry, fettering him by no specific orders.

IV. "SCOTLAND FOR EVER!"

> " Beneath their fire, in full career,
>   Rush'd on the ponderous cuirassier,
>   The lancer couch'd his ruthless spear,
>   And hurrying as to havoc near,
>   The cohorts' eagles flew.
>   In one dark torrent, broad and strong,
>   The advancing onset roll'd along,
>   Forth harbinger'd by fierce acclaim
>   That, from the shroud of smoke and flame,
>   Peal'd wildly the imperial name!"
>   —SCOTT.

THE attack of the Household and Union Brigades at Waterloo is one of the most dazzling and dramatic incidents of the great fight. For suddenness, fire, and far-reaching results, it would be difficult to parallel that famous charge in the history of war. The Household Brigade, consisting of the 1st and 2nd Life Guards, and the Dragoon Guards, with the Blues in support, moved first, Lord Uxbridge, temporarily exchanging the functions of general for those of a squadron-leader, heading the attack. They leaped the hedge, or burst through it, crossed the road—at that point of shallow depth—and met the French cuirassiers in full charge. The British were bigger men on bigger horses, and they had gained the full momentum of their charge when the two lines met. The French, to do them justice, did not shrink. The charging lines crashed together, like living and swiftly moving walls, and the sound of their impact rang sharp, sudden, deep, and long drawn out, above the din of the conflict. The

French wore armour, and carried longer swords than the British, but they were swept away in an instant, and went, a broken and shattered mass of men and horses, down the slope. Some of them were tumbled into the sand-pit, amongst the astonished Rifles there, who instantly bayoneted them. Others were swept upon the masses of their own infantry, fiercely followed by the Life Guards.

The 2nd Life Guards and the Dragoons, coming on a little in the rear, struck the right regiment of the cuirassiers and hurled them across the junction of the roads. Shaw, the famous Life Guardsman, was killed here. He was a perfect swordsman, a man of colossal strength, and is said to have cut down, through helmet and skull, no fewer than nine men in the *mêlée*. How Shaw actually died is a matter of dispute. Colonel Marten says he was shot by a cuirassier who stood clear of the *mêlée*, coolly taking pot-shots at the English Guardsmen. Captain Kelly, a brilliant soldier, who rode in the charge beside Shaw, says that Shaw was killed by a thrust through the body from a French colonel of the cuirassiers, whom Kelly himself, in return, clove through helmet and skull.

Meanwhile the Union Brigade on the left, consisting of the Royals and the Inniskillings, with the Scots Greys in support, had broken into the fight. The Royals, coming on at full speed over the crest of the ridge, broke upon the astonished vision of the French infantry at a distance of less than a hundred yards. It was an alarming vision of waving swords, crested helmets, fierce red nostrils, and galloping hoofs. The leading files tried to turn, but in an instant the Royals were upon them, cutting them down furiously. De Lacy Evans, who rode in the charge, says, "They fled like a flock of sheep." Colonel Clark Kennedy adds that the "jamb" in the French was so thick that the men could not bring down their arms or level a musket, and the Dragoons rode in the intervals between their formation, reaching forward with the stroke of their long swords, and slaying at will. More than 2000 Frenchmen flung down their arms and surrendered; and on the next morning the abandoned muskets were still lying in long straight lines and regular order, showing that the men had surrendered before their lines were broken. The charge of the Inniskillings to the left of the Royals was just as furious and just as successful. They broke on the front of Donzelot's divisions and simply ground them to powder.

The Scots Greys were supposed to be "in support"; but coming swiftly up, they suddenly saw on their left shoulder Marcognet's divisions, the extreme right of the French. At that sight the Greys swung a little off to their left, swept through the intervals of the 92nd, and smote the French battalions full in front. As the Greys rode through the intervals of the footmen — Scotch horsemen through Scotch infantry — the Scotch blood in both regiments naturally took fire. Greetings in broadest Doric flew from man to man. The pipes skirled fiercely. "Scotland for ever!" went up in a stormy shout from the kilted lines. The Greys, riding fast, sometimes jostled, or even struck down, some of the 92nd; and Armour, the rough-rider of the Greys, has told how the Highlanders shouted, "I didna think ye wad hae saired me sae!" Many of the Highlanders caught hold of the stirrups of the Greys and raced forward with them—Scotsmen calling to Scotsmen—into the ranks of the French. The 92nd, in fact, according to the testimony of their own officers, "went half mad." What could resist such a charge?

The two British cavalry brigades were by this time riding roughly abreast, the men drunk with warlike excitement and completely out of hand, and most of their officers were little better. They simply rode over D'Erlon's broken ranks. So brave were some of the French, however, that again and again a solitary soldier or officer would leap out of the ranks as the English cavalry came on, and charge them single-handed! One French private deliberately ran out as the Inniskillings came on at full gallop, knelt before the swiftly galloping line of men and horses, coolly shot the adjutant of the Inniskillings through the head, and was himself instantly trodden into a bloody pulp! The British squadrons, wildly disordered, but drunk with battle fury, and each man fighting for his "ain hand," swept across the valley, rode up to the crest of the French position, stormed through the great battery there, slew drivers and horses, and so completely wrecked the battery that forty guns out of its seventy never came into action again. Some of the men, in the rapture of the fight, broke through to the second line of the French, and told tales, after the mad adventure was over, of how they had come upon French artillery drivers, mere boys, sitting crying on their horses while the tragedy and tumult of the *mêlée* swept past them. Some of the older officers tried to rally and re-form their men; and Lord Uxbridge, by this time beginning to remember that he was a general and not a dragoon, looked round for his "supports," who, as it happened, oblivious of the duty of "supporting" anybody, were busy fighting on their own account, and were riding furiously in the very front ranks.

Then there came the French counter-stroke. The French batteries opened on the triumphant, but disordered British squadrons; a brigade of lancers smote them on the flank and rolled them up. Lord Edward Somerset, who commanded the Household Brigade, was unhorsed, and saved his life by scrambling dexterously, but ignobly, through a hedge. Sir William Ponsonby, who commanded the Union Brigade, had ridden his horse to a dead standstill; the lancers caught him standing helpless in the middle of a ploughed field, and slew him with a dozen lance-thrusts. Vandeleur's Light Cavalry Brigade was by this time moving down from the British front, and behind its steady squadrons the broken remains of the two brigades found shelter.

Though the British cavalry suffered terribly in retiring, nevertheless they had accomplished what Sir Evelyn Wood describes as "one of the most brilliant successes ever achieved by horsemen over infantry." These two brigades—which did not number more than 2000 swords—wrecked an entire infantry corps, disabled forty guns, overthrew a division of cuirassiers, took 3000 prisoners, and captured two eagles. The moral effect of the charge was, perhaps, greater than even its material results. The French infantry never afterwards throughout the battle, until the Old Guard appeared upon the scene, moved forward with real confidence against the British position. Those "terrible horsemen" had stamped themselves upon their imagination.

The story of how the eagles were captured is worth telling. Captain Clark Kennedy of the Dragoons took one. He was riding vehemently in the early stage of the charge, when he caught sight of the cuirassier officer carrying the eagle, with his covering men, trying to break through the *mêlée* and escape. "I gave the order to my men," he says, "'Right shoulders forward; attack the colours.'" He himself overtook the officer, ran him through the body, and seized the eagle. He tried to break the eagle from the pole and push it inside his coat for security, but, failing, gave it to his corporal to carry to the rear. The other colour was taken by Ewart, a sergeant of the Greys, a very fine swordsman. He overtook the officer carrying the colour, and, to quote his own story, "he and I had a hard contest for it. He made a thrust at my groin; I parried it off, and cut him down through the head. After this a lancer came at me. I threw the lance off by my right side, and cut him through the chin and upwards through the teeth. Next, a foot-soldier fired at me, and then charged me with his bayonet, which I also had the good luck to parry, and then I cut him down through the head. Thus ended the contest. As I was about to follow the regiment, the general said, 'My brave fellow, take that to the rear; you have done enough till you get quit of it.'"

V. HORSEMEN AND SQUARES

"But yet, though thick the shafts as snow,
 Though charging knights like whirlwinds go,
 Though bill-men ply the ghastly blow,
  Unbroken was the ring;
 The stubborn spearmen still made good
 Their dark impenetrable wood,
 Each stepping where his comrade stood,
  The instant that he fell.
 No thought was there of dastard flight;
 Linked in the serried phalanx tight,
 Groom fought like noble, squire like knight,
  As fearlessly and well."
—Scott.

NAPOLEON'S infantry had failed to capture either Hougoumont or La Haye Sainte, which was stoutly held by Baring and his Hanoverians. The great infantry attack on the British left had failed, and though the stubborn fight round the two farmhouses never paused, the main battle along the ridge for a time resolved itself into an artillery duel. Battery answered battery across the narrow valley, nearly four hundred guns in action at once, the gunners toiling fiercely to load and fire with the utmost speed. Wellington ordered his men to lie down on the reverse of the ridge; but the French had the range perfectly, and shells fell thickly on the ranks of recumbent men, and solid shot tore through them. The thunder of the artillery quickened; the French tirailleurs, showing great daring, crept in swarms up the British slope and shot down the British gunners at their pieces. Both Hougoumont and

La Haye Sainte were on fire at this stage of the battle. The smoke of the conflict, in an atmosphere heavy with moisture, hung like a low pall of blackest crape over the whole field; and every now and again, on either ridge, columns of white smoke shot suddenly up and fell back like gigantic and vaporous mushrooms—the effect of exploding ammunition waggons. "Hard pounding this, gentlemen," said Wellington, as he rode past his much-enduring battalions. "Let us see who will pound longest."

At four o'clock came the great cavalry attack of the French. Through the gap between, not merely the two farmhouses, but the two farmhouses plus their zone of fire—through a gap, that is, of probably not more than 1000 yards, the French, for two long hours, poured on the British line the whole strength of their magnificent cavalry, led by Ney in person. To meet the assault, Wellington drew up his first line in a long chequer of squares, five in the first line, four, covering their intervals, in the second. In advance of them were the British guns, with their sadly reduced complement of gunners. Immediately behind the squares were the British cavalry brigades; the Household Brigade, reduced by this time to a couple of squadrons; and behind them, in turn, the Dutch-Belgian infantry, who had fortitude enough not to run away, but lacked daring sufficient to fill a place on the fire-scourged edge of actual battle. When the British front was supposed to be sufficiently macadamised by the dreadful fire of the French batteries, Ney brought on his huge mass of cavalry, twenty-one squadrons of cuirassiers, and nineteen squadrons of the Light Cavalry of the Guard.

At a slow trot they came down the French slope, crossed the valley, and, closing their ranks and quickening their stride, swept up to the British line, and broke, a swirling torrent of men and horses, over the crest. Nothing could be more majestic, and apparently resistless, than their onset—the gleam of so many thousand helmets and breastplates, the acres of wind-blown horsehair crests and many-coloured uniforms, the thunder of so many galloping hoofs. Wellington had ordered his gunners, when the French cavalry reached their guns, to abandon them and run for shelter beneath the bayonets of the nearest square, and the brave fellows stood by their pieces pouring grape and solid shot into the glittering, swift-coming human target before them till the leading horses were almost within touch of the guns, when they ran and flung themselves under the steady British bayonets for safety.

The French horsemen, as they mounted the British slope, saw nothing before them but the ridge, empty of everything except a few abandoned guns. They were drunk with the rapture of victory, and squadron after squadron, as it reached the crest, broke into tempests of shouts and a mad gallop. All the batteries were in their possession; they looked to see an army in rout. Suddenly they beheld the double line of British squares—or, rather, "oblongs"—with their fringe of steady steel points; and from end to end of the line ran the zigzag of fire—a fire that never slackened, still less intermitted. The torrent and tumult of the horsemen never checked; but as they rode at the squares, the leading squadron—men and horses—smitten by the spray of lead, tumbled dead or dying to the ground. The following squadrons parted, swept past the flanks of the squares, scourged with deadly volleys, struggled through the intervals of the second line, emerged breathless and broken into the space beyond, to be instantly charged by the British cavalry, and driven back in wreck over the British slope. As the struggling mass left the crest clear, the French guns broke in a tempest of shot on the squares, while the scattered French re-formed in the valley, and prepared for a second and yet more desperate assault.

Foiled in his first attack, Ney drew the whole of Kellerman's division—thirty-seven squadrons, eleven of cuirassiers, six of carabineers, and the Red Lancers of the Guard—into the whirlpool of his renewed assault, and this time the mass, though it came forward more slowly, was almost double in area. Gleaming with lance and sword and cuirass, it undulated as it crossed the broken slopes, till it seemed a sea, shining with 10,000 points of glancing steel, in motion. The British squares, on the reverse slope, as they obeyed the order, "Prepare to receive cavalry!" and fell grimly into formation, could hear the thunder of the coming storm—the shrill cries of the officers, the deeper shouts of the men, the clash of scabbard on stirrup, the fierce tramp of the iron-shod hoofs. Squadron after squadron came over the ridge, like successive human waves; then, like a sea broken loose, the flood of furious horsemen inundated the whole slope on which the squares were drawn up. But each square, a tiny, immovable island of red, with its fringe of smoke and steel and darting flame, stood doggedly resolute. No French leader, however daring, ventured to ride home on the very bayonets. The flood of maddened men and horses swung sullenly back across the ridge, while the British gunners ran out and scourged them with grape as they rode down the slope.

From four o'clock to six o'clock this amazing scene was repeated. No less than thirteen times, it was reckoned, the French horsemen rode over the ridge, and round the squares, and swept back wrecked and baffled. In the later charges they came on at a trot, or even a walk, and they rode through the British batteries and round the squares, in the words of the Duke of Wellington, "as if they owned them." So dense was the smoke that sometimes the British could not see their foes until, through the whirling blackness, a line of lances and crested helmets, or of tossing horse-heads, suddenly broke. Sometimes a single horseman would ride up to the very points of the British bayonets and strike at them with his sword, or fire a pistol at an officer, in the hope of drawing the fire of the square prematurely, and thus giving his comrades a chance of breaking it. With such cool courage did the British squares endure the fiery rush of the French cavalry, that at last the temper of the men grew almost scornful. They would growl out, "Here come these fools again," as a fresh sweep of horsemen came on. Sometimes the French squadrons came on at a trot; sometimes their "charge" slackened down to a walk. Warlike enthusiasm had exhausted itself. "The English squares and the French squadrons," says Lord Anglesey, "seemed almost, for a short time, hardly taking notice of each other."

In their later charges the French brought up some

light batteries to the crest of the British ridge, and opened fire at point-blank distance on the solid squares. The front of the 1st Life Guards was broken by a fire of this sort, and Gronow relates how the cuirassiers made a dash at the opening. Captain Adair leaped into the gap, and killed with one blow of his sword a French officer who had actually entered the square! The British gunners always ran swiftly out when the French cavalry recoiled down the slope, remanned their guns, and opened a murderous fire on the broken French. Noting this, an officer of cuirassiers drew up his horse by a British battery, and while his men drew off, stood on guard with his single sword, and kept the gunners from remanning it till he was shot by a British infantryman. Directly the broken cavalry was clear of the ridge, the French guns opened furiously on the British lines, and men dropped thick and fast. The cavalry charges, as a matter of fact, were welcomed as affording relief from the intolerable artillery fire.

For two hours 15,000 French horsemen rode round the British squares, and again and again the ridge and rear slope of the British position was covered with lancers, cuirassiers, light and heavy dragoons, and hussars, with the British guns in their actual possession; and yet not a square was broken! A gaily dressed regiment of the Duke of Cumberland's (Hanoverian) Hussars watched the Homeric contest from the British rear, and Lord Uxbridge, as the British cavalry were completely exhausted by their dashes at the French horsemen as they broke through the chequer of the squares, rode up to them and called on them to follow him in a charge. The colonel declined, explaining that his men owned their own horses, and could not expose them to any risk of damage! These remarkable warriors, in fact, moved in a body, and with much expedition, off the field, Seymour (Lord Uxbridge's aide) taking their colonel by the collar and shaking him as a dog shakes a rat, by way of expressing his view of the performance.

VI. THE FIGHT OF THE GUNNERS

> "Three hundred cannon-mouths roar'd loud;
> And from their throats with flash and cloud
> Their showers of iron threw."
> —Scott.

ONE of the most realistic pictures of the fight at this stage is given by Captain Mercer, in command of a battery of horse artillery. Mercer was on the extreme British right during the first stage of the battle, and only got occasional glimpses of the ridge where the fight was raging—intermittent visions of French cavalry riding in furious charges, and abandoned British batteries with guns, muzzle in air, against the background of grey and whirling smoke. About three o'clock, in the height of the cavalry struggle, Fraser, who was in chief command of the horse artillery, galloped down the reverse slope to Mercer's battery, his face black with powder, his uniform torn, and brought the troop at full gallop to the central ridge, explaining as they rode the Duke's orders, that, when the French cavalry charged home, Mercer and his men should take refuge under the bayonets of the nearest square.

As they neared the crest at a gallop, Mercer describes the humming as of innumerable and gigantic gnats that filled the bullet-torn air. He found his position betwixt two squares of Brunswickers, in whose ranks the French guns were making huge gaps, while the officers and sergeants were busy literally pushing the men together. "The men," says Mercer, "were like wooden figures, semi-paralysed with the horrors of the fight about them;" and to have attempted to run to them for shelter would certainly have been the signal for the whole mass to dissolve. Through the smoke ahead, not a hundred yards distant, were the French squadrons coming on at a trot. The British guns were swung round, unlimbered, loaded with case-shot, and fire opened with breathless speed. Still the French came on; but as gun after gun came into action, their pace slowed down to a walk, till the front files could endure the terrific fire no longer. They turned round and tried to ride back. "I actually saw them," says Mercer, "using the pommels of their swords to fight their way out of the *mêlée*." Some, made desperate by finding themselves penned up at the very muzzles of the British guns, dashed through their intervals, but without thinking of using their swords. Presently the mass broke and ebbed, a flood of shattered squadrons, down the slope. They rallied quickly, however, and their helmets could be seen over the curve of the slope as the officers dressed the lines.

The French tirailleurs, meanwhile, crept up within forty yards of the battery, and were busy shooting down Mercer's gunners. Mercer, to keep his men steady, rode slowly to and fro in front of the muzzles of his guns, the men standing with lighted port-fires. The tirailleurs, almost within pistol-shot, seized the opportunity to take pot-shots at him. He shook his glove, with the word "Scélérat," at one of them; the fellow grinned, and took a leisurely aim at Mercer, the muzzle of his gun following him as he turned to and fro in his promenade before his own pieces. The Frenchman fired, and the ball passed at the back of Mercer's neck into the forehead of the leading driver of one of his guns.

But the cavalry was coming on again in solid squadrons, a column so deep that when the leading files were within sixty yards of Mercer's guns the rear of the great mass was still out of sight. The pace was a deliberate trot. "They moved in profound silence," says Mercer, and the only sound that could be heard from them, amidst the incessant roar of battle, was the low, thunder-like reverberation of the ground beneath the simultaneous tread of so many horses, through which ran a jangling ripple of sharp metallic sound, the ring of steel on steel. The British gunners, on their part, showed a stern coolness fully equal to the occasion. Every man stood steadily at his post, "the guns ready loaded with round-shot first, and a case over it; the tubes were in the vents, the port-fires glared and sputtered behind the wheels." The column was led on this time by an officer in a rich uniform, his breast covered with decorations, whose earnest gesticulations were strangely contrasted with the solemn demeanour of those to whom they were addressed. Mercer allowed the leading squadron to come within sixty yards, then lifted his glove as the signal to fire. Nearly the whole leading rank fell in an instant, while the round shot pierced the column The front, covered with struggling horses and men was impassable. Some of the braver spirits did break their way through, only to fall, man and horse, at the very muzzles of the guns. "Our guns," says Mercer "were served with astonishing activity, and men and horses tumbled before them like nine-pins." Where the horse alone was killed, the cuirassier could be seen stripping himself of his armour with desperate haste to escape. The mass of the French for a moment stood still, then broke to pieces and fled. Again they came on, with exactly the same result. So dreadful was the carnage, that on the next day, Mercer, looking back from the French ridge, could identify the position held by his battery by the huge mound of slaughtered men and horses lying in front of it. The French at last brought up a battery, which opened a flanking fire on Mercer's guns; he swung round two of his pieces to meet the attack, and the combat raged till, out of 200 fine horses in Mercer's troop, 140 lay dead or dying, and two men out of every three were disabled.

Ney's thirteen cavalry charges on the British position were magnificent, but they were a failure. They did not break a single square, nor permanently disable a single gun. Both Wellington and Napoleon are accused of having flung away their cavalry; but Wellington—or, rather, Uxbridge—by expending only 2000 sabres, wrecked, as we have seen, a French infantry corps, destroyed a battery of 40 guns, and took 3000 prisoners. Ney practically used up 15,000 magnificent horsemen without a single appreciable result. Napoleon, at St. Helena, put the blame of his wasted cavalry on Ney's hot-headed impetuosity. The cavalry attack, he said, was made without his orders; Kellerman's division joined in the attack without even Ney's orders. But that Napoleon should watch for two hours his whole cavalry force wrecking itself in thirteen successive and baffled assaults on the British squares, without his orders, is an utterly incredible supposition.

If two hours of cavalry assault, punctuated as with

flame by the fire of 200 guns, did not destroy the stubborn British line, it cannot be denied that it shook it terribly. The British ridge was strewn with the dead and dying. Regiments had shrunk to companies, companies to mere files. "Our square," says Gronow, "presented a shocking sight. We were nearly suffocated by the smoke and smell from burnt cartridges. It was impossible to move a step without treading on a wounded or slain comrade." "Where is your brigade?" Vivian asked of Lord Edward Somerset, who commanded the Life Guards. "Here," said Lord Edward, pointing to two scanty squadrons, and a long line of wounded or mutilated horses. Before nightfall the two gallant brigades that made the great cavalry charge of the morning had contracted to a single squadron of fifty files. Wellington sent an aide-de-camp to ask General Hackett, "What square of his that was which was so far in advance?" It was a mass of killed and wounded men belonging to the 30th and 73rd regiments that lay slain, yet in ranks, on the spot the square had occupied at one period of the fight, and from which it had been withdrawn. Seen through the whirling smoke, this quadrangle of corpses looked like a square of living men. The destruction wrought by the French guns on the British squares was, in brief, terrific. By a single discharge of grape upon a German square, one of its sides was completely blown away, and the "square" transfigured into a triangle, with its base a line of slaughtered men. The effect produced by cannon-shot at short range on solid masses of men was sometimes very extraordinary. Thus Croker tells how an officer received a severe wound in the shoulder, apparently from a jagged ball. When the missile was extracted, however, it turned out to be a huge human double-tooth. Its owner's head had been shattered by a cannon-ball, and the very teeth transformed into a radiating spray of swift and deadly missiles. There were other cases of soldiers being wounded by coins driven suddenly by the impact of shot from their original owners' pockets. The sustained fire of the French tirailleurs, too, wrought fatal mischief.

La Haye Sainte by this time had been captured. The brave men who held it for so many hours carried rifles that needed a special cartridge, and supplies of it failed. When the French captured the farmhouse, they were able to push some guns and a strong infantry attack close up to the British left. This was held by the 27th, who had marched from Ghent at speed, reached Waterloo, exhausted, at nine A.M., on the very day of the battle, slept amid the roar of the great fight till three o'clock, and were then brought forward to strengthen the line above La Haye Sainte. The 27th was drawn up in square, and the French skirmishers opened a fire so close and fatal, that, literally, in the space of a few minutes every second man was shot down!

VII. THE OLD GUARD

"On came the whirlwind—like the last,
But fiercest sweep of tempest blast—
On came the whirlwind—steel-gleams broke
Like lightning through the rolling smoke;
The war was waked anew."
—Scott.

NAPOLEON had expended in vain upon the stubborn British lines his infantry, his cavalry, and his artillery. There remained only the Guard! The long summer evening was drawing to a close, when, at half-past seven, he marshalled these famous soldiers for the final attack. It is a curious fact that the intelligence of the coming attack was brought to Wellington by a French cuirassier officer, who deserted his colours just before it took place. The eight battalions of the immortal Guard formed a body of magnificent soldiers, the tall stature of the men being heightened by their imposing bearskin caps. The prestige of a hundred victories played round their bayonets. Their assault had never yet been resisted. Ney and Friant led them on. Napoleon himself, as the men marched past him to the assault, spoke some fiery words of exhortation to each company—the last words he ever spoke to his Guard.

It is a matter of keen dispute whether the Guard attacked in two columns or in one. The truth seems to be that the eight battalions were arranged in echelon, and really formed one mass, though in two parallel columns of companies, with batteries of horse artillery on either flank advancing with them. Nothing could well be more majestic, nothing more menacing, than the advance of this gallant force, and it seemed as if nothing on the British ridge, with its disabled guns and shot-torn battalions, could check such an assault. Wellington, however, quickly strengthened his centre by calling in Hill's division from the extreme right, while Vivian's Light Cavalry, surrendering the extreme left to the advancing Prussians, moved, in anticipation of orders, to the same point. Adams's brigade, too, was brought up to the threatened point, with all available artillery. The exact point in the line which would be struck by the head of the Guard was barred by a battery of nine-pounders. The attack of the Guard was aided by a general infantry advance—usually in the form of a dense mass of skirmishers—against the whole British front, and so fierce was this that some Hanoverian and Nassau battalions were shaken by it into almost fatal rout. A thread of British cavalry, made up of the scanty remains of the Scots Greys and some of Vandeleur's Light Cavalry, alone kept the line from being pierced.

All interest, however, centred in the attack of the Guard. Steadily, on a slightly diagonal line, it moved up the British slope. The guns smote it fiercely; but never shrinking or pausing, the great double column moved forward. It crossed the ridge. Nothing met the eyes of the astonished French except a wall of smoke, and the battery of horse artillery, at which the gunners were toiling madly, pouring case-shot into the approaching column. One or two horsemen, one of whom was Wellington himself, were dimly seen through the smoke behind the guns. The Duke denied that he used the famous phrase, "Up Guards, and at 'em!" "What I may have said, and possibly did say," he told Croker, "was, 'Stand up, Guards!' and then gave the commanding officers the order to attack."

An officer who took part in the fight has described the scene at the critical moment when the French Old Guard appeared at the summit of the British ridge: "As the smoke cleared away, a most superb sight opened on us. A close column of the Guard, about seventies in front, and not less than six thousand strong, their drums sounding the *pas de charge*, the men shouting 'Vive l'Empereur!' were within sixty yards of us." The sudden appearance of the long red line of the British Foot Guards rising from the ground seems to have brought the French Guard to a momentary pause, and, as they hesitated, along the whole line of the British ran—and ran again, and yet again—the vivid flash of a tremendous volley. The Guard tried to deploy; their officers leaped to the front, and, with shouts and waving swords, tried to bring them on, the British line, meanwhile, keeping up "independent" firing. Maitland and Lord Saltoun simultaneously shouted the order to "Charge!" The bayonets of the British Guards fell to level, the men came forward at a run, the tramp of the charging line sounded louder and louder, the line of shining points gleamed nearer and yet nearer—the bent and threatening faces of the British came swiftly on. The nerve of the French seemed to fail; the huge battalion faltered, shrank in upon itself, and tumbled in ruin down the hill!

But this was only the leading battalion of the right

segment of the great column, and the left was still moving steadily up. The British Guards, too, who had followed the broken battalion of the French down the hill, were arrested by a cry of "Cavalry!" and fell back on the ridge in confusion, though the men obeyed instantly the commands of the officers, "Halt! Front! Re-form!" Meanwhile the left section of the huge column was moving up, the men as steady as on parade, the lofty bearskins of the Grenadiers, as they mounted the ridge, giving them a gigantic aspect. The black, elongated shadows, as the last rays of the setting sun smote the lines, ran threateningly before them. But the devoted column was practically forcing itself up into a sort of triangle of fire. Bolton's guns crossed its head, the Guards, thrown slightly forward, poured their swift volleys in waves of flame on its right shoulder, the 52nd and 71st on its left scourged it with fire, beneath which the huge mass of the French Guard seemed sometimes to pause and thrill as if in convulsion.

Then came the movement which assured victory to the British. Colborne, a soldier with a singular genius for war, not waiting for orders, made his regiment, the 52nd, bring its right shoulder forward, the outer company swinging round at the double, until his whole front was parallel with the flank of the French Guard. Adams, the general in command of the brigade, rode up and asked him what he was going to do. Colborne replied, "To make that column feel our fire," and, giving the word, his men poured into the unprotected flank of the unfortunate Guard a terrific volley. The 52nd, it should be noted, went into action with upwards of one thousand bayonets, being probably the strongest battalion in the field. Colborne had "nursed" his regiment during the fight. He formed them into smaller squares than usual, and kept them in shelter where possible, so that at this crisis the regiment was still a body of great fighting force, and its firing was of deadly volume and power. Adams swiftly brought the 71st to sustain Colborne's attack, the Guards on the other flank also moved forward, practically making a long obtuse angle of musketry fire, the two sides of which were rapidly closing in on the head of the great French column.

The left company of the 52nd was almost muzzle to muzzle with the French column, and had to press back, while the right companies were swinging round to bring the whole line parallel with the flank of the Guard; yet, though the answering fire of the Frenchmen was broken and irregular, so deadly was it—the lines almost touching each other—that, in three minutes, from the left front of the 52nd one hundred and fifty men fell! When the right companies, however, had come up into line with the left, Colborne cried, "Charge! charge!" The men answered with a deep-throated, menacing shout, and dashed at the enemy. Napoleon's far-famed Guard, the victors in a hundred fights, shrank, the mass swayed to and fro, the men in the centre commenced to fire in the air, and the whole great mass seemed to tumble, break into units, and roll down the hill!

The 52nd and 71st came fiercely on, their officers leading. Some squadrons of the 23rd Dragoons came at a gallop down the slope, and literally smashed in upon the wrecked column. So wild was the confusion, so dense the whirling smoke that shrouded the whole scene, that some companies of the 52nd fired into the Dragoons, mistaking them for the enemy; and while Colborne was trying to halt his line to remedy the confusion, Wellington, who saw in this charge the sure pledge of victory, rode up and shouted, " Never mind! go on! go on!"

Gambier, then an officer of the 52nd, gives a graphic description of how that famous regiment fought at this stage :—

"A short time before, I had seen our colonel (Colborne), twenty yards in front of the centre, suddenly disappear, while his horse, mortally wounded, sank under him. After one or two rounds from the guns, he came striding down the front with, 'These guns will destroy the regiment.'—'Shall I drive them in, sir?'— 'Do.'—'Right section, left shoulders forward!' was the word at once. So close were we that the guns only fired their loaded charges, and limbering up, went hastily to the rear. Reaching the spot on which they had stood, I was clear of the Imperial Guard's smoke, and saw three squares of the Old Guard within four hundred yards farther on. They were standing in a line of contiguous squares with very short intervals, a small body of cuirassiers on their right, while the guns took post on their left. Convinced that the regiment, when it saw them, would come towards them, I continued my course, stopped with my section about two hundred yards in front of the centre square, and sat down. They were standing in perfect order and steadiness, and I knew they would not disturb that steadiness to pick a quarrel with an insignificant section. I alternately looked at them, at the regiment, and up the hill to my right (rear), to see who was coming to help us.

"A red regiment was coming along steadily from the British position, with its left directly upon me. It reached me some minutes before the 52nd, of which the right came within twenty paces of me. Colonel Colborne then called the covering sergeants to the front, and dressed the line upon them. Up to this moment neither the guns, the squares of the Imperial Guard, nor the 52nd had fired a shot. I then saw one or two of the guns slewed round to the direction of my company and fired, but their grape went over our heads. We opened our fire and advanced; the squares replied to it, and then steadily facing about, retired. The cuirassiers advanced a few paces; our men ceased firing, and, bold in their four-deep formation, came down to a sort of elevated bayonet charge; but the cuirassiers declined the contest, and turned. The French proper right square brought up its right shoulders and crossed the *chaussée*, and we crossed it after them. Twilight had manifestly commenced, and objects were now bewildering. The first event of interest was, that getting among some French tumbrils, with the horses attached, our colonel was seen upon one, shouting 'Cut me out!' Then we came upon the hollow road beyond La Belle Alliance, filled with artillery and broken infantry. Here was instantly a wild *mêlée:* the infantry tried to escape as best they could, and at the same time turn and defend themselves; the artillery drivers turned their horses to the left and tried to scramble up the bank of the road, but the horses were immediately shot down; a young subaltern of the battery threw his sword and himself on the ground in the act of surrender; his commander, who wore the cross of the Legion of Honour, stood in defiance among his guns, and was bayoneted, and the subaltern, unwisely making a run for his liberty, was shot in the attempt. The *mêlée* at this spot placed us amid such questionable companions, that no one at that moment could be sure whether a bayonet would be the next moment in his ribs or not."

It puts a sudden gleam of humour into the wild scene to read how Colonel Sir Felton Harvey, who led a squadron of the 18th, when he saw the Old Guard tumbling into ruins, evoked a burst of laughter from his entire squadron by saying in a solemn voice, "Lord Wellington has won the battle," and then suddenly adding in a changed tone, "If we could but get the d——d fool to advance!" Wellington, as a matter of fact, had given the signal that launched his wasted and sorely tried battalions in one final and victorious advance. Vivian's cavalry still remained to the Duke—the 10th and 18th Hussars—and they, at this stage, made a charge almost as decisive as that of the Household and Union Brigades in the morning. The 10th crashed into some cuirassiers who were coming up to try and relieve the flank of the Guard, overthrew them in a moment, and then plunged into the broken French Guard itself. These veterans were retreating, so to speak, individually, all formation wrecked, but each soldier was stalking fiercely along with frowning brow and musket grasped, ready to charge any too audacious horsemen. Vivian himself relates how his orderly alone cut down five or six in swift succession who were trying to bayonet the British cavalry general. When Vivian had launched the 10th, he galloped back to the 18th, who had lost almost every officer. "My lads," he said, "you'll follow me"; to which the sergeant-major, a man named Jeffs, replied, "To h——, general, if you will lead us!" The wreck of Vandeleur's brigade, too, charged down the slope more to the left; batteries were carried, cavalry squadrons smashed, and infantry battalions tumbled into ruin. Napoleon had an entire light cavalry brigade still untouched; but this, too, was caught in the reflux of the broken masses, and swept away. The wreck of the Old Guard and the spectacle of the general advance of the British—cavalry, artillery, and infantry—seemed to be the signal for the dissolution of the whole French army.

Two squares of the French Guard yet kept their formation. Some squadrons of the 10th Hussars, under Major Howard, rode fiercely at one. Howard himself rode home, and died literally on the French bayonets; and his men rivalled his daring, and fought and died on two faces of the square. But the Frenchmen kept their ranks, and the attack failed. The other square was broken. The popular tradition that Cambronne, commanding a square of the Old Guard, on being summoned to surrender, answered, "La Garde meurt, et ne se rend pas," is pure fable. As a matter of fact, Halkett, who commanded a brigade of Hanoverians, personally captured Cambronne. Halkett was heading some squadrons of the 10th, and noted Cambronne trying to rally the Guard. In his own words, "I made a gallop for the general. When about cutting him down, he called out he would surrender, upon which he preceded me to the rear. But I had not gone many paces before my horse got shot through his body and fell to the ground. In a few seconds I got him on his legs again, and found my friend Cambronne had taken French leave in the direction from which he came. I instantly overtook him, laid hold of him by the aiguillette, and brought him back in safety, and gave him in charge of a sergeant of the Osnabruckers to deliver to the Duke."

Napoleon himself, from a spot of rising ground not far from La Haye Sainte, had watched the advance of his Guard. His empire hung on its success. It was the last fling of the dice for him. His cavalry was wrecked, his infantry demoralised, half his artillery dismounted; the Prussian guns were thundering with ever louder roar upon his right. If the Guard succeeded, the electrifying thrill of victory would run through the army, and knit it into energy once more. But if the Guard failed——!

VIII. THE GREAT DEFEAT

"And while amid their scattered band
Raged the fierce riders' bloody brand,
Recoil'd in common rout and fear,
Lancer and Guard and Cuirassier,
Horsemen and foot—a mingled host,
Their leaders fall'n, their standards lost."
—Scott.

Napoleon watched the huge black echelon of battalions mount the slope, their right section crumbled under the rush of the British Guards. Colborne and the 52nd tumbled the left flank into ruin; the British cavalry swept down upon them. Those who stood near Napoleon watched his face. It became pale as death. "Ils sont mêlés ensemble" ("they are mingled together"), he muttered to himself. He cast one hurried glance over the field, to right and left, and saw nothing but broken squadrons, abandoned batteries, wrecked infantry battalions. "Tout est perdu," he said, "sauve qui peut," and, wheeling his horse, he turned his back upon his last battlefield. His star had set!

Napoleon's strategy throughout the brief campaign was magnificent; his tactics—the detailed handling of his troops on the actual battlefield—were wretched. "We were manœuvred," says the disgusted Marbot, "like so many pumpkins." Napoleon was only forty-seven years old, but, as Wolseley says, "he was no longer the thin, sleek, active little man he had been at Rivoli. His now bloated face, large stomach, and fat and rounded legs bespoke a man unfitted for hard work on horseback." His fatal delay in pursuing Blücher on the 17th, and his equally fatal waste of time in attacking Wellington on the 18th, proved how his quality as a general had decayed. It is a curious fact that, during the battle of Waterloo, Napoleon remained for hours motionless at a table placed for him in the open air, often asleep, with his head resting on his arms. One reads with an odd sense of humour the answer which a dandy officer of the British Life Guards gave to the inquiry, "How he felt during the battle of Waterloo?" He replied that he had felt "awfully bored"! That anybody should feel " bored " in the vortex of such a drama is wonderful; but scarcely so wonderful as the fact that the general of one of the two contending hosts found it possible to go to sleep during the crisis of the gigantic battle, on which hung his crown and fate. Napoleon had lived too long for the world's happiness or for his own fame.

The story here told is that of Waterloo on its British side. No attempt is made to describe Blücher's magnificent loyalty in pushing, fresh from the defeat of Ligny, through the muddy cross-roads from Wavre, to join Wellington on the blood-stained field of Waterloo. No account, again, is attempted of Grouchy's wanderings into space, with 33,000 men and 96 guns, lazily attacking Thielmann's single corps at Wavre, while Blücher, with three divisions, was marching at speed to fling himself on Napoleon's right flank at Waterloo. It is idle to speculate on what would have happened to the British if the Prussians had not made their movement on Napoleon's right flank. The assured help of Blücher was the condition upon which Wellington made his

S

stand at Waterloo; it was as much part of his calculations as the fighting quality of his own infantry. A plain tale of British endurance and valour is all that is offered here; and what a head of wood and heart of stone any man of Anglo-Saxon race must have who can read such a tale without a thrill of generous emotion!

Waterloo was for the French not so much a defeat as a rout. Napoleon's army simply ceased to exist. The number of its slain is unknown, for its records were destroyed. The killed and wounded in the British army reached the tragical number of nearly 15,000. Probably not less than between 30,000 and 40,000 slain or wounded human beings were scattered, the night following the battle, over the two or three square miles where the great fight had raged; and some of the wounded were lying there still, uncared for, four days afterwards. It is said that for years afterwards, as one looked over the waving wheat-fields in the valley betwixt Mont St. Jean and La Belle Alliance, huge irregular patches, where the corn grew rankest and was of deepest tint, marked the gigantic graves where, in the silence and reconciliation of death, slept Wellington's ruddy-faced infantry lads and the grizzled veterans of the Old Guard. The deep cross-country road which covered Wellington's front has practically disappeared; the Belgians have cut away the banks to build up a huge pyramid, on the summit of which is perched a Belgian lion, with tail erect, grinning defiance towards the French frontier. A lion is not exactly the animal which best represents the contribution the Belgian troops made to Waterloo.

But still the field keeps its main outlines. To the left lies Planchenoit, where Wellington watched to see the white smoke of the Prussian guns; opposite is the gentle slope down which D'Erlon's troops marched to fling themselves on La Haye Sainte; and under the spectator's feet, a little to his left as he stands on the summit of the monument, is the ground over which Life Guards and Inniskillings and Scots Greys galloped in the fury of their great charge. Right in front is the path along which came Milhaud's Cuirassiers and Kellerman's Lancers, and Friant's Old Guard, in turn, to fling themselves in vain on the obstinate squares and thin red line of the British. To the right is Hougoumont, the orchard walls still pierced with loopholes made by the Guards. A fragment of brick, blackened with the smoke of the great fight, is one of the treasures of the present writer. Victors and vanquished alike have passed away, and, since the Old Guard broke on the slopes of Mont St. Jean, British and French have never met in the wrestle of battle. May they never meet again in that fashion! But as long as nations preserve the memory of the great deeds of their history, as long as human courage and endurance can send a thrill of admiration through generous hearts, as long as British blood beats in British veins, the story of the brave men who fought and died at their country's bidding at Waterloo will be one of the great traditions of the English-speaking race.

Of Wellington's part in the great fight it is difficult to speak in terms which do not sound exaggerated. He showed all the highest qualities of generalship—swift vision, cool judgment, the sure insight that forecasts each move on the part of his mighty antagonist, the unfailing resource that instantly devises the plan for meeting it. There is no need to dwell on Wellington's courage; the rawest British militia lad on the field shared that quality with him. But in the temper of Wellington's courage there was a sort of ice-clear quality that was simply marvellous. He visited every square and battery in turn, and was at every point where the fight was most bloody. Every member of his staff, without exception, was killed or wounded, while it is curious to reflect that not a member of Napoleon's staff was so much as touched. But the roar of the battle, with its swift chances of life and death, left Wellington's intellect as cool, and his nerve as steady, as though he were watching a scene in a theatre. One of his generals said to him when the fight seemed most desperate, "If you should be struck, tell us what is your plan?" "My plan," said the Duke, "consists in dying here to the last man." He told at a dinner-table, long after the battle, how, as he stood under the historic tree in the centre of his line, a Scotch sergeant came up, told him he had observed the tree was a mark for the French gunners, and begged him to move from it. Somebody at the table said, "I hope you did, sir?" "I really forget," said the Duke, "but I know I thought it very good advice at the time."

Only twice during the day did Wellington show any trace of remembering what may be called his personal interest in the fight. Napoleon had called him "a Sepoy general." "I will show him to-day," he said, just before the battle began, "how a Sepoy general can defend himself." At night, again, as he sat with a few of his surviving officers about him at supper, his face yet black with the smoke of the fight, he repeatedly leaned back in his chair, rubbing his hands convulsively, and exclaiming aloud, "Thank God! I have met him. Thank God! I have met him." But Wellington's mood throughout the whole of the battle was that which befitted one of the greatest soldiers war has ever produced in the supreme hour of his country's fate. The Duke was amongst the leading files of the British line as they pushed the broken French Guard down the slope, and some one begged him to remember what his life was worth, and go back. "The battle is won," said Wellington; "my life doesn't matter now." Dr. Hulme, too, has told how he woke the Duke early in the morning after the fight, his face grim, unwashed, and smoke-blackened, and read the list of his principal officers—name after name—dead or dying, until the hot tears ran, like those of a woman, down the iron visage of the great soldier.

As Napoleon in the gathering darkness galloped off the field, with the wreck and tumult of his shattered army about him, there remained to his life only those six ignoble years at St. Helena. But Wellington was still in his very prime. He was only forty-six years old, and there awaited him thirty-seven years of honoured life, till, "to the noise of the mourning of a mighty nation," he was laid beside Nelson in the crypt of St. Paul's, and Tennyson sang his requiem:—

> "O good grey head, which all men knew,
> O voice from which their omens all men drew,
> O iron nerve, to true occasion true;
> O fall'n at length that tower of strength
> Which stood four-square to all the winds that blew."

THE NIGHT ATTACK OFF CADIZ

" 'Captain,' they cry, 'the fight is done,
  They bid you send your sword!'
And he answered, 'Grapple her stern and bow.
They have asked for the steel. They shall have it now;
  Out cutlasses, and board!'"
—KIPLING.

ON the morning of July 3, 1801, a curious scene, which might almost be described as a sea comedy, was being transacted off the coast of Alicante. Three huge French line-of-battle ships were manœuvring and firing round a tiny little British brig-of-war. It was like three mastiffs worrying a mouse. The brig was Lord Cochrane's famous little *Speedy*, a craft so tiny that its commander could carry its entire broadside in his own pockets, and when he shaved himself in his cabin, had to put his head through the skylight and his shaving-box on the quarter-deck, in order to stand upright.

Cochrane was caught by Admiral Linois' squadron, consisting of two ships of eighty guns and one of seventy-four, on a lee shore, where escape was impossible; but from four o'clock till nine o'clock Cochrane evaded all the efforts of his big pursuers to capture him. The French ships separated on different tacks, so as to keep the little *Speedy* constantly under the fire of one or the other; and as the British

ADMIRAL SAUMAREZ

After a portrait by T. Phillips, R.A.

brig turned and dashed at one opening of the moving triangle or the other, the great ships thundered their broadsides at her. Cochrane threw his guns and stores overboard, and by the most ingenious seamanship evaded capture for hours, surviving some scores of broadsides. He could tack far more quickly than the gigantic ships that pursued him, and again and again the *Speedy* spun round on its heel and shot off on a new course, leaving its particular pursuer with sheet shivering, and nothing but space to fire into. Once, by a quick turn, he shot past one of the 80-gun ships occupied in trying to tack, and got clear. The *Desaix*, however, a seventy-four, was swiftly on the track of the *Speedy*; its tall canvas under the growing breeze gave it an advantage, and it ran down to within musket-shot of the *Speedy*, then yawed, bringing its whole broadside to bear, intending to sink its tiny foe with a single discharge. In yawing, however, the *Desaix* shot a little too far, and the weight of her broadside only smote the water, but the scattered grape cut up the *Speedy's* rigging and canvas so terribly that nothing was left but surrender.

When Cochrane went on board his captor, its gallant captain refused to take his sword, saying he "could not accept the sword of an officer who had struggled for so many hours against impossibility." Cochrane and his gallant crew were summarily packed into the Frenchman's hold, and when the French in their turn were pursued by the British line-of-battle ships, as every broadside crashed on the hull of the ship that held them captive, Cochrane and his men gave a round of exultant cheers, until the exasperated Frenchmen threatened to shoot them unless they would hold their tongues — an announcement which only made the British sailors cheer a little louder. The fight between Saumarez and Linois ended with a tragedy; but it may be said to have begun with a farce.

The presence of a French squadron in the Straits of Gibraltar at this particular moment may be explained in a few sentences. Napoleon had woven afresh the web of those naval "combinations" so often torn to fragments by British seamanship and daring. He had persuaded or bullied Spain into placing under the French flag a squadron of six line-of-battle ships, including two leviathans of 112 guns each, lying in the harbour of Cadiz. With haughty, it might almost be said with insolent daring, a couple of British seventy-fours — sometimes, indeed, only one — patrolled the entrance to Cadiz, and blockaded a squadron of ten times their own force. Napoleon's plan was to draw a strong French squadron, under Admiral Linois, from Toulon, a second Spanish squadron from Ferrol, unite these with the ships lying in Cadiz, and thus form a powerful fleet of at least fifteen ships of the line, with a garnishing of frigates.

Once having got his fleet, Napoleon's imagination— which had a strong predatory bias—hesitated betwixt two uses to which it could be turned. One was to make a dash on Lisbon, and require, under threat of an instant bombardment, the delivery of all British ships and goods lying there. This ingenious plan, it was reckoned, would fill French pockets with cash and adorn French brows with glory at one stroke. The amount of British booty at Lisbon was computed—somewhat airily—at

£200,000,000; its disappearance would send half the mercantile houses of Great Britain into the insolvency court, and, to quote a French state paper on the subject, " our fleet, without being buffeted about the sea, would return to Brest loaded with riches and covered with glory, and France would once more astonish Europe." The alternative scheme was to transport some 32,000 new troops to Egypt and restore French fortunes in that country.

Meanwhile Great Britain took energetic measures to wreck this new combination. Sir James Saumarez, in the *Cæsar*, of eighty guns, with six seventy-fours, was despatched to keep guard over Cadiz; and he had scarcely reached his station there when a boat, pulling furiously over from Gibraltar, reported that Admiral Linois' squadron had made its appearance off the Rock, beating up westward. The sails of the *Cæsar* were instantly swung round, a many-coloured flutter of bunting summoned the rest of the squadron to follow, and Saumarez began his eager chase of the French, bearing away for the Gut under a light north-west wind. But the breeze died down, and the current swept the straggling ships westward. All day they drifted helplessly, and the night only brought a breath of air sufficient to fan them through the Straits.

Meanwhile Linois had taken refuge in the tiny curve of the Spanish coast known as the roadstead of Algeciras. Linois was, perhaps, the best French seaman of his day, having, it is true, very little French dash, but endowed with a wealth of cool resolution, and a genius for defensive warfare altogether admirable. Algeciras gave Linois exactly what he wanted, an almost unassailable position. The roadstead is open, shallow, and plentifully besprinkled with rocks, while powerful shore batteries covered the whole anchorage with their zone of fire. The French admiral anchored his ships at intervals of 500 yards from each other, and so that the lines of fire from the batteries north and south crossed in front of his ships. The French squadron carried some 3000 troops, and these were at once landed, and, manning the batteries, raised them to a high degree of effectiveness. Some fourteen heavy Spanish gunboats added enormously to the strength of the French position.

The French never doubted that Saumarez would instantly attack; the precedents of the Nile and of Copenhagen were too recent to make any doubt possible. And Saumarez did exactly what his enemies expected. Algeciras, in fact, is the battle of the Nile in miniature. But Saumarez, though he had the swift daring of Nelson, lacked his warlike genius. Nelson, in Aboukir Bay, leaped without an instant's pause on the line of his enemy, but then he had his own ships perfectly in hand, and so made the leap effective. Saumarez sent his ships into the fight headlong, and without the least regard to mutual support. At 7.50 on the morning of July 6, an uncertain gust of air carried the leading British ship, the *Pompée,* round Cabrita; Hood, in the *Venerable,* lay becalmed in the offing; the flagship, with the rest of the squadron, were mere pyramids of idle canvas on the rim of the horizon.

The *Pompée* drifted down the whole French line, scorched with the fire of batteries and of gunboats, as well as by the broadsides of the great French ships, and at 8.45 dropped her anchor so close to the *Formidable*

—a ship much bigger than itself—that the Frenchman's buoy lay outside her. Then, deliberately clewing up her sails and tautening her springs, the *Pompée* opened a fire on her big antagonist so fierce, sustained, and deadly, that the latter found it intolerable, and began to warp closer to the shore. The *Audacious* and *Venerable* came slowly up into their assigned positions, and here was a spectacle of three British ships fighting four French ships and fourteen Spanish gunboats, with heavy shore batteries manned by 3000 troops thrown into the scale! At this stage, too, the *Pompée's* springs gave way, or were shot away, the current swung her round till she lay head on to the broadside of her huge antagonist, while the batteries smote her with a deadly cross-fire. A little after ten o'clock the *Cæsar* dropped anchor three cables' lengths from the *Indomptable*, and opened a fire which the French themselves described as "tremendous" upon her antagonist.

Linois found the British fire too destructive, and signalled his ships to cut or slip their cables, calculating that a faint air from the sea, which was beginning to blow, would drift them closer under the shelter of the batteries. Saumarez, too, noticed that his topsails were beginning to swell, and he instantly slipped his cable and endeavoured to close with the *Indomptable*, signalling his ships to do the same. The British cables rattled hoarsely through their hawse-holes along the whole line, and the ships were adrift; but the breeze almost instantly died away, and on the strong coast current the British ships floated helplessly, while the fire from the great shore batteries, and from the steady French decks, now anchored afresh, smote them heavily in turn. The *Pompée* lay for an hour under a concentrated fire without being able to bring a gun to bear in return, and then summoned by signal the boats of the squadron to tow her off.

Saumarez, meanwhile, had ordered the *Hannibal*, under Captain Ferris, to round the head of the French line and "rake the admiral's ship." Ferris, by fine seamanship, partly sailed and partly drifted into the post assigned to him, and then grounded hopelessly, under a plunging fire from the shore batteries, within hail of the Frenchman, itself also aground. A fire so dreadful soon reduced the unfortunate *Hannibal* to a state of wreck. Boats from the *Cæsar* and the *Venerable* came to her help, but Ferris sent them back again. They could not help him, and should not share his fate. Saumarez, as a last resource, prepared for a boat attack on the batteries, but in the whole squadron there were not enough uninjured boats to carry the marines. The British flagship itself was by this time well-nigh a wreck, and was drifting on the reefs. A flaw of wind from the shore gave the ships steerage-way, and Saumarez drew off, leaving the *Hannibal* to its fate.

Ferris fought till his masts were gone, his guns dismounted, his bulwarks riddled, his decks pierced, and one-third of his crew killed or wounded. Then he ordered the survivors to the lower decks, and still kept his flag flying for half-an-hour after the shot-torn sails of the shattered British ships had disappeared round Cabrita. Then he struck. Here was a French triumph, indeed! A British squadron beaten off, a British seventy-four captured! It is said that when the news reached Paris the city went half-mad with exultation.

Napoleon read the despatch to his ministers with eyes that danced, and almost wept, with mere gladness!

The British squadron—officers and men in such a mood as may be imagined—put into Gibraltar to refit; the *Cæsar*, with her mainmast shot through in five places, her boats destroyed, her hull pierced; while of the sorely battered *Pompée* it is recorded that she had "not a mast, yard-spar, shroud, rope, or sail" which was not damaged by hostile shot. Linois, meanwhile, got his grounded ships and his solitary prize afloat, and summoned the Cadiz squadron to join him. On the 9th these ships—six sail of the line, two of them giants of 112 guns each, with three frigates—went triumphantly, with widespread canvas and many-coloured bunting, past Gibraltar, where the shattered British squadron was lying, and cast anchor beside Admiral Linois in Algeciras Bay.

The British were labouring, meanwhile, with fierce energy, to refit their damaged ships under shelter of the guns of Gibraltar. The *Pompée* was practically destroyed, and her crew were distributed amongst the other ships. Saumarez himself regarded the condition of his flagship as hopeless, but his captain, Brenton, begged permission to at least attempt to refit her. He summoned his crew aft, and told the men the admiral proposed to leave the ship behind, and asked them "what they thought about it." The men gave a wrathful roar, punctuated, it is to be feared, with many sea-going expletives, and shouted, "All hands to work day and night till she's ready!" The whole crew, down to the very powder-boys, actually worked while daylight lasted, kept it up, watch and watch, through the night, and did this from the evening of the 6th to the noon of the 12th! Probably no ship that ever floated was refitted in shorter time. In that brief period, to quote the "Naval Register," she "shifted her mainmast; fished and secured her foremast, shot through in several places; knotted and spliced the rigging, which had been cut to pieces, and bent new sails; plugged the shot-holes between wind and water; completed with stores of all kinds, anchors and cables, powder and shot, and provisions for four months."

On Sunday, July 12, 1801, the French and Spanish ships in Algeciras Bay weighed anchor, formed their line of battle as they came out, off Cabrita Point, and, stately and slow, with the two 112-gun Spaniards as a rearguard, bore up for Cadiz. An hour later the British ships warped out of the mole in pursuit. It was an amazing sight: a squadron of five sail of the line, which had been completely disabled in an action only five days before, was starting, fresh and refitted, in pursuit of a fleet double its own number, and more than double its strength! All Gibraltar crowded to watch the ships as, one by one, they cleared the pierhead. The garrison band blew itself hoarse playing "Britons, strike home," while the *Cæsar's* band answered in strains as shrill with "Come, cheer up, my lads, 'tis for glory we steer." Both tunes, it may be added, were simply submerged beneath the cheers which rang up from mole-head and batteries and dock-walls. Just as the *Cæsar* drifted, huge and stately, past the pier-head, a boat came eagerly pulling up to her. It was crowded with jack-tars, with bandaged heads and swathed arms. A cluster of the *Pompée's* wounded, who escaped from the hospital, bribed a boatman to pull them out to the flagship, and clamoured to be taken on board!

Saumarez had strengthened his squadron by the addition of the *Superb*, with the *Thames* frigate, and at twenty minutes to nine P.M., vainly searching the black horizon for the lights of the enemy, he hailed the *Superb*, and ordered its captain, Keats, to clap on all sail and attack the enemy directly he overtook them. Saumarez, in a word, launched a single seventy-four against a fleet! Keats was a daring sailor; his ship was, perhaps, the fastest British seventy-four afloat, and his men were instantly aloft spreading every inch of canvas. Then, like a huge ghost, the *Superb* glided ahead and vanished in the darkness. The wind freshened; the blackness deepened; the lights of the British squadron died out astern. But a wide sprinkle of lights ahead became visible; it was the Spanish fleet! Eagerly the daring *Superb* pressed on, with slanting decks and men at quarters, but with lights hidden. At midnight the rear ships of the Spanish squadron were under the larboard bow of the *Superb* —two stupendous three-deckers, with lights gleaming through a hundred port-holes—while a French two-decker to larboard of both the Spanish giants completed the line.

Keats, unseen and unsuspected, edged down with his solitary seventy-four, her heaviest guns only 18-pounders, on the quarter of the nearest three-decker. He was about to fling himself, in the gloom of the night, on three great ships, with an average of 100 guns each! Was ever a more daring feat attempted? Silently through the darkness the *Superb* crept, her canvas glimmering ghostly white, till she was within some 300 yards of the nearest Spaniard. Then out of the darkness to windward there broke on the astonished and drowsy Spaniards a tempest of flame, a whirlwind of shot. Thrice the *Superb* poured her broadside into the huge and staggering bulk of her antagonist. With the second broadside the Spaniard's topmast came tumbling down; with the third, so close was the flame of the *Superb's* guns, the Spanish sails—dry as touchwood with lying for so many months in the sunshine of Cadiz—took fire.

Meanwhile a dramatic incident occurred. The two great Spaniards commenced to thunder their heavy broadsides into each other! Many of the *Superb's* shots had struck the second and more distant three-decker. Cochrane, indeed, says that the *Superb* passed actually betwixt the two gigantic Spaniards, fired a broadside, larboard and starboard, into both, and then glided on and vanished in the darkness. It is certain that the *San Hermenegildo*, finding her decks torn by a hurricane of shot, commenced to fire furiously through the smoke and the night at the nearest lights. They were the lights of her own consort! She, in turn, fired at the flash of the guns tormenting her. So, under the black midnight skies, the two great Spanish ships thundered at each other, flame answering flame. They drifted ever closer. The fire of the *Real Carlos* kindled the sails of the sister ship; the flames leaped and danced to the very mast-heads; and, still engaged in a fiery wrestle, they blew up in succession, and out of their united crews of 2000 men only a little over 200 were picked up!

The *Superb*, meanwhile, had glided ahead, leaving the three-deckers to destroy each other, and opened fire at pistol-shot distance on the French two-decker, and in thirty minutes compelled her to strike. In less than two hours of a night action, that is, this single English seventy-four had destroyed two Spanish three-deckers of 112 guns each, and captured a fine French battle-ship of 74 guns!

The British ships by this time were coming up in the rear, with every inch of canvas spread. They swept past the amazing spectacle of the two great Spaniards destroying each other, and pressed on in chase of the enemy. The wind rose to a gale. In the grey dawn the *Cæsar* found herself, with all her sister ships, far astern, except the *Venerable*, under Hood, which was hanging on the quarter of the rearmost French ship, the *Formidable*, a magnificent ship of 80 guns, with a gallant commander, and carrying quite too heavy metal for Hood. Hood, however, the most daring of men, exchanged broadsides at pistol-shot distance with his big antagonist, till his ship was dismasted, and was drifted by the current on the rocky shoals off San Pedro. The *Cæsar* came up in time to enable its disgusted crew to see ship after ship of the flying enemy disappear safely within the sheltering batteries of Cadiz.

TRAFALGAR

I. THE STRATEGY

> "Uprose the soul of him a star
>   On that brave day of Ocean days;
> It rolled the smoke from Trafalgar
>   To darken Austerlitz ablaze.
> Are we the men of old, its light
>   Will point us under every sky
> The path he took; and must we fight,
>   Our Nelson be our battle-cry!
>
> He leads: we hear our Seaman's call
>   In the roll of battles won;
> For he is Britain's Admiral
>   Till setting of her sun."
>   —GEORGE MEREDITH.

THAT Trafalgar was a great British victory, won by splendid seamanship and by magnificent courage, everybody knows. On October 21, 1805, Nelson, with twenty-seven line-of-battle ships, attacked Villeneuve, in command of a combined fleet of thirty-three line-of-battle ships. The first British gun was fired at 12.10 o'clock; at 5 o'clock the battle was over; and within those five hours the combined fleets of France and Spain were simply destroyed. No fewer than eighteen ships of the line were captured, burnt, or sunk; the rest were in flight, and had practically ceased to exist as re fighting force. But what very few people realise is that

NELSON

After the portrait by HOPPNER *in the possession of the Queen*

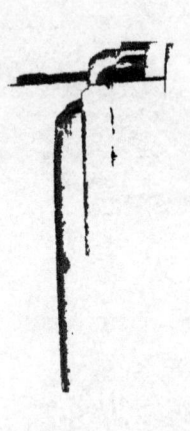

Trafalgar is only the last incident in a great strategic conflict—a warfare of brains rather than of bullets—which for nearly three years raged round a single point. For that long period the warlike genius of Napoleon was pitted in strategy against the skill and foresight of a cluster of British sailors; and the sailors won. They beat Napoleon at his own weapons. The French were not merely out-fought in the shock of battling fleets, they were out-generalled in the conflict of plotting and warlike brains which preceded the actual fight off Cape Trafalgar.

The strategy which preceded Trafalgar represents Napoleon's solitary attempt to plan a great campaign on the tossing floor of the sea. "It has an interest wholly unique," says Mahan, "as the only great naval campaign ever planned by this foremost captain of modern times." And it is a very marvellous fact that a cluster of British sailors—Jervis and Barham (a salt eighty years old) at the Admiralty, Cornwallis at Brest, Collingwood at Cadiz, and Nelson at Toulon—guessed all Napoleon's profound and carefully hidden strategy, and met it by even subtler plans and swifter resolves than those of Napoleon himself. The five hours of gallant fighting off Cape Trafalgar fill us with exultant pride. But the intellectual duel which preceded the shock of actual battle, and which lasted for nearly three years, is, in a sense, a yet more splendid story. Great Britain may well honour her naval leaders of that day for their cool and profound strategy, as much as for the unyielding courage with which such a blockade as, say, that of Brest by Cornwallis was maintained for years, or such splendid daring as that which Collingwood showed when, in the *Royal Sovereign*, he broke Villeneuve's line at Trafalgar.

When in 1803 the war which brought to an end the brief peace of Amiens broke out, Napoleon framed a great and daring plan for the invasion of England. French plans for the invasion of England were somewhat numerous a century or so ago. The Committee of Public Safety in 1794, while keeping the guillotine busy in the Place de la Révolution, had its own little plan for extending the Reign of Terror, by means of an invasion, to England; and on May 27 of that year solemnly appointed one of their number to represent the Committee in England "when it was conquered." The member chosen was citizen Bon Saint André, the same hero who, in the battle of the 1st of June, fled in terror to the refuge of the French flagship's cock-pit when the *Queen Charlotte*, with her triple lines of guns, came too alarmingly near. But Napoleon's plans for the same object in 1803 were definite, formidable, profound. Great Britain was the one barrier in the path of his ambition. "Buonaparte," says Green, in his "Short History of the English People," "was resolute to be master of the western world, and no notions of popular freedom or sense of popular right ever interfered with his resolve.... England was now the one country where freedom in any sense remained alive.... With the fall of England, despotism would have been universal throughout Europe; and it was at England that Buonaparte resolved to strike the first blow in his career of conquest. Fifteen millions of people, he argued, must give way to forty millions."

So he formed the vast camp at Boulogne, in which

were gathered 130,000 veterans. A great flotilla of boats was built, each boat being armed with one or two guns, and capable of carrying 100 soldiers. More than 1000 of such boats were built, and concentrated along twenty miles of the Channel coast, and at four different ports. A new port was dug at Boulogne, to give shelter to the main division of this flotilla, and great and powerful batteries erected for its protection. The French soldiers were exercised in embarking and disembarking till the whole process could be counted by minutes. "Let us," said Napoleon, "be masters of the Straits for six hours, and we shall be masters of the world."

When since the days of William the Conqueror were the shores of Great Britain menaced by such a peril? "There is no difficulty," said Moltke, "in getting an army into England; the trouble would be to get it out again." And, no doubt, Englishmen, fighting on their own soil and for their own hearths, would have given an invader a very rough time of it. But let it be remembered that Napoleon was a military genius of the first order, and that the 130,000 soldiers waiting on the heights above Boulogne to leap on British soil were, to quote Mahan, "the most brilliant soldiery of all time." They were the men who afterwards won Austerlitz, who struck down Prussia with a single blow at Jena, who marched as victors through the streets of Vienna and of Berlin, and fought their way to Moscow. Imagine such an army, with such a leader, landed on the green fields of Kent! In that case there might have been an English Austerlitz or Friedland. London might have shared the fate of Moscow. If Napoleon had succeeded, the fate of the world would have been changed, and Toronto and

Cape Town, Melbourne and Sydney and Auckland might have been ruled by French prefects.

Napoleon himself was confident of success. He would reach London, he calculated, within four days of landing, and then he would have issued decrees abolishing the House of Lords, proclaiming a redistribution of property, and declaring England a republic. "You would never have burned your capital," he said to O'Meara at St. Helena; "you are too rich and fond of money." The London mob, he believed, would have joined him, for, as he cynically argued, "the *canaille* of all nations are nearly alike."

Even Napoleon would probably have failed, however, in subduing Great Britain, and would have remained a prisoner where he came intending to be a conqueror. As he himself said when a prisoner on his way to St. Helena, "I entered into no calculation as to the manner in which I was to return"! But in the battles which must have been fought, how many English cities would have perished in flames, how many English rivers would have run red with the blood of slain men! "At Waterloo," says Alison, "England fought for victory; at Trafalgar for existence."

But "the streak of silver sea" guarded England, and for more than two years Napoleon framed subtle plans and organised vast combinations which might give him that brief six hours' command of the Strait which was all he needed, as he thought, to make himself the master of the world. The flotilla could not so much as get out of the ports, in which the acres of boats lay, in a single tide, and one half of the army of invasion must lie tossing—and, it may be suspected, dreadfully sea-sick—for hours outside these ports, waiting for the other half to get afloat. Then there remained forty miles of sea to cross. And what would happen if, say, Nelson and Collingwood, with a dozen 74-gun ships, got at work amongst the flotilla? It would be a combat between wolves and sheep. It was Nelson's chief aspiration to have the opportunity of "trying Napoleon on a wind," and the attempt to cross the Straits might have given him that chance. All Napoleon's resources and genius were therefore strained to give him for the briefest possible time the command of the Channel; and the skill and energy of the British navy were taxed to the utmost to prevent that consummation.

Now, France, as a matter of fact, had a great fleet, but it was scattered, and lying imprisoned, in fragments, in widely separated ports. There were twelve ships of the line in Toulon, twenty in Brest, five in Rochefort, yet other five in Ferrol; and the problem for Napoleon was, somehow, to set these imprisoned squadrons free, and assemble them for twenty-four hours off Boulogne. The British policy, on the other hand, was to maintain a sleepless blockade of these ports, and keep the French fleet sealed up in scattered and helpless fragments. The battle for the Straits of Dover, the British naval chiefs held, must be fought off Brest and Ferrol and Toulon; and never in the history of the world were blockades so vigilant, and stern, and sleepless maintained.

Nelson spent two years battling with the fierce north-westers of the Gulf of Lyons, keeping watch over a great French squadron in Toulon, and from May 1803 to August 1805 left his ship only three times, and for less than an hour on each occasion. The watch kept by Cornwallis off Brest, through summer and winter, for nearly three years, Mahan declares, has never, for constancy and vigilance, been excelled, perhaps never equalled, in the history of blockades. The hardship of these long sea-watches was terrible. It was waging a fight with weariness and brain-paralysing monotony, with cold and scurvy and tempest, as well as with human foes. Collingwood was once twenty-two months at sea without dropping anchor. In seventeen years of sea service—between 1793 and 1810—he was only twelve months in England.

The wonder is that the seamen of that day did not grow web-footed, or forget what solid ground felt like! Colingwood tells his wife in one letter that he had "not seen a green leaf on a tree" for fourteen months! By way of compensation, these long and stern blockades developed such a race of seamen as perhaps the world has never seen before or since; exhaustless of resource, hardy, tireless, familiar with every turn of sea life, of iron frame and an iron courage which neither tempest nor battle could shake. Great Britain, as a matter of fact, won her naval battles, not because she had better ships or heavier guns than her enemies, but only because she trained a finer race of seamen. Says Brenton, himself a gallant sailor of the period, "I have seen Spanish line-of-battle ships twenty-four hours unmooring; as many minutes are sufficient for a well-manned British ship to perform the same operation. When, on any grand ceremony, they found it necessary to cross their top-gallant yards in harbour, they began the day before; we cross ours in one minute from the deck."

But it was these iron blockades that in the long-run thwarted the plans of Napoleon and changed the fate of the world. Cornwallis off Brest, Collingwood off Rochefort, Pellew off Ferrol, Nelson before Toulon, fighting the wild gales of the Bay of Biscay and the fierce north-westers of the Gulf of Lyons, in what Mahan calls "that tremendous and sustained vigilance which reached its utmost tension in the years preceding Trafalgar," really saved England. "Those far-distant, storm-beaten ships, upon which the Grand Army never looked," says Mahan, "stood between it and the dominion of the world."

An intellect so subtle and combative as Napoleon's was, of course, strained to the utmost to break or cheat the British blockades, and the story of the one crafty ruse after another which he employed to beguile the British leaders is very remarkable. Even more remarkable, perhaps, is the manner in which these plain-minded, business-like British seamen, for whose mental powers Napoleon cherished the deepest contempt, fathomed his plans and shattered his combinations.

Napoleon's first plot was decidedly clever. He gathered in Brest 20,000 troops, ostensibly for a descent upon Ireland. This, he calculated, would preoccupy Cornwallis, and prevent him moving. The Toulon fleet was to run out with the first north-west wind, and, as long as a British look-out ship was in sight, would steer east, as though making for Egypt; but when beyond sight of British eyes the fleet was to swing round, run through the Straits, be joined off Cadiz by the Rochefort squadron, and sweep, a great fleet of at least sixteen sail of the line, past the Scilly Islands to Boulogne. Napoleon calculated that Nelson would be racing in the direction of Egypt, Cornwallis would be redoubling his vigilance before Brest, at the exact moment the great Boulogne flotilla was carrying its 130,000 invading Frenchmen to Dover! Napoleon put the one French admiral as to whose resolve and daring he was sure—Latouche Tréville—in command of the Toulon fleet; but before the moment for action came Tréville died, and Napoleon had to fall back upon a weaker man, Villeneuve.

He changed his plans to suit the qualities of his new admiral—the Toulon and Rochefort squadrons were to break out, sail separately to a rendezvous in the West Indies, and, once joined, spread havoc through the British possessions there. "I think," wrote Napoleon, "that the sailing of these twenty ships of the line will oblige the English to despatch over thirty in pursuit." So the blockades everywhere would be weakened, and the Toulon and Rochefort squadrons, doubling back to Europe, were to raise the blockade off Ferrol and Brest, and the Brest squadron was to land 18,000 troops, under Augereau, in Ireland, while the Grand Army of Boulogne was to cross the Straits, with Napoleon at its head. Thus Great Britain and Ireland would be invaded simultaneously.

The trouble was to set the scheme going by the release of the Toulon and Rochefort squadrons. Nelson's correspondence shows that he guessed Napoleon's strategy. If the Toulon fleet broke loose, he wrote, he was sure its course would be held for the Atlantic, and thither he would follow it. In the meanwhile he kept guard so steadfastly that the great French strategy could not get itself started. In December 1804 war broke out betwixt Britain and Spain, and this gave Napoleon a new ally and a new fleet. Napoleon found he had nearly sixty line-of-battle ships, French or Spanish, to weave into his combinations, and he framed—to use Mahan's words—" upon lines equal, both in boldness and scope, to those of the Marengo and Austerlitz campaigns, the immense strategy which resulted in Trafalgar." The Toulon and Rochefort squadrons, as before, were to break out separately, rendezvous in the West Indies, return by a different route to European waters, pick up the French and Spanish ships in Ferrol, and then sweep through the narrow seas.

The Rochefort squadron duly escaped; Villeneuve, too, in command of the Toulon squadron, aided by the weather, evaded Nelson's watchfulness and disappeared towards the east. Nelson, however, suspected the real plan, and with fine insight took up a position which must have intercepted Villeneuve; but that admiral found the weather too rough for his ships, and ran back into Toulon. "These gentlemen," said Nelson, " are not accustomed to a Gulf of Lyons gale. We have faced them for twenty-one months, and not lost a spar!" The Rochefort squadron was, of course, left by its own success wandering in space, a mere cluster of sea-vagrants.

By March 1805, Napoleon had a new combination prepared. In the ports between Brest and Toulon were scattered no less than sixty-seven French or Spanish ships of the line. Ganteaume, with his squadron, was to break out from Brest; Villeneuve, with his, from

Toulon; both fleets were to rendezvous at Martinique, return by an unusual route, and appear off Boulogne, a great fleet of thirty-five French ships of the line.

About the end of June the Toulon fleet got safely out—Nelson being, for once, badly served by his frigates—picked up additional ships off Cadiz, and disappeared on its route to the West Indies. Nelson, misled by false intelligence, first went eastward, then had to claw back through the Straits of Gibraltar in the teeth of strong westerly gales, and plunged over the horizon in fierce pursuit of Villeneuve. But the watch kept by Cornwallis over Ganteaume in Brest was so close and stern that escape was impossible, and one-half of Napoleon's combination broke down. Napoleon despatched swift ships on Villeneuve's track, summoning him back to Ferrol, where he would find a squadron of fifteen French and Spanish ships ready to join him. Villeneuve, Napoleon believed, had thoroughly deceived Nelson. "Those boasted English," he wrote, "who claim to know of everything, know nothing of it," *i.e.* of Villeneuve's escape and course. But the "boasted English," as a matter of fact, did know all about it, and in place of weakening their forces in the Bay of Biscay, strengthened them. Meanwhile Nelson, with ten ships of the line, was hard on the track of Villeneuve with eighteen. At Barbadoes, Nelson was sent a hundred miles out of his course by false intelligence, and that hundred miles just enabled Villeneuve to double back towards Europe.

Nelson divined this plan, and followed him with the fiercest energy, sending off, meanwhile, his fastest brig to warn the Admiralty. Villeneuve, if he picked up the Ferrol and Rochefort squadrons, would arrive off Brest with forty line-of-battle ships; if he raised the blockade, and added Ganteaume's squadron to his own, he might appear off Boulogne with sixty great ships! Napoleon calculated on British blunders to aid him. "We have not to do with a far-sighted, but with a very proud Government," he wrote. The blunder Napoleon hoped the British Admiralty would make was that of weakening the blockading squadrons in order to pursue Villeneuve's fleet, and thus release the imprisoned French squadrons, making a great concentration possible.

But this was exactly the blunder into which the Admiralty refused to be tempted. When the news that Villeneuve was on his way back to Europe reached the Admiralty, the First Lord, Barham, an old sailor, eighty years of age, without waiting to dress himself, dictated orders which, without weakening the blockades at any vital point, planted a fleet, under Sir Robert Calder, west of Finisterre, and right in Villeneuve's track; and if Calder had been Nelson, Trafalgar might have been fought on July 22, instead of October 21. Calder fought, and captured two of Villeneuve's ships, but failed to prevent the junction of Villeneuve's fleet with the squadron in Ferrol, and was court-martialled for his failure—victory though he called it. But this partial failure does not make less splendid the promptitude shown by the British Admiralty. "The English Admiralty," Napoleon reasoned, "could not decide the movements of its squadron in twenty-four hours." As a matter of fact, Barham decided the British strategy in almost as many minutes!

Meanwhile Nelson had reached the scene; and, like his ship, worn out with labours, sailed for Portsmouth, for what proved his last visit to England. On August 13, Villeneuve sailed from Ferrol with twenty-nine ships. He had his choice between Brest, where Cornwallis was keeping guard, with Boulogne beyond, and where Napoleon was watching eagerly for the white topsails of his fleet; or Cadiz, where Collingwood with a tiny squadron held the Spanish fleet strictly bottled up.

Villeneuve's true course was Boulogne, but Cornwallis lay in his path with over thirty sail of the line, and Villeneuve's nerve failed him. On August 21 he swung round and bore up for Cadiz; and with the turn of the helm which swung Villeneuve's ship away from Boulogne, Napoleon's last chance of invading England vanished. Villeneuve pushed Collingwood's tiny squadron aside and entered Cadiz, where the combined fleet now numbered nearly forty ships of the line, and Collingwood, with delightful coolness, solemnly resumed his blockade—four ships, that is, blockading forty! Napoleon gave way to a tempest of rage when his fleet failed to appear off Boulogne, and he realised that the British sailors he despised had finally thwarted his strategy. A French writer has told how Daru, his secretary, found him walking up and down his cabinet with agitated steps. With a voice that shook, and in half-strangled exclamations, he cried, "What a navy! What sacrifices for nothing! What an admiral! All hope is gone! That Villeneuve, instead of entering the Channel, has taken refuge in Ferrol. It is all over. He will be blockaded there." Then with that swift and terrible power of decision in which he has never been surpassed, he flung the long-cherished plan of invading England out of his brain, and dictated the orders which launched his troops on the road which led to Austerlitz and Jena, and, beyond, to the flames of Moscow and the snows of the great retreat, and which finally led Napoleon himself to St. Helena. Villeneuve's great fleet meanwhile lay idle in Cadiz, till, on October 20, the ill-fated French admiral led his ships out to meet Nelson in his last great sea-fight.

II. HOW THE FLEETS MET

"Wherever the gleams of an English fire
  On an English roof-tree shine,
Wherever the fire of a youth's desire
  Is laid upon Honour's shrine,
Wherever brave deeds are treasured and told,
  In the tale of the deeds of yore,
Like jewels of price in a chain of gold
  Are the name and the fame he bore.

Wherever the track of our English ships
  Lies white on the ocean foam,
His name is sweet to our English lips
  As the names of the flowers at home;
Wherever the heart of an English boy
  Grows big with a deed of worth,
Such names as his name have begot the same,
  Such hearts will bring it to birth."
—E. NESBIT.

IT was the night of October 20, 1805, a night moonless and black. In the narrow waters at the western throat of the Straits of Gibraltar, at regular intervals of three minutes through the whole night, the deep voice of a gun broke out and swept, a pulse of dying sound, almost to either coast, while at every half-hour a rocket soared aloft and broke in a curve of stars in the black sky. It was one of Nelson's repeating frigates signalling to the British fleet, far off to the south-west, Villeneuve's movements. Nelson for more than a week had been trying to daintily coax Villeneuve out of Cadiz, as an angler might try to coax a much-experienced trout from the cool depths of some deep pool. He kept the main body of his fleet sixty leagues distant—west of Cape St. Mary—but kept a chain of frigates within signalling distance of each other betwixt Cadiz and himself. He allowed the news that he had detached five of his line-of-battle ships on convoy duty to the eastward to leak through to the French admiral, but succeeded in keeping him in ignorance of the fact that he had called in under his flag five ships of equal force from the westward.

On October 19, Villeneuve, partly driven by hunger, and by the news that a successor was on the road from Paris to displace him, and partly tempted by the belief that he had before him a British fleet of only twenty-one ships of the line, crept out of Cadiz with thirty-three ships of the line—of which three were three-deckers—and seven frigates. Nelson had twenty-seven sail of the line with four frigates. The wind was light, and all through the 20th, Villeneuve's fleet, formed in seven columns—the *Santissima Trinidad* towering like a giant amongst them—moved slowly eastward. Nelson would not alarm his foe by making too early an appearance over the sky-line. His frigates signalled to him every few minutes, through sixty miles of sea-air, the enemy's movements; but Nelson himself held aloof till Villeneuve was too far from Cadiz to make a dash back to it and safety. All through the night of the 20th, Villeneuve's great fleet—a procession of mighty phantoms—was dimly visible against the Spanish coast, and the British frigates sent the news in alternate pulses of sound and flame to Nelson, by this time eagerly bearing up from Cape St. Mary.

The morning of the 21st broke misty, yet bright. The sea was almost like a floor of glass. The faintest of sea-airs blew. A lazy Atlantic swell rolled at long intervals towards the Straits, and the two fleets at last were visible to each other. Villeneuve's ships stretched a waving and slightly curved line, running north and south, with no regularity of order. The British fleet, in two compact and parallel columns, half a mile apart, came majestically on from the west. The ships in each column followed each other so closely that sometimes the bow of one was thrust past the quarter of the ship in advance of it. Nelson, in the *Victory*, headed one column, Collingwood, in the *Royal Sovereign*, led the other, and each flagship, it was to be noted, led with a clear interval between itself and its supports.

Villeneuve had a tactician's brain, and his battle-plan was admirable. In a general order, issued just before leading out his fleet, he told his captains, "There is nothing to alarm us in the sight of an English fleet. Their 64-gun ships have not 500 men on board; they are not more brave than we are; they are harassed by a two-years' cruise; they have fewer motives to fight well!" Villeneuve explained that the enemy would attack in column, the French would meet the attack in close line of battle; and, with a touch of Nelson's spirit, he urged his captains to take every opportunity of boarding, and warned them that every ship not under fire would be counted a defaulter.

Nelson's plan was simple and daring. The order of sailing was to be the order of battle. Collingwood leading one column, and he the other, would pierce the enemy's lines at points which would leave some twelve of the enemy's ships to be crushed betwixt the two British lines. Nelson, whose brooding genius forecast every changing eddy of battle, gave minute instructions on a score of details. To prevent mistakes amid the smoke and the fight, for example, he had the hoops on the masts of every British ship painted yellow; every ship was directed to fly a St. George's ensign, with the Union Jack at the fore-topmast, and another flying from the top-gallant stays. That he would beat the enemy's fleet he calmly took for granted, but he directed that every effort should be made to capture its commander-in-chief. Nelson crowned his instructions with the characteristic remark, that "in case signals were obscure, no captain can do wrong if he places his ship alongside of an enemy."

By twelve o'clock the two huge fleets were slowly approaching each other: the British columns compact, grim, orderly; the Franco-Spanish line loose, but magnificently picturesque, a far-stretching line of lofty hulls, a swaying forest of sky-piercing masts. They still preserve the remark of one prosaic British sailor, who, surveying the enemy through an open port, offered the comment, "What a fine sight, Bill, yon ships would make at Spithead!"

It is curious to reflect how exactly both British and French invert on sea their land tactics. French infantry attack in column, and are met by British infantry in line; and the line, with its steadfast courage and wide front of fire, crushes the column. On sea, on the other hand, the British attack in column, and the French meet the attack in line; but the column wins. But it must be admitted that the peril of this method of attack is enormous. The leading ship approaches, stem on, to a line of fire which, if steady enough, may

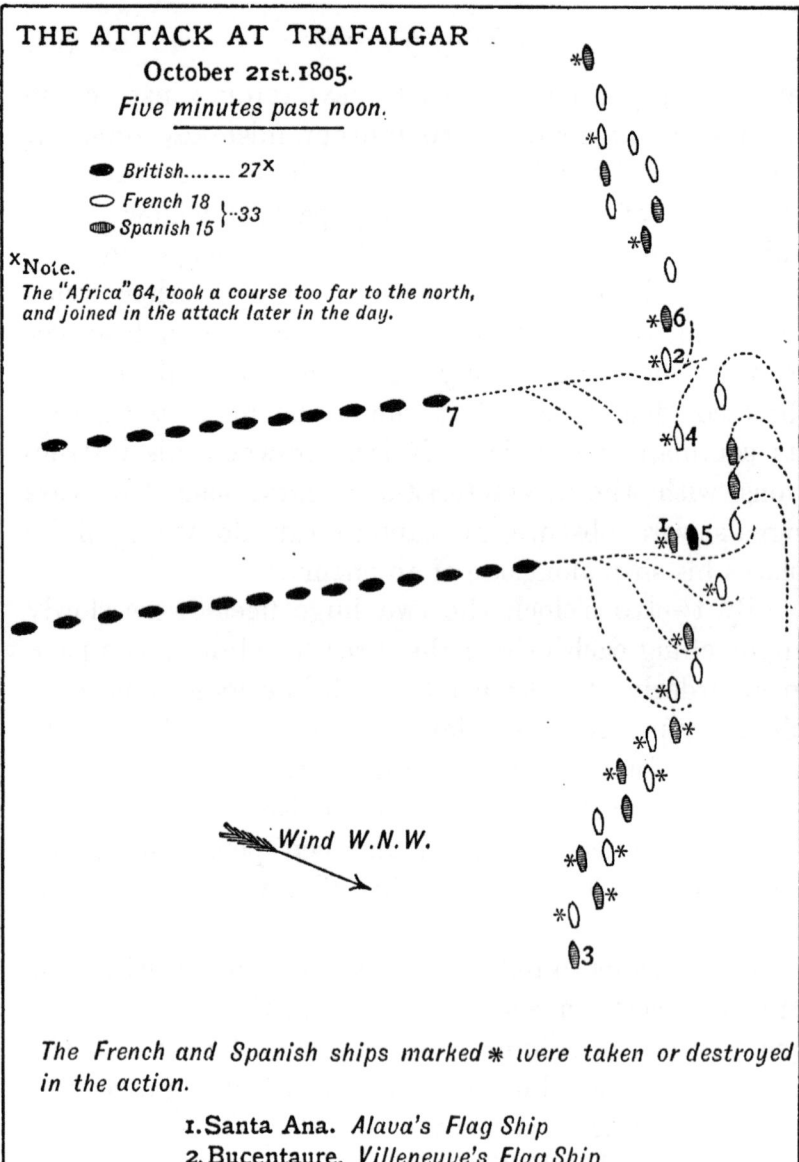

THE ATTACK AT TRAFALGAR

October 21st. 1805.

Five minutes past noon.

- British....... 27 ˣ
- ○ French 18 ⎫ ..33
- ⬬ Spanish 15 ⎭

ˣ Note.
The "Africa" 64, took a course too far to the north, and joined in the attack later in the day.

Wind W.N.W.

The French and Spanish ships marked * were taken or destroyed in the action.

1. Santa Ana. *Alava's Flag Ship*
2. Bucentaure. *Villeneuve's Flag Ship*
3. Principe de Asturias. *Gravina's Flag Ship*
4. Redoutable
5. Royal Sovereign. *Collingwood's Flag Ship*
6. Santisima Trinidad.
7. Victory. *Nelson's Flag Ship*

from Mahan's "Life of Nelson" Walker & Boutall sc.

well crush her by its concentration of flame. Attack in column, in fact, means that the leading ships are sacrificed to secure victory for the ships in the rear. The risks of this method of attack at Trafalgar were enormously increased by the light and uncertain quality of the wind. Collingwood, in the *Royal Sovereign*, and Nelson, in the *Victory*, as a matter of fact, drifted slowly rather than sailed, stem on to the broadsides of their enemy. The leading British ships, with their stately heights of swelling canvas, moved into the raking fire of the far-stretching Franco-Spanish line at a speed of about two knots an hour. His officers knew that Nelson's ship, carrying the flag of the commander-in-chief, as it came slowly on, would be the mark for every French gunner, and must pass through a tempest of flame before it could fire a shot in reply; and Blackwood begged Nelson to let the *Téméraire*—" the fighting *Téméraire*"—take the *Victory's* place at the head of the column. "Oh yes, let her go ahead," answered Nelson, with a queer smile; and the *Téméraire* was hailed, and ordered to take the lead. But Nelson meant that the *Téméraire* should take the *Victory's* place only if she could, and he watched grimly to see that not a sheet was let fly or a sail shortened to give the *Téméraire* a chance of passing; and so the *Victory* kept its proud and perilous lead.

Collingwood led the lee division, and had the honour of beginning the mighty drama of Trafalgar. The *Royal Sovereign* was newly coppered, and, with every inch of canvas outspread, got so far ahead of her followers, that after Collingwood had broken into the French line, he sustained its fire, unhelped, for nearly twenty minutes before the *Belleisle*, the ship next following, could fire a gun for his help.

Of Collingwood, Thackeray says, "I think, since Heaven made gentlemen, it never made a better one than Cuthbert Collingwood," and there was, no doubt, a knightly and chivalrous side to Collingwood worthy of King Arthur's round table. But there was also a side of heavy-footed common-sense, of Dutch-like frugality, in Collingwood, a sort of wooden-headed unimaginativeness which looks humorous when set against the background of such a planet-shaking fight as Trafalgar. Thus on the morning of the fight he advised one of his lieutenants, who wore a pair of boots, to follow his example and put on stockings and shoes, as, in the event of being shot in the leg, it would, he explained, "be so much more manageable for the surgeon." And as he walked the break of his poop in tights, silk stockings, and buckled shoes, leading, in his single ship, an attack on a fleet, he calmly munched an apple. To be able to munch an apple when beginning Trafalgar is an illustration of what may be called the quality of wooden-headed unimaginativeness in Collingwood. And yet Collingwood had a sense of the scale of the drama in which he was taking part. "Now, gentlemen," he said to his officers, "let us do something to-day which the world may talk of hereafter." Collingwood, in reality, was a great man and a great seaman, and in the battle which followed he "fought like an angel," to quote the amusingly inappropriate metaphor of Blackwood.

The two majestic British columns moved slowly on, the great ships, with ports hauled up and guns run out, following each other like a procession of giants. "I suppose," says Codrington, who commanded the *Orion*, "no man ever before saw such a sight." And the element of humour was added to the scene by the spectacle of the tiny *Pickle*, a duodecimo schooner, gravely hanging on to the quarter of an 80-gun ship—as an actor in the fight describes it—" with the boarding-nettings up, and her tompions out of her four guns—about as large and as formidable as two pairs of Wellington boots."

Collingwood bore down to the fight a clear quarter of a mile ahead of the next ship. The fire of the enemy, like so many spokes of flame converging to a centre, broke upon him. But in silence the great ship moved ahead to a gap in the line between the *Santa Anna*, a huge black hulk of 112 guns, and the *Neptune*, of 74. As the bowsprit of the *Royal Sovereign* slowly glided past the stern of the *Santa Anna*, Collingwood, as Nelson had ordered all his captains, cut his studding-sails loose, and they fell, a cloud of white canvas, into the water. Then as the broadside of the *Royal Sovereign* fairly covered the stern of the *Santa Anna*, Collingwood spoke. He poured with deadly aim and suddenness, and at pistol-shot distance, his whole broadside into the Spaniard's stern. The tempest of shot swept the unhappy *Santa Anna* from end to end, and practically destroyed that vessel. Some 400 of its crew are said to have been killed or wounded by that single discharge! At the same moment Collingwood discharged his other broadside at the *Neptune*, though with less effect; then swinging round broadside to broadside on the Spanish ship, he swept its decks again and again with his guns. The first broadside had practically done the Spaniard's business; but its captain, a gallant man, still returned what fire he could. All the enemy's ships within reach of Collingwood had meanwhile opened on him a dreadful fire; no fewer than five line-of-battle ships were emptying their guns upon the *Royal Sovereign* at one time, and it seemed marvellous that the British ship was not shattered to mere splinters by the fire poured from so many quarters upon her. It was like being in the heart of a volcano. Frequently, it is said, the British saw the flying cannon-balls meet in mid-air. The seamen fell fast, the sails were torn, the bulwarks shattered, the decks ran red with blood. It was at that precise moment, however, that Collingwood said to his captain, "What would not Nelson give to be here!" While at the same instant Nelson was saying to Hardy, "See how that noble fellow Collingwood takes his ship into action!"

The other ships of Collingwood's column were by this time slowly drifting into the fight. At a quarter past twelve the *Belleisle*, the next ship, ranged under the stern of the unfortunate *Santa Anna*, and fired her larboard guns, double shotted, into that ship, with the result that her three masts fell over the side. She then steered for the *Indomptable*, an 80-gun ship, and sustained at the same moment the fire of two Spanish seventy-fours. Ship after ship of Collingwood's column came steadily up, and the roar of the battle deepened as in quick-following crashes each new line-of-battle ship broke into the thunder of broadsides.

Nelson, leading the weather column, steered a trifle to the northward, as the slowly moving line of the enemy pointed towards Cadiz. Nelson had given his last orders. At his mainmast head was flying, fast belayed, the signal,

"Engage the enemy more closely." Nelson himself walked quietly to and fro on the little patch of clear plank, scarcely seven yards long, on the quarter-deck of the *Victory*, whence he could command the whole ship, and he wore the familiar threadbare frock uniform coat, bearing on the left breast four tarnished and lack-lustre stars. Then came the incident of the immortal signal. "We must give the fleet," said Nelson to Blackwood, "something by way of a fillip." After musing a while, he said, "Suppose we signal, 'Nelson confides that every man will do his duty'?" Some one suggested "England" instead of "Nelson," and Nelson at once caught at the improvement. The signal-officer explained that the word "confide" would have to be spelt, and suggested instead the word "expects," as that was in the vocabulary. So the flags on the masthead of the *Victory* spelt out the historic sentence to the slowly moving fleet. That the signal was "received with cheers" is scarcely accurate. The message was duly acknowledged, and recorded in the log of every ship, but perhaps not one man in every hundred of the actors at Trafalgar knew at the moment that it had been sent. But the message rings in British ears yet, across ninety years, and will ring in the ears of generations yet unborn.

Nelson led his column on a somewhat slanting course into the fight. He was bent on laying himself alongside the flagship of the enemy, and he knew that this must be one of the three great line-of-battle ships near the huge *Santissima Trinidad*. But there was no sign to show which of the three carried Villeneuve. At half-past twelve the ships upon which the *Victory* was moving began to fire single shots at her slowly drifting hulk to discover whether she was within range. The seventh of these shots, fired at intervals of a minute or so, tore a rent through the upper canvas of the *Victory*—a rent still to be seen in the carefully preserved sail. A couple of minutes of awful silence followed. Slowly the *Victory* drifted on its path, and then no fewer than eight of the great ships upon which the *Victory* was moving broke into such a tempest of shot as perhaps never before was poured on a single ship. One of the first shots killed Scott, Nelson's secretary; another cut down eight marines standing in line on the *Victory's* quarter-deck; a third passed between Nelson and Hardy as they stood side by side. "Too warm work to last long, Hardy," said Nelson, with a smile. Still the *Victory* drifted majestically on its fiery path without an answering gun.

The French line was irregular at this point, the ships lying, in some instances, two or three deep, and this made the business of "cutting" the line difficult. As Nelson could not pick out the French flagship, he said to Hardy, "Take your choice, go on board which you please;" and Hardy pointed the stem of the *Victory* towards a gap between the *Redoutable*, a 74-gun ship, and the *Bucentaure*. But the ship moved slowly. The fire upon it was tremendous. One shot drove a shower of splinters upon both Nelson and Hardy; nearly fifty men and officers had been killed or wounded; the *Victory's* sails were riddled, her studding-sail booms shot off close to the yard-arm, her mizzen-topmast shot away. At one o'clock, however, the *Victory* slowly moved past the stern of the *Bucentaure*, and a

68-pounder carronade on its forecastle, charged with a round shot and a keg of 500 musket balls, was fired into the cabin windows of the French ship. Then, as the great ship moved on, every gun of the remaining fifty that formed its broadside—some of them double and treble loaded—was fired through the Frenchman's cabin windows.

The dust from the crumpled woodwork of the *Bucentaure's* stern covered the persons of Nelson and the group of officers standing on the *Victory's* quarter-deck, while the British sailors welcomed with a fierce shout the crash their flying shot made within the Frenchman's hull. The *Bucentaure*, as it happened—though Nelson was ignorant of the fact—was the French flagship; and after the battle its officers declared that by this single broadside, out of its crew of nearly 1000 men, nearly 400 were struck down, and no less than twenty guns dismounted!

But the *Neptune*, a fine French 80-gun ship, lay right across the water-lane up which the *Victory* was moving, and it poured upon the British ship two raking broadsides of the most deadly quality. The *Victory*, however, moved on unflinchingly, and the *Neptune*, fearing to be run aboard by the British ship, set her jib and moved ahead; then the *Victory* swung to starboard on to the *Redoutable*. The French ship fired one hurried broadside, and promptly shut her lower-deck ports, fearing the British sailors would board through them. No fewer, indeed, than five French line-of-battle ships during the fight, finding themselves grinding sides with British ships, adopted the same course—an expressive testimony to the enterprising quality of British sailors. The *Victory*, however, with her lower-deck guns actually touching the side of the *Redoutable*, still kept them in full and quick action; but at each of the lower-deck ports stood a sailor with a bucket of water, and when the gun was fired—its muzzle touching the wooden sides of the *Redoutable*—the water was dashed upon the ragged hole made by the shot, to prevent the Frenchman taking fire and both ships being consumed.

The guns on the upper deck of the *Victory* speedily swept and silenced the upper deck of the *Redoutable*, and as far as its broadsides were concerned, that ship was helpless. Its tops, however, were crowded with marksmen, and armed with brass coehorns, firing langrage shot, and these scourged with a pitiless and most deadly fire the decks of the *Victory*, while the *Bucentaure* and the gigantic *Santissima Trinidad* also thundered on the British flagship.

III. HOW THE VICTORY WAS WON

> "All is over and done.
> Render thanks to the Giver;
> England, for thy son
> Let the bell be toll'd.
> Render thanks to the Giver,
> And render him to the mould.
> Under the cross of gold
> That shines over city and river,
> There he shall rest for ever
> Among the wise and the bold."
> —TENNYSON.

NELSON'S strategy at Trafalgar is described quaintly, but with real insight, in a sentence which a Spanish novelist, Don Perez Galdos, puts into the mouth of one of his characters: "Nelson, who, as everybody knows, was no fool, saw our long line and said, 'Ah, if I break through that in two places, and put the part of it between the two places between two fires, I shall grab every stick of it.' That was exactly what the confounded fellow did. And as our line was so long that the head couldn't help the tail, he worried us from end to end, while he drove his two wedges into our body." It followed that the flaming vortex of the fight was in that brief mile of sea-space, between the two points where the parallel British lines broke through Villeneuve's swaying forest of masts. And the tempest of sound and flame was fiercest, of course, round the two ships that carried the flags of Nelson and Collingwood. As each stately British liner, however, drifted—rather than sailed—into the black pall of smoke, the roar of the fight deepened and widened until the whole space between the *Royal Sovereign* and the *Victory* was shaken with mighty pulse-beats of sound that marked the furious and quick-following broadsides.

The scene immediately about the *Victory* was very remarkable. The *Victory* had run foul of the *Redoutable*, the anchors of the two ships hooking into each other. The concussion of the broadsides would, no doubt, have driven the two hulls apart, but that the *Victory's* studding-sail boom iron had fastened, like a claw, into the leech of the Frenchman's fore-topsail. The *Téméraire*, coming majestically up through the smoke, raked the *Bucentaure*, and closed with a crash on the starboard side of the *Redoutable*, and the four great ships lay in a solid tier, while between their huge grinding sides came, with a sound and a glare almost resembling the blast of an exploding mine, the flash, the smoke, the roar of broadside after broadside.

In the whole heroic fight there is no finer bit of heroism than that shown by the *Redoutable*. She was only a 74-gun ship, and she had the *Victory*, of 100 guns, and the *Téméraire*, of 98, on either side. It is true these ships had to fight at the same time with a whole ring of antagonists; nevertheless, the fire poured on the *Redoutable* was so fierce that only courage of a steel-like edge and temper could have sustained it. The gallant French ship was semi-dismasted, her hull shot through in every direction, one-fourth of her guns were dismounted. Out of a crew of 643, no fewer than 522 were killed or wounded. Only 35, indeed, lived to reach England as prisoners. And yet she fought on. The fire from her great guns, indeed, soon ceased, but the deadly splutter of musketry from such of her tops as were yet standing was maintained; and, as Brenton put it, "there was witnessed for nearly an hour and a half the singular spectacle of a French 74-gun ship engaging a British first and second rate, with small-arms only."

As a matter of fact, the *Victory* repeatedly ceased firing, believing that the *Redoutable* had struck, but still the venomous and deadly fire from the tops of that vessel continued; and it was to this circumstance, indeed, that Nelson owed his death. He would never put small-arms men in his own tops, as he believed their fire interfered with the working of the sails, and, indeed, ran the risk of igniting them. Thus the French marksmen that crowded the tops of the *Redoutable* had it all their own way; and as the distance was short, and their aim deadly, nearly every man on the poop, quarter-deck, and forecastle of the *Victory* was shot down.

Nelson, with Hardy by his side, was walking backwards and forwards on a little clear space of the *Victory's* quarter-deck, when he suddenly swung round and fell face downwards on the deck. Hardy picked him up. "They have done for me at last, Hardy," said Nelson; "my backbone is shot through." A musket bullet from the *Redoutable's* mizzen-top—only fifteen yards distant—had passed through the forepart of the epaulette, smashed a path through the left shoulder, and lodged in the spine. The evidence seems to make it clear that it was a chance shot that wrought the fatal mischief. Hardy had twice the bulk of Nelson's insignificant figure, and wore a more striking uniform, and would certainly have attracted the aim of a marksman in preference to Nelson.

Few stories are more pathetic or more familiar than that of Nelson's last moments. As they carried the dying hero across the blood-splashed decks, and down the ladders into the cock-pit, he drew a handkerchief over his own face and over the stars on his breast, lest the knowledge that he was struck down should discourage his crew. He was stripped, his wound probed, and it was at once known to be mortal. Nelson suffered greatly; he was consumed with thirst, had to be fanned with sheets of paper; and he kept constantly pushing away the sheet, the sole covering over him, saying, "Fan, fan," or "Drink, drink," and one attendant was constantly employed in drawing the sheet over his thin limbs and emaciated body. Presently Hardy, snatching a moment from the fight raging on the deck, came to his side, and the two comrades clasped hands. "Well, Hardy, how goes the battle?" Nelson asked. He was told that twelve or fourteen of the enemy's ships had struck. "That is well," said Nelson, "but I had bargained for twenty." Then his seaman's brain forecasting the change of weather, and picturing the battered ships with their prizes on a lee shore, he exclaimed emphatically, "Anchor! Hardy, anchor!" Hardy hinted that Collingwood would take charge of affairs. "Not while I live, I hope, Hardy," said the dying chief, trying to raise himself on his bed. "No! do you anchor, Hardy."

Many of Nelson's expressions, recorded by his doctor, Beatty, are strangely touching. "I am a dead man, Hardy," he said. "I am going fast. It will all be over with me soon." "O *Victory, Victory*," he said, as the great ship shook to the roar of her own guns, "how you distract my poor brain!" "How dear is life to all men!" he said, after a pause. He begged that "his carcass might be sent to England, and not thrown overboard." So in the dim cock-pit, with the roar of the great battle —bellow of gun, and shout of cheering crews—filling all the space about him, and his last thoughts yet busy for his country, the soul of the greatest British seaman passed away. "Kiss me, Hardy," was one of his last sentences. His last intelligible sentence was, "I have done my duty; I praise God for it."

It may interest many to read the prayer which Nelson wrote—the last record, but one, he made in his diary—and written as the final act of preparation for Trafalgar: "May the great God, whom I worship, grant to my country, and for the benefit of Europe in general, a great and glorious victory; and may no misconduct in any one tarnish it; and may humanity after victory be the predominant feature in the British fleet. For myself individually, I commit my life to Him that made me, and may His blessing alight on my endeavours for serving my country faithfully. To Him I resign myself, and the just cause which is entrusted to me to defend. Amen, Amen, Amen."

Nelson's plan allowed his captains a large discretion in the choice of their antagonists. Each British ship had to follow the wake of her leader till she reached the enemy's line, then her captain was free to choose his own foe—which, naturally, was the biggest Frenchman or Spaniard in sight. And the huge *Santissima Trinidad*, of course, attracted the eager attention of the ships that immediately followed the *Victory*. The Spaniard carried 140 guns, and in that swaying continent of fighting ships, towered like a giant amongst dwarfs. The *Neptune*, the *Leviathan*, and the *Conqueror*, in turn, hung on the quarter or broadside of the gigantic Spaniard, scourged it with fire, and then drifted off to engage in a fiery wrestle with some other antagonist. By half-past two the Spanish four-decker was a mastless wreck. The *Neptune* at that moment was hanging on her bow, the *Conqueror* on her quarter. "This tremendous fabric," says an account written by an officer on board the *Conqueror*, "gave a deep roll, with a swell to leeward, then back to windward, and on her return every mast went by the board, leaving her an unmanageable hulk on the water. Her immense topsails had every reef out, her royals were sheeted home but lowered, and the falling of this majestic mass of spars, sails, and rigging plunging into the water at the muzzles of our guns, was one of the most magnificent sights I ever beheld. Directly after this a Spaniard waved an English union over the lee gangway of the *Santissima Trinidad* in token of surrender; whereupon the *Conqueror*, scorning to waste time in taking possession of even a four-decker that had no longer any fight in it, pushed off in search of a new foe; while the *Neptune's* crew proceeded to shift the tattered topsails of their ship for new ones, with as much coolness as though in a friendly port.

The *Africa*, sixty-four, less than half the size of the Spaniard, presently came slowly up through the smoke, and fired into the Spanish ship; then seeing no flag flying, sent a lieutenant on board the mastless hulk to take possession. The Englishman climbed to the quarter-deck, all black with smoke and bloody with slaughter, and asked the solitary officer he found there whether or not the *Santissima Trinidad* had surrendered. The ship, as a matter of fact, was drifting into the centre of a cluster of French and Spanish ships; so the Spaniard replied, "Non, non," at the same time pointing to the friendly ships upon which they were drifting. The Englishman had only half-a-dozen men with him, so he coolly returned to his boat, and the *Santissima Trinidad* drifted like a log upon the water till half-past five P.M., when the *Prince* put a prize crew on board.

Perez Galdos has given a realistic picture—quoted in the *Cornhill Magazine*—of the scenes within the gloomy recesses of the great Spanish four-decker as the British ships hung on her flanks and wasted her with their fire: "The English shot had torn our sails to tatters. It was as if huge invisible talons had been dragging at them. Fragments of spars, splinters of wood, thick hempen cables cut up as corn is cut by the sickle, fallen blocks, shreds of canvas, bits of iron, and hundreds of other things that had been wrenched away by the enemy's fire, were piled along the deck, where it was scarcely possible to move about. From moment to moment men fell—some into the sea; and the curses of the combatants mingled with groans of the wounded, so that it was often difficult to decide whether the dying were blaspheming God or the fighters were calling upon Him for aid. I helped in the very dismal task of carrying the wounded into the hold, where the surgeons worked. Some died ere we could convey them thither; others had to undergo frightful operations ere their worn-out bodies could get an instant's rest. It was much more satisfactory to be able to assist the carpenter's crew in temporarily stopping some of the holes torn by shot in the ship's hull. . . . Blood ran in streams about the deck; and, in spite of the sand, the rolling of the ship carried it hither and thither until it made strange patterns on the planks. The enemy's shot, fired, as they were, from very short range, caused horrible mutilations. . . . The ship creaked and groaned as she rolled, and through a thousand holes and crevices in her strained hull the sea spurted in and began to flood the hold. The *Trinidad's* people saw the commander-in-chief haul down his flag; heard the *Achille* blow up and hurl her six hundred men into eternity; learnt that their own hold was so crowded with wounded that no more could be received there. Then, when all three masts had in succession been brought crashing down, the defence collapsed, and the *Santissima Trinidad* struck her flag."

The dreadful scenes on the decks of the *Santissima Trinidad* might almost have been paralleled on some of the British ships. Thus the *Belleisle*, Collingwood's immediate supporter, sustained the fire of two French and one Spanish line-of-battle ships until she was dismasted. The wreck of her mizzen-mast covered her larboard guns, her mainmast fell upon the break of the poop; her larboard broadside was thus rendered useless; and just then another French line-of-battle ship, the *Achille*, took her position on the *Belleisle's* larboard quarter, and opened on her a deadly fire, to which the British ship could not return a shot. This scene lasted for nearly an hour and a half, but at half-past three the *Swiftsure* came majestically up, passed under the *Belleisle's* stern —the two crews cheering each other, the *Belleisle's* men waving a Union Jack at the end of a pike to show they were still fighting, while an ensign still flew from the stump of the mainmast—and the fury with which the *Swiftsure* fell upon the *Achille* may be imagined. The *Defiance* about the same time took off the *Aigle*, and the *Polyphemus* the *Neptune*, and the much-battered *Belleisle* floated free. Masts, bowsprit, boats, figure-head— all were shot away; her hull was pierced in every direction; she was a mere splintered wreck.

The *Téméraire* fought a battle almost as dreadful. The *Africa*, a light ship carrying only sixty-four guns, chose as her antagonist the *Intrépide*, a French seventy-four, in weight of broadside and number of crew almost double her force. How dreadful were the damages sustained by the British ship in a fight so unequal and so stubborn may be imagined; but she clung to her big antagonist until, the *Orion* coming up, the *Intrépide* struck.

At three P.M. the firing had begun to slacken, and ship after ship of the enemy was striking. At a quarter past two the *Algeziras* struck to the *Tonnant*, and fifteen minutes afterwards the *San Juan*—the *Tonnant* was fighting both ships — also hailed that she surrendered. Lieutenant Clement was sent in the jolly-boat, with two hands, to take possession of the Spanish seventy-four, and the boat carrying the gallant three was struck by a shot and swamped. The sailors could swim, but not the lieutenant; the pair of tars succeeded in struggling back with their officer to the *Tonnant;* and as that ship had not another boat that would float, she had to see her prize drift off. The *Colossus*, in like manner, fought with the French *Swiftsure* and the *Bahama*—each her own size—and captured them both! The *Redoutable* had surrendered by this time, and a couple of midshipmen, with a dozen hands, had climbed from the *Victory's* one remaining boat through the stern ports of the French ship. The *Bucentaure*, Villeneuve's flagship, had her fate practically sealed by the first tremendous broadside poured into her by the *Victory*. With fine courage, however, the French ship maintained a straggling fire until both the *Leviathan* and the *Conqueror*, at a distance of less than thirty yards, were pouring a tempest of shot into her. The French flagship then struck, and was taken possession of by a tiny boat's crew from the *Conqueror* consisting of three marines and two sailors. The marine officer coolly locked the powder magazine of the Frenchman, put the key in his pocket, left two of his men in charge of the surrendered *Bucentaure*, put Villeneuve and his two captains in his boat with his two marines and himself, and went off in search of the *Conqueror*. In the smoke and confusion, however, he could not find that ship, and so carried the captured French admiral to the *Mars*. Hercules Robinson has drawn a pen picture of the unfortunate French admiral as he came on board the British ship: "Villeneuve was a tallish, thin man, a very tranquil, placid, English-looking Frenchman; he wore a long-tailed uniform coat, high and flat collar, corduroy pantaloons of a greenish colour with stripes two inches wide, half-boots with sharp toes, and a watch-chain with long gold links. Majendie was a short, fat, jocund sailor, who found a cure for all ills in the Frenchman's philosophy, "Fortune de la guerre" (though this was the third time the goddess had brought him to England as a prisoner); and he used to tell our officers very tough stories of the 'Mysteries of Paris.'"

By five o'clock the roar of guns had died almost into silence. Of thirty-three stately battle-ships that formed the Franco-Spanish fleet four hours earlier, one had vanished in flames, seventeen were captured as mere blood-stained hulks, and fifteen were in flight; while Villeneuve himself was a prisoner. But Nelson was dead. Night was falling. A fierce south-east gale was blowing. A sea—such a sea as only arises in shallow waters—ugly, broken, hollow, was rising fast. In all directions ships dismantled, with scuppers crimson with blood, and sides jagged with shot-holes, were rolling their tall, huge hulks in the heavy sea; and the shoals of Trafalgar were only thirteen miles to leeward! The fight with tempest and sea during that terrific night was almost more dreadful than the battle with human foes during the day. Codrington says, the gale was so furious that "it blew away the top main-topsail, though it was close-reefed, and the fore-topsail after it was clewed up ready for furling." They dare not set a storm staysail, although now within six miles of the reef. The *Redoutable* sank at the stern of the ship towing it; the *Bucentaure* had to be cut adrift, and went to pieces on the shoals. The wind shifted in the night and enabled the shot-wrecked and storm-battered ships to claw off the shore; but the fierce weather still raged, and on the 24th the huge *Santissima Trinidad* had to be cut adrift. It was night; wind and sea were furious; but the boats of the *Ajax* and the *Neptune* succeeded in rescuing every wounded man on board the huge Spaniard. The boats, indeed, had all put off when a cat ran out on the muzzle of one of the lower-deck guns and mewed plaintively, and one of the boats pulled back, in the teeth of wind and sea, and rescued poor puss!

Of the eighteen British prizes, fourteen sank, were wrecked, burnt by the captors, or recaptured; only four reached Portsmouth. Yet never was the destruction of a fleet more absolutely complete. Of the fifteen ships that escaped Trafalgar, four were met in the open sea on November 4 by an equal number of British ships, under Sir Richard Strahan, and were captured. The other eleven lay disabled hulks in Cadiz till—when France and Spain broke into war with each other—they were all destroyed. Villeneuve's great fleet, in brief, simply vanished from existence! But Napoleon, with that courageous economy of truth characteristic of him, summed up Trafalgar in the sentence: "The storms occasioned to us the loss of a few ships after a battle imprudently fought"! Trafalgar, as a matter of fact, was the most amazing victory won by land or sea through the whole Revolutionary war. It permanently changed the course of history; and it goes far to justify Nelson's magnificently audacious boast, "The fleets of England are equal to meet the world in arms!"

THE END

Printed by BALLANTYNE, HANSON & Co.
Edinburgh & London

Smith, Elder, & Co.'s New Books

In 2 vols with Portraits, crown 8vo, 15s. net.

THE LETTERS OF ELIZABETH BARRETT BROWNING.

Edited, with Biographical Additions, by

FREDERIC G. KENYON.

NEW AND CHEAPER EDITION OF MRS. BROWNING'S COMPLETE WORKS.
Complete in 1 volume, with Portrait and Facsimile of the MS. of a "Sonnet from the Portuguese." Large crown 8vo, bound in cloth, with gilt top, 7s. 6d.

THE POEMS OF ELIZABETH BARRETT BROWNING.
⁎ This edition is uniform with the two-volume edition of Robert Browning's complete works.

NEW ILLUSTRATED EDITION OF "THE GREY LADY."
With 12 Full-page Illustrations by Arthur Rackham. Crown 8vo, 6s.

THE GREY LADY. By Henry Seton Merriman, Author of "The Sowers," "With Edged Tools," "In Kedar's Tents," &c.

CHEAP POPULAR EDITION OF "MARCELLA."
Crown 8vo, bound in limp cloth, 2s. 6d.

MARCELLA. By Mrs. Humphry Ward. Cheap Popular Edition.

FRIENDSHIP'S GARLAND. By Matthew Arnold. Second Edition. Small crown 8vo, bound in white cloth, 4s. 6d.

DEEDS THAT WON THE EMPIRE. By the Rev. W. H. Fitchett. With 11 Plans and 16 Portraits. Crown 8vo, 6s.

THE STORY OF THE CHURCH OF EGYPT: being an Outline of the History of the Egyptians under their successive Masters from the Roman Conquest until now. By E. L. Butcher, Author of "A Strange Journey," "A Black Jewel," &c. In 2 vols. crown 8vo, 16s. [*Immediately.*]

THE LIFE OF SIR JOHN HAWLEY GLOVER, R.N., G.C.M.G. By Lady Glover. Edited by the Right Hon Sir Richard Temple, Bart., G.C.S.I., D.C.L., LL.D., F.R.S. With Portrait and Maps. Demy 8vo, 14s. [*Nearly ready.*]

THE AUTOBIOGRAPHY OF ARTHUR YOUNG. With Selections from his Correspondence. Edited by M. Betham-Edwards. With 2 Portraits and 2 Views. Large crown 8vo, 12s. 6d. [*Nearly ready.*]

THE WAR OF GREEK INDEPENDENCE, 1821-1835. By W. Alison Phillips, M.A., late Scholar of Merton College, Senior Scholar of St. John's College, Oxford. With Map. Large crown 8vo, 7s. 6d.

TWELVE YEARS IN A MONASTERY. By Joseph McCabe, late Father Antony, O.S.F. Large crown 8vo, 7s. 6d.

ITALIAN LITERATURE. By the late John Addington Symonds. 2 vols. large crown 8vo, 15s. (Vols. IV. and V. of the New and Cheaper Edition of "The Renaissance in Italy" in 7 vols.) [*In November.*]

STUDIES IN BOARD SCHOOLS. By Charles Morley. Crown 8vo, 6s.
"A work which all who are interested in the work and possibilities of the School Board should hasten to read."—*Daily Mail.*

ELECTRIC MOVEMENTS IN AIR AND WATER. With Theoretical Inferences. By Lord Armstrong, C.B., F.R.S., LL.D., &c. With Autotype Plates. Imperial 4to, £1, 10s.

ISABELLA THE CATHOLIC, QUEEN OF SPAIN: Her Life, Reign, and Times, 1451-1504. By M. le Baron de Nervo. Translated from the Original French by Lieut.-Colonel Temple-West (Retired). With Portraits. Demy 8vo, 12s. 6d.

GABRIELE VON BÜLOW, Daughter of Wilhelm von Humboldt. A Memoir compiled from the Family Papers of Wilhelm von Humboldt and his Children, 1791-1887. Translated by Clara Nordlinger. With Portraits and a Preface by Sir Edward B. Malet, G.C.B., G.C.M.G., &c. Demy 8vo, 16s.

POT-POURRI FROM A SURREY GARDEN. By Mrs. C. W. Earle. With an Appendix by Lady Constance Lytton. Seventh Edition. Large crown 8vo, 7s. 6d.

London: SMITH, ELDER, & CO., 15 Waterloo Place, S.W.

SMITH, ELDER, & CO.'S PUBLICATIONS

SIR CHARLES HALLÉ'S LIFE AND LETTERS. Being an Autobiography (1819-60), with Correspondence and Diaries. Edited by his Son, C. E. HALLÉ, and his Daughter MARIE HALLÉ. With 2 Portraits. Demy 8vo, 16s.

"The volume is one of the most interesting of recent contributions to the literature of music. ... A strong sense of humour is manifest in the autobiography as well as in the letters, and there are some capital stories scattered up and down the volume."—*Times.*

THE MEMOIRS OF BARON THIÉBAULT (late Lieutenant-General in the French Army). With Recollections of the Republic, the Consulate, and the Empire. Translated and condensed by A. J. BUTLER, M.A., Translator of the "Memoirs of Marbot." 2 vols., with 2 Portraits and 2 Maps. Demy 8vo, 28s.

"Mr. Butler's work has been admirably done. ... These memoirs abound in varied interest, and, moreover, they have no little literary merit. ... For solid history, bright sketches of rough campaigning, shrewd studies of character, and lively anecdote, these memoirs yield in no degree to others."—*Times.*

PREHISTORIC MAN AND BEAST. By the Rev. H. N. HUTCHINSON, Author of "Extinct Monsters," "Creatures of Other Days," &c. With a Preface by Sir HENRY HOWORTH, M.P., F.R.S., and 10 full-page Illustrations. Small demy 8vo, 10s. 6d.

"A striking picture of living men and conditions as they once existed. ... It combines graphic description with scientific accuracy, and is an admirable example of what a judicious use of the imagination can achieve upon a basis of established facts."—*Knowledge.*

A YEAR IN THE FIELDS. Selections from the Writings of JOHN BURROUGHS. With Illustrations from Photographs by CLIFTON JOHNSON. Crown 8vo, 6s.

"The book is an excellent example of its kind, pleasant, chatty, and readable. ... Fresh and graphic, instinct with country sights, scents, and sounds."—*Land and Water.*

"The book is pleasant reading, and Mr. Burroughs is a true lover of Nature."—*Athenæum.*

THE MONEY-SPINNER, and other Character Notes. By H. SETON MERRIMAN, Author of "The Sowers," "With Edged Tools," &c., and S. G. TALLENTYRE. With 12 full-page Illustrations by ARTHUR RACKHAM. Second Edition. Crown 8vo, 6s.

"We have many bad books, and many goody-goody books, but few good books; this is one of them.'—Mr. JAMES PAYN in the *Illustrated London News.*

SELECTED POEMS OF WALTER VON DER VOGELWEIDE THE MINNESINGER. Done into English Verse by W. ALISON PHILLIPS, M.A., late Scholar of Merton College, and Senior Scholar of St. John's College, Oxford. With 6 full-page Illustrations. Small 4to, 10s. 6d. net.

"There is in the outpourings of the famous Minnesinger a freshness and a spontaneity that exercise an irresistible charm. ... Mr. Phillips deserves thanks from all lovers of poetry for bringing him before the world again in so acceptable a form."—*Times.*

HISTORY IN FACT AND FICTION. By the Hon. A. S. G. CANNING, Author of "Lord Macaulay: Essayist and Historian," "The Philosophy of Charles Dickens," &c. Crown 8vo, 6s.

"An intensely interesting book. ... I do not think that I ever saw the difficulties of the Eastern question in so clear a light as I did after reading the short chapter which Mr. Canning devotes to it."—*Pall Mall Gazette.*

THROUGH LONDON SPECTACLES. By CONSTANCE MILMAN. Crown 8vo, 3s. 6d.

"Altogether a very pleasant and companionable little book."—*Spectator.*

MY CONFIDENCES: An Autobiographical Sketch, Addressed to my Descendants. By FREDERICK LOCKER-LAMPSON. Edited by AUGUSTINE BIRRELL, Q C., M.P. Second Edition. With 2 Portraits. 8vo, 15s.

THE MAMELUKE OR SLAVE DYNASTY OF EGYPT, 1260-1517 A.D. By Sir WILLIAM MUIR, K.C.S.I., LL.D., D.C.L., Ph.D. (Bologna), Author of "The Life of Mahomet," "Mahomet and Islam," "The Caliphate," &c. With 12 full-page Illustrations and a Map. 8vo, 10s. 6d.

THE BROWNINGS FOR THE YOUNG. Edited by FREDERIC G. KENYON, late Fellow of Magdalen College, Oxford. Small fcap. 8vo, cloth, 1s.; or with gilt edges, 1s. 4d.

THE LIFE AND LETTERS OF ROBERT BROWNING. By Mrs. SUTHERLAND ORR. With Portrait and Steel Engraving of Mr. Browning's Study in De Vere Gardens. Second Edition. Crown 8vo, 12s. 6d.

LONDON: SMITH, ELDER, & CO., 15 WATERLOO PLACE, S.W.

ROBERT BROWNING'S WORKS
AND "LIFE AND LETTERS"

THE COMPLETE WORKS OF ROBERT BROWNING. Edited and Annotated by AUGUSTINE BIRRELL, Q.C., M.P., and FREDERIC G. KENYON. In 2 vols. large crown 8vo, bound in cloth, gilt top, with a Portrait-Frontispiece to each volume, 7s. 6d. per volume.

⁎ An Edition has also been printed on Oxford India Paper. This can be obtained only through booksellers, who will furnish particulars as to price, &c.

UNIFORM EDITION OF THE WORKS OF ROBERT BROWNING. Seventeen Volumes, small crown 8vo, lettered separately, or in set binding, price 5s. each. This edition contains Three Portraits of Mr Browning, at different periods of life, and a few illustrations.

CONTENTS OF THE VOLUMES

1. PAULINE: and SORDELLO.
2. PARACELSUS: and STRAFFORD.
3. PIPPA PASSES: KING VICTOR AND KING CHARLES: THE RETURN OF THE DRUSES: and A SOUL'S TRAGEDY. With a Portrait of Mr. Browning.
4. A BLOT IN THE 'SCUTCHEON: COLOMBE'S BIRTHDAY: and MEN AND WOMEN.
5. DRAMATIC ROMANCES: and CHRISTMAS-EVE AND EASTER-DAY.
6. DRAMATIC LYRICS: and LURIA.
7. IN A BALCONY: and DRAMATIS PERSONÆ. With a Portrait of Mr. Browning.
8. THE RING AND THE BOOK. Books 1 to 4. With Two Illustrations.
9. THE RING AND THE BOOK. Books 5 to 8.
10. THE RING AND THE BOOK. Books 9 to 12. With a Portrait of Guido Franceschini.
11. BALAUSTION'S ADVENTURE: PRINCE HOHENSTIEL-SCHWANGAU, Saviour of Society: and FIFINE AT THE FAIR.
12. RED COTTON NIGHT-CAP COUNTRY: and THE INN ALBUM.
13. ARISTOPHANES' APOLOGY, including a Transcript from Euripides, being the Last Adventure of Balaustion: and THE AGAMEMNON OF ÆSCHYLUS.
14. PACCHIAROTTO, and How he Worked in Distemper: with other Poems: LA SAISIAZ: and THE TWO POETS OF CROISIC.
15. DRAMATIC IDYLS, First Series: DRAMATIC IDYLS, Second Series: and JOCOSERIA.
16. FERISHTAH'S FANCIES: and PARLEYINGS WITH CERTAIN PEOPLE OF IMPORTANCE IN THEIR DAY. With a Portrait of Mr. Browning.
17. ASOLANDO: Fancies and Facts; and BIOGRAPHICAL AND HISTORICAL NOTES TO THE POEMS.

A SELECTION FROM THE POETICAL WORKS OF ROBERT BROWNING. FIRST SERIES, crown 8vo, 3s. 6d. SECOND SERIES, crown 8vo, 3s. 6d.

POCKET VOLUME OF SELECTIONS FROM THE POETICAL WORKS OF ROBERT BROWNING. Small fcap. 8vo, bound in half-cloth, with cut or uncut edges, price 1s.

THE LIFE AND LETTERS OF ROBERT BROWNING. By Mrs. SUTHERLAND ORR. With Portrait, and Steel Engraving of Mr. Browning's Study in De Vere Gardens. SECOND EDITION, crown 8vo, 12s. 6d.

LONDON: SMITH, ELDER, & CO., 15 WATERLOO PLACE, S.W.

WORKS OF ELIZABETH BARRETT BROWNING

THE POEMS OF ELIZABETH BARRETT BROWNING. New and Cheaper Edition. Complete in One Volume, with Portrait and Facsimile of the MS. of "A Sonnet from the Portuguese." Large crown 8vo, bound in cloth, with gilt top, 7s. 6d.

** *This Edition is uniform with the Two-Volume Edition of Robert Browning's Complete Works.*

THE POETICAL WORKS OF ELIZABETH BARRETT BROWNING. Uniform Edition. Six Volumes, in set binding, small crown 8vo, 5s. each.

Volume 6, "Aurora Leigh," can also be had bound as a separate volume.

This Edition is uniform with the Seventeen-Volume Edition of Mr. Robert Browning's Works. It contains the following Portraits and Illustrations:—

Portrait of Elizabeth Barrett Moulton-Barrett at the age of nine.
Coxhoe Hall, County of Durham.
Portrait of Elizabeth Barrett Moulton-Barrett in early youth.
Portrait of Mrs. Browning, Rome, February 1859.
Hope End, Herefordshire.
Sitting Room of Casa Guidi, Florence.
"May's Love,"—Facsimile of Mrs. Browning's Handwriting.
Portrait of Mrs. Browning, Rome, March 1859.
Portrait of Mrs. Browning, Rome, 1861.
The Tomb of Mrs. Browning in the Cemetery at Florence.

A SELECTION FROM THE POETRY OF ELIZABETH BARRETT BROWNING. First Series, crown 8vo, 3s. 6d. Second Series, crown 8vo, 3s. 6d.

POEMS. Small fcap. 8vo, half-cloth, cut or uncut edges, 1s.

EXTRACT FROM PREFATORY NOTE BY MR. ROBERT BROWNING.

"In a recent 'Memoir of Elizabeth Barrett Browning,' by John H. Ingram, it is observed that 'such essays on her personal history as have appeared, either in England or elsewhere, are replete with mistakes or misstatements.' For these he proposes to substitute 'a correct if short memoir:' but, kindly and appreciative as may be Mr. Ingram's performance, there occur not a few passages in it equally 'mistaken and misstated.'"

London: SMITH, ELDER, & CO., 15 Waterloo Place, S.W.

W. M. THACKERAY'S WORKS

THE LIBRARY EDITION

Twenty-four Volumes, Large Crown 8vo, 7s. 6d. each, with Illustrations by the Author, RICHARD DOYLE, and FREDERICK WALKER.

Sets in cloth, £9; or, in half-Russia, £13, 13s.

VANITY FAIR. A NOVEL WITHOUT A HERO. Two Volumes. With Forty Steel Engravings and 149 Woodcuts by the Author.

THE HISTORY OF PENDENNIS: HIS FORTUNES AND MISFORTUNES: HIS FRIENDS AND HIS GREATEST ENEMY. Two Volumes. With Forty-eight Steel Engravings and numerous Woodcuts by the Author.

THE NEWCOMES: MEMOIRS OF A MOST RESPECTABLE FAMILY. Two Volumes. With Forty-eight Steel Engravings by RICHARD DOYLE, and numerous Woodcuts.

THE HISTORY OF HENRY ESMOND, ESQ.: A COLONEL IN THE SERVICE OF HER MAJESTY QUEEN ANNE. With Eight Illustrations by GEORGE DU MAURIER, and numerous Woodcuts.

THE VIRGINIANS: A TALE OF THE LAST CENTURY. Two Volumes. With Forty-eight Steel Engravings and numerous Woodcuts by the Author.

THE ADVENTURES OF PHILIP ON HIS WAY THROUGH THE WORLD, SHOWING WHO ROBBED HIM, WHO HELPED HIM, AND WHO PASSED HIM BY. To which is prefixed A SHABBY GENTEEL STORY. Two Volumes. With Twenty Illustrations by the Author and FREDERICK WALKER.

THE PARIS SKETCH-BOOK OF MR. M. A. TITMARSH AND THE MEMOIRS OF MR. C. J. YELLOWPLUSH. With Illustrations by the Author.

THE MEMOIRS OF BARRY LYNDON, ESQ., WRITTEN BY HIMSELF: WITH THE HISTORY OF SAMUEL TITMARSH AND THE GREAT HOGGARTY DIAMOND. With Illustrations by the Author.

THE IRISH SKETCH-BOOK: AND NOTES OF A JOURNEY FROM CORNHILL TO GRAND CAIRO. With Illustrations by the Author.

THE BOOK OF SNOBS; SKETCHES AND TRAVELS IN LONDON; AND CHARACTER SKETCHES. With Illustrations by the Author.

BURLESQUES:— Novels by Eminent Hands—Adventures of Major Gahagan—Jeames's Diary—A Legend of the Rhine—Rebecca and Rowena—The History of the Next French Revolution—Cox's Diary. With Illustrations by the Author and RICHARD DOYLE.

CHRISTMAS BOOKS OF M. A. TITMARSH:— Mrs. Perkins's Ball—Dr. Birch—Our Street—The Kickleburys on the Rhine—The Rose and the Ring. With Twenty-four Illustrations by the Author.

BALLADS AND TALES. With Illustrations by the Author.

THE FOUR GEORGES; THE ENGLISH HUMORISTS OF THE EIGHTEENTH CENTURY. With Portraits and other Illustrations.

ROUNDABOUT PAPERS. To which is added the SECOND FUNERAL OF NAPOLEON. With Illustrations by the Author.

DENIS DUVAL; LOVEL THE WIDOWER; AND OTHER STORIES. With Illustrations by FREDERICK WALKER and the Author.

CATHERINE, a Story; LITTLE TRAVELS; THE FITZBOODLE PAPERS; CRITICAL REVIEWS; AND THE WOLVES AND THE LAMB. Illustrations by the Author, and a Portrait.

MISCELLANEOUS ESSAYS, SKETCHES, AND REVIEWS. With Illustrations by the Author.

CONTRIBUTIONS TO "PUNCH." With 132 Illustrations by the Author.

THE POPULAR EDITION

Complete in Thirteen Volumes, Crown 8vo, with Frontispiece to each Volume, price 5s. each.

Sets, handsomely bound in scarlet cloth, gilt top, price £3, 5s.; or in half-morocco, gilt, price £5, 10s.

1.—**VANITY FAIR.**

2.—**THE HISTORY OF PENDENNIS.**

3.—**THE NEWCOMES.**

4.—**ESMOND AND BARRY LYNDON.**

5.—**THE VIRGINIANS.**

6.—**THE ADVENTURES OF PHILIP,** to which is prefixed A SHABBY GENTEEL STORY.

7.—**PARIS, IRISH, AND EASTERN SKETCHES:—** Paris Sketch-Book — Irish Sketch-Book — Cornhill to Cairo.

8.—**HOGGARTY DIAMOND, YELLOWPLUSH PAPERS, AND BURLESQUES:—** The Great Hoggarty Diamond—Yellowplush Papers—Novels by Eminent Hands—Jeames's Diary—Adventures of Major Gahagan—A Legend of the Rhine—Rebecca and Rowena—The History of the Next French Revolution—Cox's Diary—The Fatal Boots.

9.—**THE BOOK OF SNOBS, AND SKETCHES OF LIFE AND CHARACTER:—** The Book of Snobs—Sketches and Travels in London—Character Sketches—Men's Wives—The Fitzboodle Papers—The Bedford Row Conspiracy—A Little Dinner at Timmins's.

10.—**ROUNDABOUT PAPERS AND LECTURES:—** Roundabout Papers—The Four Georges—The English Humorists of the Eighteenth Century—The Second Funeral of Napoleon.

11.—**CATHERINE, &c.** Catherine—Lovel the Widower—Denis Duval—Ballads—The Wolves and the Lamb—Critical Reviews—Little Travels and Roadside Sketches.

12.—**CHRISTMAS BOOKS:—** Mrs. Perkins's Ball — Dr. Birch — Our Street — The Kickleburys on the Rhine—The Rose and the Ring.

13.—**MISCELLANEOUS ESSAYS, SKETCHES, AND REVIEWS; CONTRIBUTIONS TO "PUNCH."**

LONDON: SMITH, ELDER, & CO., 15 WATERLOO PLACE, S.W.

WORKS BY F. ANSTEY.

THE TALKING HORSE; and other Tales.
Popular Edition. Crown 8vo. 6s. Cheap Edition. Crown 8vo. limp red cloth, 2s. 6d.

From THE SATURDAY REVIEW.—'A capital set of stories, thoroughly clever and witty, often pathetic, and always humorous.'

From THE ATHENÆUM.—'The grimmest of mortals, in his most surly mood, could hardly resist the fun of "The Talking Horse."'

THE GIANT'S ROBE.
Popular Edition. Crown 8vo. 6s. Cheap Edition. Crown 8vo. limp red cloth, 2s. 6d.

From THE PALL MALL GAZETTE.—'The main interest of the book, which is very strong indeed, begins when Vincent returns, when Harold Caffyn discovers the secret, when every page threatens to bring down doom on the head of the miserable Mark. Will he confess? Will he drown himself? Will Vincent denounce him? Will Caffyn inform on him? Will his wife abandon him?—we ask eagerly as we read and cannot cease reading till the puzzle is solved in a series of exciting situations.'

THE PARIAH.
Popular Edition. Crown 8vo. 6s. Cheap Edition. Crown 8vo. limp red cloth, 2s. 6d.

From THE SATURDAY REVIEW.—'In "The Pariah" we are more than ever struck by the sharp intuitive perception and the satirical balancing of judgment which makes the author's writings such extremely entertaining reading. There is not a dull page—we might say, not a dull sentence—in it. . . . The girls are delightfully drawn, especially the bewitching Margot and the childish Lettice. Nothing that polish and finish, cleverness, humour, wit, and sarcasm can give us is left out.'

VICE VERSÂ; or, a Lesson to Fathers.
Cheap Edition. Crown 8vo. limp red cloth, 2s. 6d.

From THE SATURDAY REVIEW.—'If ever there was a book made up from beginning to end of laughter, and yet not a comic book, or a "merry" book, or a book of jokes, or a book of pictures, or a jest book, or a tomfool book, but a perfectly sober and serious book, in the reading of which a sober man may laugh without shame from beginning to end, it is the book called "Vice Versâ; or, a Lesson to Fathers." . . We close the book, recommending it very earnestly to all fathers in the first instance, and their sons, nephews, uncles, and male cousins next.'

A FALLEN IDOL.
Cheap Edition. Crown 8vo. limp red cloth, 2s. 6d.

From THE TIMES.—'Will delight the multitudinous public that laughed over "Vice Versâ." . . . The boy who brings the accursed image to Champion's house, Mr. Bales, the artist's factotum, and above all Mr. Yarker, the ex-butler who has turned policeman, are figures whom it is as pleasant to meet as it is impossible to forget.'

LYRE AND LANCET.
With 24 Full-page Illustrations. Square 16mo. 3s.

From THE SPEAKER.—'Mr. Anstey has surpassed himself in "Lyre and Lancet." . . . One of the brightest and most entertaining bits of comedy we have had for many a day.'

From THE GLOBE.—'The little book is amusing from beginning to end.'

From THE SCOTSMAN.—'The story makes most delightful reading, full of quiet fun.'

London: SMITH, ELDER, & CO., 15 Waterloo Place.

ILLUSTRATED EDITION OF THE
LIFE AND WORKS OF CHARLOTTE BRONTË
(CURRER BELL) AND HER SISTERS
EMILY and ANNE BRONTË
(ELLIS AND ACTON BELL).

In Seven Volumes, large crown 8vo. handsomely bound in cloth, price 5s. each.

1. JANE EYRE. By CHARLOTTE BRONTË. With Five Illustrations.
2. SHIRLEY. By CHARLOTTE BRONTË. With Five Illustrations.
3. VILLETTE. By CHARLOTTE BRONTË. With Five Illustrations.
4. THE PROFESSOR, and POEMS. By CHARLOTTE BRONTË. With Poems by her Sisters and Father. With Five Illustrations.
5. WUTHERING HEIGHTS. By EMILY BRONTË. AGNES GREY. By ANNE BRONTË. With a Preface and Biographical Notice of both Authors by CHARLOTTE BRONTË. With Five Illustrations.
6. THE TENANT OF WILDFELL HALL. By ANNE BRONTË. With Five Illustrations.
7. LIFE OF CHARLOTTE BRONTË. By Mrs. GASKELL. With Seven Illustrations.

*** The Volumes are also to be had in small post 8vo. limp green cloth, or cloth boards, gilt top, price 2s. 6d. each. And in small fcp. 8vo. bound in half cloth, with Frontispiece to each volume, cut or uncut edges, price 1s. 6d. each; or the Set bound in cloth, with gilt top, in gold-lettered cloth case, 12s. 6d.

ILLUSTRATED EDITION OF
MRS. GASKELL'S NOVELS AND TALES.

In Seven Volumes, bound in cloth, each containing Four Illustrations, price 3s. 6d. each.

CONTENTS OF THE VOLUMES:

VOL. I. WIVES AND DAUGHTERS. | VOL. III. SYLVIA'S LOVERS.
VOL. II. NORTH AND SOUTH. | VOL. IV. CRANFORD.

Company Manners—The Well of Pen-Morpha—The Heart of John Middleton -Traits and Stories of the Huguenots—Six Weeks at Heppenheim—The Squire's Story—Libbie Marsh's Three Eras—Curious if True—The Moorland Cottage—The Sexton's Hero—Disappearances—Right at Last—The Manchester Marriage—Lois the Witch—The Crooked Branch.

VOL. V. MARY BARTON.

Cousin Phillis—My French Master—The Old Nurse's Story—Bessy's Troubles at Home—Christmas Storms and Sunshine.

VOL. VI. RUTH.

The Grey Woman—Morton Hall—Mr. Harrison's Confessions—Hand and Heart.

VOL. VII. LIZZIE LEIGH.

A Dark Night's Work—Round the Sofa—My Lady Ludlow—An Accursed Race—The Doom of the Griffiths—Half a Lifetime Ago—The Poor Clare—The Half-Brothers.

*** The Volumes are also to be had in small post 8vo. limp green cloth, or cloth boards, gilt top, price 2s. 6d. each: and in Eight Volumes, small fcp. 8vo. bound in half-cloth, cut or uncut edges, price 1s. 6d. each; or the Set bound in cloth, with gilt top, in gold-lettered cloth case, 14s.

London: SMITH, ELDER, & CO., 15 Waterloo Place.

SMITH, ELDER, & CO.'S POPULAR LIBRARY.

Fcp. 8vo. limp green cloth; or cloth boards, gilt top. **2s. 6d. each.**

By the Sisters BRONTË.

JANE EYRE. By Charlotte Brontë.
SHIRLEY. By Charlotte Brontë.
VILLETTE. By Charlotte Brontë.
THE TENANT OF WILDFELL HALL. By Anne Brontë.
WUTHERING HEIGHTS. By Emily Brontë. AGNES GREY. By Anne Brontë
With Preface and Memoir of the Sisters, by Charlotte Brontë.
THE PROFESSOR. By Charlotte Brontë. To which are added the Poems of Charlotte, Emily, and Anne Brontë.

By Mrs. GASKELL.

WIVES AND DAUGHTERS
NORTH AND SOUTH.
SYLVIA'S LOVERS.
CRANFORD, AND OTHER TALES.

MARY BARTON, AND OTHER TALES,
RUTH, AND OTHER TALES.
LIZZIE LEIGH, AND OTHER TALES.
LIFE OF CHARLOTTE BRONTË.

By LEIGH HUNT.

IMAGINATION AND FANCY; or, Selections from the English Poets.
THE TOWN: Its Memorable Characters and Events. Illustrated.
AUTOBIOGRAPHY OF LEIGH HUNT.
MEN, WOMEN, AND BOOKS; a Selection of Sketches, Essays, and Critical Memoirs.
WIT AND HUMOUR: Selected from the English Poets.
A JAR OF HONEY FROM MOUNT HYBLA; or, Sweets from Sicily in Particular, and Pastoral Poetry in General.
TABLE TALK. To which are added IMAGINARY CONVERSATIONS OF POPE AND SWIFT.

Uniform with the above.

THE SMALL HOUSE AT ALLINGTON. By Anthony Trollope.
THE CLAVERINGS. By Anthony Trollope.
FRAMLEY PARSONAGE. By Anthony Trollope.
ROMOLA. By George Eliot.
TRANSFORMATION. By Nathaniel Hawthorne.
DEERBROOK. By Harriet Martineau.
HOUSEHOLD EDUCATION. By Harriet Martineau.
LECTURES ON THE ENGLISH HUMOURISTS OF THE EIGHTEENTH CENTURY. By W. M. Thackeray.

PAUL THE POPE AND PAUL THE FRIAR. By T. A. Trollope.
THE ROSE-GARDEN. By the Author of 'Unawares.'
CHRONICLES OF DUSTYPORE. A Tale of Modern Anglo-Indian Society. By the Author of 'Wheat and Tares.'
IN THE SILVER AGE. By Holme Lee.
CARITÀ. By Mrs. Oliphant.
WITHIN THE PRECINCTS. By Mrs. Oliphant.
SOME LITERARY RECOLLECTIONS. By James Payn.
EXTRACTS FROM THE WRITINGS OF W. M. THACKERAY.
FALLING IN LOVE; with other Essays. By Grant Allen.

Also the following in limp red cloth, crown 8vo, 2s. 6d. each.

A BRIDE FROM THE BUSH. By E. W. Hornung.
THE STORY OF ABIBAL THE TSOURIAN. Edited by Val C. Prinsep, A.R.A.
HOLIDAY PAPERS. Second Series. By the Rev. Harry Jones.
VICE VERSÂ. By F. Anstey.
A FALLEN IDOL. By F. Anstey.
THE PARIAH. By F. Anstey.

THE TALKING HORSE; and other Tales. By F. Anstey.
THE GIANT'S ROBE. By F. Anstey.
THE VAGABONDS. By Margaret L. Woods.
THE MARTYRED FOOL. By D. Christie Murray.
GRANIA: The Story of an Island. By the Hon. Emily Lawless.
THE DISAPPEARANCE OF GEORGE DRIFFELL. By James Payn.

London: SMITH, ELDER, & CO., 15 Waterloo Place.

SMITH, ELDER, & CO.'S POPULAR LIBRARY—*continued*

Fcp. 8vo. Pictorial Covers, 2s. each; or limp red cloth, 2s. 6d. each.

By HENRY SETON MERRIMAN.

| WITH EDGED TOOLS | THE SLAVE OF THE LAMP. |
| FROM ONE GENERATION TO ANOTHER. | |

By the Author of 'Molly Bawn.'

MOLLY BAWN.	DORIS.	FAITH & UNFAITH.
PHYLLIS.	PORTIA.	LADY BRANKSMERE
MRS. GEOFFREY.	BEAUTY'S DAUGHTERS.	LOYS, LORD BERRES
AIRY FAIRY LILIAN.	GREEN PLEASURE AND	FORD, and other Tales
ROSSMOYNE.	GREY GRIEF.	UNDERCURRENTS.

By GEORGE GISSING.

| DEMOS: a Story of Socialist Life in England. | A LIFE'S MORNING. | THE NETHER WORLD. |
| | THYRZA. | NEW GRUB STREET. |

By the Author of 'Mehalah.'

| MEHALAH: a Story of the Salt Marshes. | THE GAVEROCKS. | RICHARD CABLE, THE LIGHTSHIPMAN. |
| COURT ROYAL. | JOHN HERRING: a West of England Romance. | |

By W. E. NORRIS.

| HEAPS OF MONEY. | MADEMOISELLE DE MERSAC. | NO NEW THING. |
| MATRIMONY. | | ADRIAN VIDAL. |

By HAMILTON AIDÉ.

| IN THAT STATE OF LIFE. | PENRUDDOCKE. | MR. AND MRS. FAULCONBRIDGE. |
| | MORALS AND MYSTERIES. | |

By the Author of 'John Halifax, Gentleman.'

| ROMANTIC TALES. | DOMESTIC STORIES. |

By HOLME LEE.

AGAINST WIND AND TIDE.	MAUDE TALBOT.
SYLVAN HOLT'S DAUGHTER.	COUNTRY STORIES.
KATHIE BRANDE.	KATHERINE'S TRIAL.
WARP AND WOOF.	MR. WYNYARD'S WARD.
ANNIS WARLEIGH'S FORTUNES.	THE BEAUTIFUL MISS BARRINGTON.
THE WORTLEBANK DIARY.	
BASIL GODFREY'S CAPRICE.	BEN MILNER'S WOOING.

Uniform with the above.

GRASP YOUR NETTLE. By E. Lynn Linton.
AGNES OF SORRENTO. By Mrs. H. B. Stowe.
TALES OF THE COLONIES. By C. Rowcroft.
LAVINIA. By the Author of 'Dr. Antonio' &c.
HESTER KIRTON. By Katharine S. Macquoid.
BY THE SEA. By Katharine S. Macquoid.
THE HOTEL DU PETIT ST. JEAN.
VERA. By the Author of 'The Hôtel du Petit St. Jean.'
SIX MONTHS HENCE. By the Author of 'Behind the Veil' &c.
THE STORY OF THE PLÉBISCITE. By MM. Erckmann-Chatrian.
GABRIEL DENVER. By Oliver Madox Brown.

TAKE CARE WHOM YOU TRUST. By Compton Reade.
PEARL AND EMERALD. By R. E. Francillon.
ISEULTE. By the Author of 'The Hôtel du Petit St. Jean.'
A GARDEN OF WOMEN. By Sarah Tytler.
BRIGADIER FREDERIC. By MM. Erckmann-Chatrian.
FOR PERCIVAL. By Margaret Veley.
LOVE THE DEBT. By Richard Ashe King ('Basil').
RAINBOW GOLD. By D. Christie Murray.
THE HEIR OF THE AGES. By James Payn.
LOLA: a Tale of the Rock. By Arthur Griffiths.
FRENCH JANET. By Sarah Tytler.

THE COUNTY: a Story of Social Life.
BEHIND THE VEIL. By the Author of 'Six Months Hence.'
THE RAJAH'S HEIR. By a New Writer.
A DRAUGHT OF LETHE. By Roy Tellet, Author of 'The Outcasts.'
EIGHT DAYS: a Tale of the Indian Mutiny. By R. E. Forrest.
A WOMAN OF THE WORLD. By F. Mabel Robinson.
THE NEW RECTOR. By Stanley J. Weyman.
DARK: a Tale of the Down Country. By Mrs. Stephen Batson.
STANHOPE OF CHESTER: a Mystery. By Percy Andreae.

London: SMITH, ELDER, & CO., 15 Waterloo Place.

RURAL ENGLAND

"*A series of books of really incomparable freshness and interest.*"—ATHENÆUM.

"*Books unsurpassed in power of observation and sympathy with natural objects by anything that has appeared since the days of Gilbert White.*"—DAILY NEWS.

WORKS BY THE LATE RICHARD JEFFERIES

THE GAMEKEEPER AT HOME; or, Sketches of Natural History and Rural Life. New Edition, with all the Illustrations of the former Edition. Crown 8vo, 5s.

"Delightful sketches. The lover of the country can hardly fail to be fascinated whenever he may happen to open the pages. It is a book to read and keep for reference, and should be on the shelves of every country gentleman's library."—*Saturday Review.*

ROUND ABOUT A GREAT ESTATE. New Edition. Crown 8vo, 5s.

"To read a book of his is really like taking a trip into some remote part of the country, where the surroundings of life remain very much what they were thirty or forty years ago. Mr. Jefferies has made up a very pleasant volume."—*Globe.*

WILD LIFE IN A SOUTHERN COUNTY. New Edition. Crown 8vo, 6s.

"A volume which is worthy of a place beside White's 'Selborne.' In closeness of observation, in power of giving a picture far beyond the power of a mere word-painter, he is the equal of the Selborne rector—perhaps his superior. This is a book to read and to treasure."—*Athenæum.*

THE AMATEUR POACHER. New Edition. Crown 8vo, 5s.

"Unsurpassed in power of observation and sympathy with natural objects by anything that has appeared since the days of Gilbert White."—*Daily News.*

"We have rarely met with a book in which so much that is entertaining is combined with matter of real practical worth."—*Graphic.*

HODGE AND HIS MASTERS. New Edition. Crown 8vo, 7s. 6d.

"The one great charm of Mr. Jefferies' writings may be summed up in the single word 'graphic.' He has a rare power of description, and in 'Hodge and his Masters' we find plenty of good reading."—*Standard.*

"Mr. Jefferies knows his ground well and thoroughly, and writes with much of his wonted straightforwardness and assurance. . . . Pleasant and easy reading throughout."—*Athenæum.*

WOODLAND, MOOR, AND STREAM: Being the Notes of a Naturalist. Edited by J. A. OWEN. Third Edition. Crown 8vo, 5s.

"As a specimen of word-painting, the description of the quaint old fishing village close to the edge of the North Kent marshes can hardly be surpassed. . . . The book is capitally written, full of good stories, and thoroughly commendable."—*Athenæum.*

FOREST TITHES, and other Studies from Nature. By the Author of "Woodland, Moor, and Stream," &c. Edited by J. A. OWEN. Crown 8vo, 5s.

"The book should be read. It is full of the spirit of the South Country, and as we read it we seem to hear again the clack of the millwheel, the cry of the water-fowl, and the splash of fish."—*Spectator.*

ALL THE YEAR WITH NATURE. By P. ANDERSON GRAHAM. Crown 8vo, 5s.

"Of the twenty-eight papers composing the volume there is not one which does not brim over with love of nature, observation of her by-paths, and power of sympathetic expression."—*Observer.*

LONDON: SMITH, ELDER, & CO., 15 WATERLOO PLACE, S.W.

"A work absolutely indispensable to every well-furnished library."
—*The Times.*

Royal 8vo. Price 15s. each net, in cloth; or in half-morocco, marbled edges, 20s. net.

VOLUMES 1-52 (ABBADIE-SMIRKE) OF THE
DICTIONARY OF NATIONAL BIOGRAPHY
Edited by LESLIE STEPHEN and SIDNEY LEE

Volume I. was published on January 1st, 1885, and a further Volume will be issued quarterly until the completion of the work.

NOTE.—A Full Prospectus of "The Dictionary of National Biography," with Specimen Pages, may be had upon application.

FROM A RECENT NOTICE OF THE WORK IN "THE WORLD."

"The present instalment of this really great work is fully equal in every respect to its predecessors. Mr. Sidney Lee and his staff of contributors, indeed, have left nothing undone which the reader could wish or expect them to do, and the publishers may be congratulated on the approaching conclusion of an enterprise of which the success is as conspicuous as its merits, and in the department of literature to which it belongs unparalleled and unprecedented."

TRUTH.—"I am glad you share my admiration for Mr. Stephen's *magnum opus*—THE MAGNUM OPUS OF OUR GENERATION—'The Dictionary of National Biography.' A dictionary of the kind had been attempted so often before by the strongest men—publishers and editors—of the day, that I hardly expected it to succeed. No one expected such a success as it has so far achieved."

THE ATHENÆUM.—"The latest volumes of Mr. Stephen's Dictionary are FULL OF IMPORTANT AND INTERESTING ARTICLES. . . . Altogether the volumes are good reading. What is more important, the articles, whether they are on small or great personages, are nearly all up to the high standard which has been set in the earlier portions of the work, and occasionally above it."

SATURDAY REVIEW.—"From the names we have cited it will be seen that great pains have been taken with that portion of the Dictionary which relates to modern times, and this has been rightly done; for often nothing is more difficult than to find a concise record of the life of a man who belonged to our own times or to those just preceding them. Consistently enough, the Editor has been careful to keep the work reasonably up to date."

THE SPECTATOR.—"As each volume of the Dictionary appears, its merits become more conspicuous. . . . The book ought to commend itself to as wide a circle of buyers as the 'Encyclopædia Britannica.'"

THE MANCHESTER EXAMINER AND TIMES.—"We extend a hearty welcome to the latest instalment of a most magnificent work, in which both the editing and the writing appear still to improve."

THE QUARTERLY REVIEW.—"A 'DICTIONARY OF NATIONAL BIOGRAPHY' OF WHICH THE COUNTRY MAY BE JUSTLY PROUD, which, though it may need correcting and supplementing, will probably never be superseded, and which, in unity of conception and aim, in the number of the names inserted, in fulness and accuracy of details, in the care and precision with which the authorities are cited, and in the bibliographical information given, will not only be immeasurably superior to any work of the kind which has been produced in Great Britain, but will as far surpass the German and Belgian biographical dictionaries now in progress as these two important undertakings are in advance of the two great French collections, which until lately reigned supreme in the department of Biography."

The Rev. Dr. JESSOP in the *Nineteenth Century*.—"The greatest literary undertaking that has ever been carried out in England. . . . We shall have a Dictionary of National Biography such as no other nation in Europe can boast of, and such as can never be wholly superseded, though it will need to be supplemented for the requirements of our posterity."

THE LANCET.—"The usefulness, fulness, and general accuracy of this work become more and more apparent as its progress continues. It is a classic work of reference as such, WITHOUT ANY COMPEER IN ENGLISH OR PERHAPS ANY OTHER LANGUAGE."

THE PALL MALL GAZETTE.—"As to the general execution, we can only repeat the high praise which it has been our pleasing duty to bestow on former volumes. To find a name omitted that should have been inserted is well-nigh impossible."

LONDON: SMITH, ELDER, & CO., 15 WATERLOO PLACE, S.W.

POPULAR NOVELS.

Each Work complete in One Volume, crown 8vo, price Six Shillings.

IN KEDAR'S TENTS. By HENRY SETON MERRIMAN. Fourth Edition.

THE GREY LADY. By HENRY SETON MERRIMAN. With 12 full-page Illustrations by ARTHUR RACKHAM.

THE MILLS OF GOD. By FRANCIS H. HARDY.

UNCLE BERNAC: a Memory of the Empire. By A. CONAN DOYLE. With 12 full-page Illustrations. Second Edition.

THE WAYS OF LIFE: Two Stories. By Mrs. OLIPHANT.

THE LADY GRANGE. By ALEXANDER INNES SHAND.

RODNEY STONE. By A. CONAN DOYLE. With 8 full-page Illustrations.

SIR GEORGE TRESSADY. By Mrs. HUMPHRY WARD. Third Edition.

CLEG KELLY, ARAB OF THE CITY. By S. R. CROCKETT. Thirty-second Thousand.

THE SOWERS. By HENRY SETON MERRIMAN. Fourteenth Edition.

THE WHITE COMPANY. By A. CONAN DOYLE. Seventeenth Edition.

MARCELLA. By Mrs. HUMPHRY WARD. Sixteenth Edition.

ROBERT ELSMERE. By Mrs. HUMPHRY WARD. Twenty-seventh Edition.

THE HISTORY OF DAVID GRIEVE. By Mrs. HUMPHRY WARD. Ninth Edition.

GERALD EVERSLEY'S FRIENDSHIP; a Study in Real Life. By the Rev. J. E. C. WELLDON. Fourth Edition.

THE BORDERER. By ADAM LILBURN.

UNDER THE CIRCUMSTANCES. By ARCHIE ARMSTRONG.

GILBERT MURRAY. By A. E. HOUGHTON.

OUT OF THE DARKNESS. By PERCY FENDALL and FOX RUSSELL.

THE YOUNG CLANROY: a Romance of the '45. By the Rev. COSMO GORDON LANG.

CAPTAIN CASTLE: a Tale of the China Seas. By CARLTON DAWE. With a Frontispiece.

THE WARDLAWS. By E. RENTOUL ESLER.

KATE GRENVILLE. By LORD MONKSWELL.

DISTURBING ELEMENTS. By MABEL C. BIRCHENOUGH.

IN SEARCH OF QUIET: a Country Journal. By WALTER FRITH.

KINCAID'S WIDOW. By SARAH TYTLER.

THE MARTYRED FOOL. By D. CHRISTIE MURRAY.

A FATAL RESERVATION. By R. O. PROWSE.

THE VAGABONDS. By Mrs MARGARET L. WOODS, Author of "A Village Tragedy," &c.

ONE OF THE BROKEN BRIGADE. By CLIVE PHILLIPPS-WOLLFY.

JAN an Afrikander. By ANNA HOWARTH.

DEBORAH OF TOD'S. By Mrs. HENRY DE LA PASTURE.

GRANIA: the Story of an Island. By the Hon. EMILY LAWLESS.

THE SIGNORA: a Tale. By PERCY ANDREAE.

STANHOPE OF CHESTER: a Mystery. By PERCY ANDREAE.

THE MASK AND THE MAN. By PERCY ANDREAE.

A FALLEN IDOL. By F. ANSTEY.

THE GIANT'S ROBE. By F. ANSTEY.

THE PARIAH. By F. ANSTEY.

THE TALKING HORSE, and Other Tales. By F. ANSTEY.

NEW GRUB STREET. By GEORGE GISSING.

THYRZA. By GEORGE GISSING.

THE NETHER WORLD. By GEORGE GISSING.

DEMOS: a Story of Socialist Life in England. By GEORGE GISSING.

RICHARD CABLE, the Lightshipman. By the Author of "Mehalah," &c.

THE GAVEROCKS. By the Author of "Mehalah," "John Herring," &c.

A WOMAN OF THE WORLD. By F. MABEL ROBINSON.

EIGHT DAYS. By R. E. FORREST.

A DRAUGHT OF LETHE. By ROY TELLET.

THE RAJAH'S HEIR. By a NEW AUTHOR.

OLD KENSINGTON. By Miss THACKERAY.

THE VILLAGE ON THE CLIFF. By Miss THACKERAY.

FIVE OLD FRIENDS AND A YOUNG PRINCE. By Miss THACKERAY.

TO ESTHER, and Other Sketches. By Miss THACKERAY.

BLUEBEARD'S KEYS, and Other Stories. By Miss THACKERAY.

THE STORY OF ELIZABETH; TWO HOURS; FROM AN ISLAND. By Miss THACKERAY.

TOILERS AND SPINSTERS. By Miss THACKERAY.

MISS ANGEL; FULHAM LAWN. By Miss THACKERAY.

MISS WILLIAMSON'S DIVAGATIONS. By Miss THACKERAY.

MRS. DYMOND. By Miss THACKERAY.

LLANALY REEFS. By Lady VERNEY, Author of "Stone Edge," &c.

LETTICE LISLE. By Lady VERNEY. With 3 Illustrations.

LONDON: SMITH, ELDER, & CO., 15 WATERLOO PLACE, S.W.

**PLEASE DO NOT REMOVE
CARDS OR SLIPS FROM THIS POCKET**

UNIVERSITY OF TORONTO LIBRARY

```
DA      Fitchett, William Henry
65          Deeds that won the
F54     empire
```